DMT AND THE
SOUL OF PROPH

"Not since Huxley's landmark *The Doors of Perception* has such a profound treatise emerged exploring the nexus of consciousness, the brain, and mind-altering substances. Strassman accomplishes this tour de force by wisely inverting the vector of the field of neurotheology to that of theoneurology. This book exemplifies rigorous science and keen historical analysis and is a significant contribution to human welfare. A delight to read, a sparkling exercise in clarity."

LARRY DOSSEY, M.D., AUTHOR OF *ONE MIND*

"This book is a revelation. Strassman has written a daring and remarkable book that connects contemporary psychedelic explorers with the roots of the Jewish prophetic tradition. Here is a book that shows us how this ancient model of prophecy might provide an elegant and powerful language for the ennobling of our journey toward expanded consciousness."

RABBI SHEFA GOLD, AUTHOR OF *THE MAGIC OF HEBREW CHANT*

"A very surprising and refreshing book. Strassman is unique and opens up completely new perspectives. I have learned a lot from this well-written book, and I am sure that other readers will do so too. Strassman took me far beyond familiar ways of thinking about the brain, minds, and interactions with nonhuman intelligences."

RUPERT SHELDRAKE, PH.D., AUTHOR OF *SCIENCE SET FREE*

"As Rick Strassman's extraordinary new book explains, the Hebrew prophetic tradition provides an unexpectedly powerful lens for wrestling with the meaning of our psychedelic experiences. Strassman's model of theoneurology provides the proper context for viewing the religious importance of our mystic visions."

ALEX GREY, ARTIST, AUTHOR, AND COFOUNDER OF
CoSM, CHAPEL OF SACRED MIRRORS

"This engagingly written book will be of interest to those with primary interest in religious experience as well as those with primary interest in psychedelic experience and altered states of consciousness."

ROLAND R. GRIFFITHS, PH.D.,
PROFESSOR OF PSYCHIATRY AND NEUROSCIENCE,
JOHNS HOPKINS UNIVERSITY SCHOOL OF MEDICINE

"People interested in DMT, hallucinogens, spirituality, monotheistic religion, Buddhism, consciousness studies, and philosophy will find this book stimulating. I commend Strassman for his bold attempt to bridge science and religion, thereby risking attack from both sides. This is the kind of book that will advance knowledge . . . A deep and intense study outside the usual boundaries of education."

JEREMY NARBY, PH.D., ANTHROPOLOGIST AND
AUTHOR OF *THE COSMIC SERPENT*

"This book is deeply compelling, groundbreaking, thought provoking, and important. Rick Strassman set the bar very high with his brilliant *DMT: The Spirit Molecule,* but *DMT and the Soul of Prophecy* comfortably surpasses it by taking the work forward in exciting and unexpected directions. Highly recommended."

GRAHAM HANCOCK, AUTHOR OF *FINGERPRINTS OF THE GODS*

"By utilizing the worldview of the medieval Jewish philosophers, Strassman has presented this often emotionally laden and controversial subject in such a rational and scientific manner that even the skeptic and agnostic among us will be pleasantly surprised at how intriguing the confluence of God, the Hebrew Bible, and psychedelic endogenous DMT can be."

RABBI JOEL DAVID BAKST, AUTHOR OF *THE JERUSALEM STONE OF
CONSCIOUSNESS—DMT, KABBALAH & THE PINEAL GLAND*

"This is a brilliant, perceptive, and illuminating book. Strassman states that the best way to understand the DMT experience is to see how closely it follows the experience of Old Testament prophets and vice versa. I was surprised to find out he was right."

JAMES FADIMAN, PH.D.,
AUTHOR OF *THE PSYCHEDELIC EXPLORER'S GUIDE*

"A stimulating work that, while controversial, will be of interest to students of the Bible and human thought."

RABBI NORMAN STRICKMAN, PH.D.,
ASSISTANT PROFESSOR OF JUDAIC STUDIES, TUORO COLLEGE

"Dr. Strassman's theoneurology theory is a coherent and successful undertaking by a uniquely qualified and situated medical researcher of altered states of consciousness."

ALEX S. KOHAV, PH.D., AUTHOR OF *THE SÔD HYPOTHESIS*

DMT AND THE
SOUL OF PROPHECY

A New Science of Spiritual Revelation in the Hebrew Bible

RICK STRASSMAN, M.D.

Park Street Press
Rochester, Vermont • Toronto, Canada

Park Street Press
One Park Street
Rochester, Vermont 05767
www.ParkStPress.com

SUSTAINABLE FORESTRY INITIATIVE — Certified Sourcing
www.sfiprogram.org
SFI-00854

Text stock is SFI certified

Park Street Press is a division of Inner Traditions International

Library of Congress Cataloging-in-Publication Data

Strassman, Rick, 1952–
  DMT and the soul of prophecy : a new science of spiritual revelation in the
Hebrew Bible / Rick Strassman, M.D.
      pages cm
  Includes bibliographical references and index.
  Summary: "Naturally occurring DMT may produce prophecy-like states
of consciousness and thus represent a bridge between biology and religious
experience" — Provided by publisher.
  ISBN 978-1-59477-342-6 (pbk.) — ISBN 978-1-62055-168-4 (e-book)
  1. Hallucinogenic drugs and religious experience. 2. Dimethyltryptamine. 3.
Prophecy—Judaism. 4. Bible. Old Testament—Criticism, interpretation, etc. I.
Title.
  BL65.D7S77 2014
  204'.2—dc23
                                                                    2014012115

Printed and bound in the United States by Lake Book Manufacturing, Inc.
The text stock is SFI certified. The Sustainable Forestry Initiative® program
promotes sustainable forest management.

10 9 8 7 6 5 4 3 2 1

Text design and layout by Debbie Glogover
This book was typeset in Garamond Premier Pro with Papyrus and Gil Sans
display fonts

To send correspondence to the author of this book, mail a first-class letter to the
author c/o Inner Traditions • Bear & Company, One Park Street, Rochester, VT
05767, and we will forward the communication, or contact the author directly at
www.rickstrassman.com.

In memory of
Daniel X. Freedman, M.D. (1921–1993)
Willis Harman, Ph.D. (1918–1997)

I spoke with the prophets and multiplied visions, and through the prophets I assumed likenesses.

Hosea 12:11

Contents

PART IV

Mechanisms:
Spiritual and Material

PART V

The Past, Present,
and Future of Prophecy

Acknowledgments

Friends, colleagues, study partners, and mentors have provided encouragement, advice, fact-checking, and careful reading as I wound my way through the labyrinth of ideas concerning Hebrew Bible prophecy. These include Ralph Abraham, Ph.D.; Sarah Afkami; Holly Avila; Lisa Baker; Rabbi Joel Bakst; Steve Barker, Ph.D.; Lorenzo Bello; Mark and Celina Bennett; Tai and Satara Bixby; Cindy Blount; Jeffrey Bronfman; Nicholas Cozzi, Ph.D.; Boa Cowee; Hanna Dettman; Aaron and Emily Ellingsen; James Fadiman, Ph.D.; Tadeo Feijão, M.D.; Ede Frecksa, M.D.; Ren Geertsen; Neal Goldsmith, Ph.D.; Jon Graham; Allyson and Alex Grey; Roland Griffiths, Ph.D.; Jeffrey Guss, M.D.; Mark Hoffman; Beatriz Labate, Ph.D.; Wendy Kout; Ariana Kramer; Haim Kreisel, Ph.D.; Jeffrey Kripal, Ph.D.; Jeffrey Lieb, M.D.; Jonathan Lisansky, M.D.; Jeremy Narby, Ph.D.; members of the Nucleo Santa Fe of the União do Vegetal; Clifford Qualls, Ph.D.; Bob Schrei; Mitch Schultz; Barbara Scott; Jonathan Sobol; Avi Solomon; Lily Springer, Ph.D.; Leanna Standish, N.D., Ph.D.; Andrew Stone; Marc Strassman; Rabbi H. Norman Strickman, Ph.D.; Martina Swart; Alexandre Tannous; members of the Taos Minyan; Donna Thomson; Robert Weisz, Ph.D.; and Rabbi Michael Ziegler. I wish to express special appreciation to the dedicated readers who reviewed and commented on all or nearly all of the chapters. Despite their best efforts, I am certain that errors have crept into the book, and those errors are entirely my responsibility. Finally, I would like to offer my gratitude for an especially timely grant from the Aurora Foundation.

BIBLICAL ABBREVIATIONS

Amos	Amos	Judg.	Judges
I Chron.	I Chronicles	I Kings	I Kings
2 Chron.	2 Chronicles	2 Kings	2 Kings
Dan.	Daniel	Lam.	Lamentations
Deut.	Deuteronomy	Lev.	Leviticus
Eccles.	Ecclesiastes	Mal.	Malachi
Esther	Esther	Mic.	Micah
Exod.	Exodus	Nah.	Nahum
Ezek.	Ezekiel	Neh.	Nehemiah
Ezra	Ezra	Num.	Numbers
Gen.	Genesis	Obad.	Obadiah
Hab.	Habakkuk	Prov.	Proverbs
Hag.	Haggai	Ps. (pl. Pss.)	Psalms
Hosea	Hosea	Ruth	Ruth
Isa.	Isaiah	I Sam.	I Samuel
Jer.	Jeremiah	2 Sam.	2 Samuel
Job	Job	Song of Songs	Song of Songs
Joel	Joel		
Jon.	Jonah	Zech.	Zechariah
Josh.	Joshua	Zeph.	Zephaniah

Books of the Hebrew Bible

Names, Abbreviations, and Versification

Names of the books of the Hebrew Bible and their standard abbreviations appear on page xii. The versification of the biblical text may vary between Jewish translations of the Hebrew Bible and Christian translations as, for example, the King James Version. In this book I use only Jewish translations of the Hebrew Bible, my primary references being works by the Jewish Publication Society, Judaica Press, and ArtScroll/Mesorah Publications. Please refer to the appendix for the publication details of these sources. The appendix also contains lists of post-biblical writings from both rabbinic and nonrabbinic sources, brief sketches of some of the most important contributors to the field, and a bibliography representing more than 2,000 years of creative interaction with the Hebrew Bible.

Prologue

A Hebrew Prophet in Babylonia and a DMT Volunteer in New Mexico

In mid-sixth-century BCE* Babylonia,† the Hebrew prophet Ezekiel experienced a vision that came upon him while he stood by the river's shore. Ezekiel was among the exiles from Judea, the Southern Kingdom of ancient Israel. He and his comrades were beginning a seventy-year sojourn in their conquerors' homeland after their armies destroyed the First (or Solomon's) Temple and the rest of Jerusalem in 597 BCE. We know nothing about Ezekiel before his prophetic mission, a mission he carried out with relentless passion. He both raged against his people for their role in Jerusalem's downfall as well as offered hope for a future redemption. The Book of Ezekiel begins with this vision:

> *A stormy wind was coming from the north, a great cloud with flashing fire and a brilliance surrounding it . . . and from its midst, a*

---

*BCE means "before the common era" and is the nondenominational equivalent of BC, or "before Christ." Similarly, CE means "common era" and is used instead of AD, which means "*anno Domini,*" or "in the year of the Lord."

†Babylonia is present-day Iraq.

semblance of four Chayot.* . . . And as for the appearance of the Chayot, their appearance was like fiery coals, burning like the appearance of torches. . . . There was a brilliance to the fire, and from the fire went forth lightning. . . . Then I heard the sound of their wings like the sound of great waters . . . the sound of the words like the sound of a company. . . . I fell upon my face and I heard a voice speaking, . . . "Son of man, stand on your feet and I will speak to you." (Ezek. 1:1–2:1)†

Nearly 2,500 years later and halfway around the world, I injected Leo,‡ a human research volunteer, with the powerful psychedelic drug dimethyltryptamine, or DMT. The setting was the General Clinical Research Center of the University of New Mexico Hospital in Albuquerque in what was the first new American human research with psychedelic drugs in a generation. I have previously written about this study in *DMT: The Spirit Molecule*.[1] Hundreds of plants produce DMT. So does the human body. Thus it is an *endogenous* psychedelic substance, one that the body makes on its own. My long-standing interest in the biology of spiritual experience had finally culminated in this project studying the effects of DMT, effects I speculated might resemble naturally occurring spiritual states of consciousness.

Leo was a psychologist in his mid-thirties and reported the following to us after the drug effects had worn off:

Large crystalline prisms appeared, a wild display of lights shooting off into all directions. . . . My body felt cool and light. Was I about to faint? . . . My mind was completely full of some sort of sound, like the aftereffects of a large ringing bell. . . . Out of the raging

---

*Hebrew for "living things."
†The convention "Book X:Y" refers to a particular book, chapter, and verse in the Hebrew Bible (the "Old Testament"). Here the notation indicates Ezekiel, chapter 1, verse 1, to chapter 2, verse 1.
‡This volunteer's pseudonym is "Saul" in *DMT: The Spirit Molecule*, but because Saul is also the name of a biblical figure, I changed his pseudonym to "Leo."

colossal waterfall of flaming color expanding into my visual field, the roaring silence, and an unspeakable joy, they stepped, or rather, emerged. Welcoming, curious, they almost sang, . . . "Now do you see? Now do you see?" (DMT, 344)*

The similarities between the two men's descriptions are striking: a "rush" of wind or physical lightness, a mind-filling auditory experience, feelings so powerful as to cause a falling down or near faint, and the appearance of creatures emerging out of an amorphous, intensely dynamic background of preternaturally bright, flashing, and flaming colors. Both sets of beings' spoken voices also possess a noteworthy authority and power.

How are we to understand these impressive similarities? What do they mean? What are their implications, both theoretical and practical? Do Ezekiel's and Leo's visions consist of the same "stuff"? If so, what is it? And if not, how do they differ? And most important, what do their visions mean? What can we learn about ourselves and about the natural, social, and spiritual worlds from their experiences?

In formulating a set of answers to these and many other related questions in *DMT and the Soul of Prophecy*, I will present a new scientific model for spiritual experience that bridges the Hebrew Bible and contemporary psychiatry. This model is *theoneurology*, and it uses for a bridge a modern reinterpretation of medieval Jewish metaphysics. A remarkable collection of medieval authors used this metaphysical system to explain Hebrew Bible prophecy—the paradigmatic spiritual experience of their time—taking into account both the science and theology of their day. It is a model that explains how God affects the world through the natural laws of science. As interest in the biology of spirituality continues to grow and new research findings in the field emerge, reexamining the medieval Jewish philosophers' approach to spirituality seems especially timely because of its synthesis of scientific and Western religious sensibilities.

---

*(DMT, pg.) refers to my book DMT: The Spirit Molecule, followed by the page number on which these excerpts appear.

Theoneurology provides a counterpoint to the present research model of *neurotheology,* which proposes that the brain *generates* spiritual experience.[2] In contrast, the theoneurological approach asserts instead that the brain is the *agent through which* God communicates with humans. This new model incorporates the findings of contemporary brain science while providing a more expansive understanding of the organizing principles for which those objective data provide evidence. Integrating theological notions into a biomedical model of spiritual experience also may provide meaning for such experiences beyond their solely adaptive biological or social consequences.

The striking similarities that I will demonstrate between the prophetic and DMT states suggest common underlying mechanisms, both biological and metaphysical. As these shared features and theoretical mechanisms become clearer, I begin to build a case for a contemporary renaissance of prophetic experience. This project proposes combining the enduring teachings of the Hebrew Bible with the powerful consciousness-altering effects of the psychedelic drugs.

ORGANIZATION OF THIS BOOK

In Part I, I review my DMT research: its scientific and cultural contexts, what led me to design the study and how I performed it, its results, the problems those results posed for my initial hypotheses, and how I began to search for additional models to explain those findings. Concluding that DMT administration led to an awareness of what we currently call spiritual levels of existence, I decided to seek answers using spiritual models, taking my search outside of conventional scientific ones. I then describe how I came to the Hebrew Bible's model of prophecy as a way to understand the DMT effect in ways not possible within Buddhism or Latin American shamanism. Because I know so much more about Buddhism, I emphasize its strengths and weaknesses more than those of Latin American shamanism in this and subsequent parts of the book.

Part II introduces the structure and content of the Hebrew Bible and emphasizes its notions of God and of prophecy. Here I recruit the assistance of the medieval Jewish philosophers and introduce the reader to their metaphysical models.

Part III makes up the bulk of this project. In it I carefully compare and contrast the DMT and prophetic states, using my bedside notes of volunteers' reports of their DMT sessions and the record of prophetic experiences in the Hebrew Bible. I show that while the phenomenology of the two states is extraordinarily similar, major differences appear with respect to the information each state contains. The prophetic message is much richer and more highly articulated, especially in the case of the canonical prophets.

I then describe that prophetic message through which we learn certain things about God and our relationship with the spiritual world. The Hebrew Bible also teaches guidelines for how to relate to each other and the natural world, and introduces us to the enigmatic notions of the "end of days," "world to come," and "messiah." In this section I also discuss the concept of false prophecy, one that is extraordinarily relevant to the thesis of this book. That is, how do we know if our or others' experiences are "true" or "false," deluded or insightful, useful or detrimental?

Part IV addresses mechanisms of action; that is, explanations for how the DMT and prophetic states either resemble each other or do not. I propose that those resemblances and disparities reflect shared or disparate biological as well as metaphysical processes underlying both states. In keeping with the theoneurological emphasis in this book, I focus primarily on metaphysical models for prophecy and then apply them to the DMT experience.

Part V begins with the question of whether prophecy, as the Hebrew Bible understands it, still exists. Critiquing the rabbinic notion of "the end of prophecy" using our theoneurological model, I suggest how prophecy may or may not be our birthright. If it is our birthright, then certain suggestions for future studies and practices logically follow from our knowledge of the relevant metaphysical and biological mechanisms. If prophecy no longer exists, this does not prevent our working on becoming more qualified so as to increase the likelihood of its occurrence in the future.

PART I

From Psychedelic Drugs to the Hebrew Bible

1 Setting the Stage

What is prophecy? And what are the psychedelic drugs? In this introductory chapter, I will lay the groundwork for the material that follows, ideas and information that will lead us on a journey taking in a vast religious, intellectual, and scientific landscape.

PROPHECY

The Hebrew Bible, or the "Old Testament," considers prophecy to be the highest spiritual experience humans may attain. In the prophetic state one communicates with God or God's angels, hears voices, sees visions, feels extraordinary emotions and physical sensations, and receives novel and valuable insights of a personal or collective nature. This definition of prophecy is much broader than the conventional one of foretelling or predicting. Prediction may occur in prophecy, but it doesn't always or even frequently occur, and when it does occur, its accuracy often is uncertain. And one may accurately predict without having recourse to prophecy.

The Hebrew Bible is a prophetic text. It recounts innumerable prophetic episodes in dozens of biblical figures. Those who conveyed its legal, poetic, and wisdom content received this information while in a state of prophecy. Even the text's historical narratives, according to some, required a prophet to accurately record them. And those who redacted the text, the ancient sages of Israel, partook of prophecy-like states on a regular basis. The Hebrew Bible emerged from the mind of prophecy and therefore is a prophetic text.

While the phenomenological characteristics of prophecy, including its visions and voices, are extraordinarily compelling, they do not explain why the Hebrew Bible has exerted such an enduring and pervasive influence on civilization. Rather, the prophetic message is responsible. This message derives from God and serves God's purposes, some of which we understand and some we don't.

Prophecy, or direct communication with God, began with the first humans, Adam and Eve, and a particular form of prophecy, what is called canonical prophecy, flourished during the monarchical era of Israel. This period began in the ancient Kingdom of Israel in the mid-eleventh century BCE, a time and place in which the canonical prophets found worthy targets for their ethical and moral teachings in the corrupt royalty and in general society. These figures left behind books bearing their names: Isaiah, Ezekiel, Jeremiah, and others. According to the rabbinical authorities of the early common era, prophecy "ended" in the mid-fifth century BCE—the early period of the Second Temple in Jerusalem. These clerical leaders made this declaration for a variety of reasons, theological and political. However, prophecy appears to have continued after its supposed end, albeit no longer within the mainstream of normative Judaism.

PSYCHEDELIC DRUGS

Since Ezekiel's time, medical science has also ventured into the visionary realms, in this case through the effects of the psychedelic drugs. These unique mind-altering compounds, of which LSD* is the prototype, affect all facets of human consciousness in a relatively consistent manner. They modify perception, mood, thought processes, physical sensations, and will in ways that strikingly parallel stories we encounter when reading the Hebrew Bible. One perceives visions and voices,

---

*Lysergic acid diethylamide

experiences extreme emotions and somatic sensations, and attains new insights into personal, social, and spiritual issues.

To date, however, the aesthetic contents of the Western psychedelic drug experience have had a much greater impact on our culture than the message conveyed. We see abundant evidence of this influence in "psychedelic" art, music, and technology. As yet, however, no cogent Western model of "psychedelic" spirituality has emerged, particularly one incorporating traditional Western religious beliefs and practices.

As with prophecy, the Western psychedelic drug experience burst into the larger culture and affected it in a highly public manner. These substances were the object of a tremendous amount of medical-psychiatric research in the 1950s and 1960s. In addition, millions of young people experienced their effects in non-research settings, settings that also were associated with major social upheaval, including anti-government protests against the wars in Southeast Asia and reexamination of fundamental sexual mores. Psychedelic drugs also seem to have disappeared after declarations of their banishment by the authorities, in this case the political and scientific rather than the clerical authorities, and legitimate human studies ended with the enactment of legal restrictions in the 1960s and 1970s. And in the final analogy to prophecy, the use of psychedelic drugs continued playing an important role in our culture even after this proclamation, albeit outside the mainstream scientific and public arena. That situation is now changing with the resumption of medical research with these drugs. The psychedelic drug research renaissance now provides us with an opportunity to revisit critical elements related to both psychedelic drugs and the religious experience.

THE THEONEUROLOGICAL MODEL
AND ITS IMPLICATIONS

In this book I present a new scientific model that joins the prophetic and psychedelic experiences by proposing that their shared phenomenology reflects shared mechanisms. These mechanisms of action—how experiences take place, or "how they work"—are biological *and* spiritual. Another way of phrasing this is that the mechanisms are physical and metaphysical. The objective data are manifestations of currently invisible metaphysical processes whose presence we infer from the observable phenomena.

I propose that the common biological denominator is the presence of elevated levels of DMT in the brains of individuals in both states. In prophecy, I hypothesize that DMT levels rise endogenously, and this mediates certain features of the experience. In my New Mexico research subjects, brain levels of DMT rose because I injected into their bloodstream large doses of the pure compound.

The common spiritual or metaphysical mechanisms involve what the medieval Jewish philosophers refer to as the "faculties" of the mind. One of these is the *imaginative* faculty, in which emerge the phenomenological contents—visions, voices, emotions, and so forth—of the experience. This is prophecy's form, or "body." The other is the *rational* faculty, whereby one interprets and communicates the information those contents convey. This message is prophecy's essential nature, its "soul."

This model also adds to the discussion the involvement of God, who is the ultimate arbiter of whether someone attains prophecy. While one may possess through birth or training high-functioning rational and imaginative faculties, these only determine one's qualifications for prophecy, not its attainment. This model is theocentric inasmuch as God is the initiating and organizing principle, rather than brain anatomy and function assuming this role. It proposes that changes in brain function are the means by which God communicates with us, rather than proposing that changes in brain function create the impression of such communication. It is a top-down rather than a bottom-up model.

There are practical implications of a theoneurological understanding of prophecy. These emerge from speculating how the prophetic and DMT states' resemblance to each other reflects similar mechanisms of action.

1. If the prophetic state possesses "psychedelic" features, the psychedelic drug experience may help facilitate one's understanding of the prophetic text. One's mind begins resembling that out of which the prophetic text, the Hebrew Bible, emerged. That mind is the mind of prophecy.

2. The Hebrew Bible's prophetic tradition may help understand and guide the contemporary Western psychedelic drug experience. Knowledge of the Hebrew Bible's message, one consisting of specific terms, concepts, and narratives, may provide a novel, while at the same time traditional, Western religious cognitive matrix within which to understand and apply the spiritual properties of the psychedelic experience.*

WHY A NEW MODEL?

I began my psychedelic drug research in 1990 hypothesizing that DMT administration would occasion states of consciousness with spiritual characteristics. If the effects of exogenous DMT replicated features of non-drug-induced spiritual experience, this would be consistent with a role for elevated endogenous DMT in these non-drug states. While contemporary psychopharmacological research models informed the design of my project, I also brought to it a specific spiritual orientation that had grown out of decades of lay Zen Buddhist study and practice. However, at the end of my research in 1995, I concluded that neither psychopharmacology nor Buddhism provided an adequate model for my volunteers' experiences.

Two features of the DMT state were responsible for this lack. One was the overwhelming and unshakeable sense of the reality of those experiences. Taking this conviction at face value is inconsistent with

---

*The psychedelic experience, with its unique constellation of effects, may result from non-drug methods. These include drumming, chanting, prolonged hyperventilation, fasting, sleep deprivation, and others. However, the psychedelic drugs are the most reliable means of inducing this syndrome. How any of these non-drug methods affect endogenous psychedelic chemistry is a critical research question.

Buddhism's and brain sciences' belief that their nature is wholly illusory, or hallucinatory. The other was the highly interactive and relational quality of volunteers' experiences. This contrasted with the unitive nature of Zen enlightenment, in which one's individuality drops away in a concept-free and imageless state. I thus began searching for alternative scientific and religious models, and this search ultimately led me to the Hebrew Bible and its notion of prophecy.

Twenty years ago, if someone had suggested turning to the Hebrew Bible for a model for the DMT experience, I would have been highly skeptical. Decades had passed since I had engaged with the Jewish tradition. More relevant, I had never considered the Hebrew Bible a source of insight into spiritual states in general, and certainly not into the psychedelic drug effect in particular. However, in seeking the best possible interpretation and application of my findings, the words of two of my original DMT mentors continually pushed me toward whatever direction seemed most promising.

Daniel X. Freedman, M.D., one of the fathers of modern American psychiatry, questioned the relevance of psychedelic drug research using the refrain "If so, so what?"[1] What does the psychedelic experience mean? Why should these drugs' effects concern us? What are they good for? The other mentor was Willis Harman, Ph.D., an engineer by training as well as a seminal figure in the use of LSD for enhancing creativity.[2] Indirectly providing some exegesis* to Dr. Freedman's cryptic mantra, he challenged me one day on a fateful walk along the central California coast by asserting: "At the very least, we must enlarge the discussion about psychedelics." While neither suggested looking at Hebrew Bible prophecy to help explicate the psychedelic drug experience,† remembering their challenging words of encouragement inspired me to embark on and persist in this project.

---

*Interpretation of text, especially biblical.

†I later learned that Dr. Freedman did consider religion a more useful discipline than psychiatry in understanding and utilizing these drugs' effects.[3]

WHAT THIS BOOK
DOES NOT PROPOSE

I wish to forestall several misunderstandings that might arise from what you have so far read. First, I am not claiming that Hebrew Bible figures experienced prophecy by ingesting psychedelic plants or drugs. There is little, if any, evidence in the text for this idea. More important, the presence of endogenous psychedelics such as DMT, ones that the body makes on its own, militates against the necessity of demonstrating the use of exogenous substances.

Second, I am not a DMT zealot, declaring that "endogenous DMT alone causes prophecy." I have chosen DMT as my model compound because we know more about its effects and biological mechanisms than about any other endogenous psychedelic substance. The state it occasions does share many features with the prophetic one. However, as we will see, the fit is not perfect with respect to the two states' phenomenology, and is rather poor when it comes to their message content. In addition, no data yet exist regarding endogenous DMT activity in non-drug-induced altered mental states such as dreams, near-death, or any type of spiritual experience, let alone prophecy. Finally, DMT, or any other endogenous or exogenous agent, does not "cause" prophecy. It may be one of the elements involved in God communicating with humans but is no more the cause of prophecy than the television set is the "cause" of the content of a television show. That content originates outside of the physical device and is thus a higher-order phenomenon.

THE RISKS AND BENEFITS OF
AMATEUR HEBREW BIBLE SCHOLARSHIP

This book lacks the imprimatur that would attach to it if I possessed formal academic or theological training in biblical studies. Even with such training, the vastness of the field of prophecy would have precluded my attaining anywhere near the mastery of the literature that

I had obtained regarding the psychedelic drugs when I wrote *DMT: The Spirit Molecule*. However, I have dedicated myself to an ever-deepening, mostly self-directed, course of Hebrew Bible study since 1998, and I believe I have learned enough to begin sharing some of my findings and conclusions.

My status as a Hebrew Bible studies amateur, pursuing the field for love and not for money or institutional fealty, provides certain advantages that were unavailable while writing *DMT: The Spirit Molecule*. Here, I may speculate more freely, because I am not adhering to any particular institution's or organization's credo. While I attempted to distinguish between fact and conjecture in *DMT: The Spirit Molecule*, my scientific credentials and affiliations led a significant number of readers to assume the factual nature of many speculative ideas.* I hope my unaffiliated and non-credentialed status makes this less likely here.

THE CONTROVERSIAL
NATURE OF THIS PROJECT

DMT and the Soul of Prophecy represents a departure from the clinical and research communities I have inhabited for many years. It also enters into a field—biblical studies—that receives little consideration and not a little antagonism from scientific and medical colleagues. Therefore, it is with some anxiety that I await responses from the scientific and medical communities outside of whose objective rigor I now stand some distance and from the biblically oriented spiritual communities, from whom I have had no formal training and with whom I have neither affiliation nor allegiance. Paradoxically, straddling both worlds has made it easier for me to attempt to resolve apparent conflicts between theology and science. It has made it easier

---

*For example, my speculations that elevations of endogenous DMT occur in dreams and near-death states, that DMT and the pineal gland play a role in attaining "personhood" during fetal development, and others.

to emphasize and build upon commonalities in methods, observations, theories, and goals relevant to both.

Nevertheless, the model I present is bound to raise objections from both scientific and religious readers. A theoneurological model requires that we take into account the God of the Hebrew Bible, a God who uses the brain as an agent rather than a God produced as an epiphenomenon of brain physiology. The God of the Hebrew Bible is externally existent and essentially incomprehensible, possesses certain expectations for our beliefs and behaviors, and through the operation of cause and effect metes out consequences for how we live our lives. This model at first blush may be unpalatable to a secular scientific audience. However, it may at the same time ease the dissonance that exists in the minds of those scientifically inclined individuals whose religious beliefs and practices play an important role in their personal lives. As such it may provide a greater integration of those beliefs into their scientific pursuits.

Those with a primarily faith-based approach to the Hebrew Bible may chafe at what they consider a medicalization of a revered spiritual tradition. Perhaps they will see my hypotheses interpreting away any validity to prophecy, inaccurately concluding that my model proposes: "It's just your brain on DMT." This is certainly not my intention, and in fact, my intention is nearly the opposite. I am attempting to explicate how God and humans relate to each other in the prophetic state at the interface of matter and spirit using the tools of metaphysics. This is far from saying that God is a phantom of our minds. Rather, God constituted our mind-brain complex so that we can communicate with the spiritual world, and DMT may be part of how that communication takes place. Therefore, I hope that those of a religious bent will find their faith even stronger as a result of seriously considering the ideas in this book.

I also anticipate resistance from some in the psychedelic subculture because of my emphasis on a Western religious tradition, which most have spurned. From its inception, the psychedelic community has struggled to balance hedonism with idealism, and it appears to me that over the last several decades, hedonism has come out ahead as the primary motivation to use these compounds. Among those taking psychedelic drugs for their spiritual properties, most are partial to Eastern religious or Latin American shamanic models rather than Western biblical ones. There is strong resistance to the suggestion that the Hebrew Bible, particularly with its concept of God, might aid in the development of a cogent psychedelic spirituality. I believe that here, too, just the opposite is the case, and hope to use my extensive background in the psychedelic research field to buttress this notion.

FOR WHOM THIS BOOK IS INTENDED

The more overtly spiritual considerations I present in *DMT and the Soul of Prophecy* may lose some prospective readers who found *DMT: The Spirit Molecule* of interest. However, I wish to broaden this book's appeal to additional readers. For example, prophecy attracts many people due to its relationship with prediction, particularly within the context of apocalyptic, messianic, or utopian "end of times" forecasting. Learning about the original broader meaning of prophecy and its deeper spiritual implications will enlarge these readers' appreciation of prophecy as more than simply divination or prognostication.

The burgeoning field of neurotheology, and of scientific study of spirituality in general, is making great strides in understanding biological concomitants of religious experience. At the same time, there exists a clear gap between the physiology and the moral and ethical messages these states contain. Evolutionary biology may provide one answer to "If so, so what?" That answer is: "Religious experience is good for you." Here, the theoneurological model offers scientifically minded readers additional conceptual tools, ones that possess a higher level of abstraction than is currently the case. It does this by answering, "Prophecy is how God communicates with humans." At the same time, it is absolutely consistent with the goals, methods, and findings of science.

I am also addressing this book to those whose non-drug-induced visionary experiences have inspired them to find a suitable religious system outside of the Western mainstream. I receive many e-mails from such individuals, who describe experiencing DMT-like states without ever partaking of the drug, most commonly during meditation or dreamlike states at the borderlands of wakefulness. Latin American shamanic and Eastern religious models address these types of altered states directly, which is part of their appeal. The Hebrew Bible and its concept of prophecy may provide a useful alternative framework by which to understand these phenomena.

While the psychedelic community may object to the God- and Hebrew Bible–oriented perspective of this book, they nevertheless are one of my target audiences. This group possesses a relatively inchoate and inarticulate view of these drugs' spiritual potential. Therefore, I wish to demonstrate to such prospective readers how the notion of Hebrew Bible prophecy, with its familiar vocabulary, concepts, and narratives, provides a viable, culturally and psychologically compatible alternative to Latin American shamanic and Eastern religious systems.

New readers forming potentially the largest group are those interested in my discussion of Hebrew Bible prophecy in the context of a novel science-based theory of spirituality. Some new Jewish, Christian, and Muslim readers may already study and revere the text.* They especially may appreciate the extensive references to their sacred text and the discussion of how a theoneurological model sheds new light on prophetic experience. Others may wish to approach the material from the perspective of atheism, agnosticism, or simply curiosity about a venerable religious experience that has exerted millennia of profound influence throughout the world.

Finally, I wish to introduce all my readers to the writings of the

---

*My exclusive attention to Hebrew Bible prophecy and its subsequent explication by Jewish thinkers is not a sign of disrespect for or disinterest in Islamic and Christian prophecy. It has taken me many years to begin understanding just the Hebrew Bible and Jewish views of prophecy. Perhaps I will address Islamic and Christian prophecy in future editions.

medieval Jewish philosophers. This remarkable cadre of thinkers has shown me how to begin reconciling science and faith in a manner I previously had been completely ignorant of. If one simply gains an appreciation of these outstanding individuals by virtue of reading this book, I will have accomplished a worthy goal.

Sigmund Freud struggled to understand the Jewish religion and, in particular, the mind of Moses, its greatest prophet. The following excerpt from his *Moses and Monotheism* resonated with my own anxieties about writing *DMT and the Soul of Prophecy:*

> At this point I expect to hear the reproach . . . that I have built up this edifice of conjectures with too great a certainty, for which no adequate grounds are to be found in the material itself. I think this reproach would be unjustified. I've already stressed the element of doubt in the introduction, put a query in front of the brackets, so to speak, and can therefore save myself the trouble of repeating it at each point inside the brackets.[4]

2 Defining Our Terms

Having already introduced words such as *consciousness, spiritual, religion,* and so forth, I believe it is important at this early juncture to address their definitions because many discussions of spiritual experiences quickly lose focus due to disagreements regarding what we are in fact talking about. To assist me in this task, I reached for my dictionary early in this project.*

CONSCIOUSNESS

General Definition

Consciousness is the aggregate of the contents and processes of mental function, such as perception, mood, and thinking. It also refers to that which is aware of some object, impression, state, or influence. Thus *awareness* is a common synonym for *consciousness.* The dictionary distinguishes between the two terms by suggesting that *awareness* attends to something outside of oneself, whereas *consciousness* attends to the inner working of one's own mind.

---

*The dictionary upon which I primarily rely is the *Funk & Wagnalls Standard Dictionary of the English Language, International Edition* (New York: Funk & Wagnalls, 1963). Because the meanings of words may change over time, I also have referred to the *Random House Webster's Unabridged Dictionary,* 2nd ed. (New York: Random House Reference, 2005) and *The American Heritage Dictionary of the English Language,* 5th ed. (New York: Houghton Mifflin Harcourt, 2011). It is reassuring to note how minor the differences are among the three dictionaries' definitions, even across the span of forty to fifty years.

Altered States of Consciousness

An altered state of consciousness is a condition in which one or more of the functions or properties of consciousness, such as perception or sense of bodily integrity, differs from those that constitute "normal" consciousness. This baseline reference state is awake and alert, the "normal waking state," and allows us to know where we are, when our experience is taking place, and the difference between our self and someone or something else. Examples of common altered states of consciousness are anesthesia, dreaming sleep, and alcohol intoxication.[1]

SPIRITUAL

The definition for *spiritual* encompasses a somewhat broader spectrum than that of consciousness. *Spiritual* refers to anything, including thoughts, feelings, or images, possessing the highest qualities of the human mind. Related terms are *holy, sacred, religious,* and *pure.* These words allude to the difference between the spiritual and the everyday, bestial, or carnal. *Spiritual* may also refer to things that are incorporeal, immaterial, or invisible. Those with a theological bent would include more specifically the immaterial nature of humans; that is, their soul or spirit. And even more specifically, *spiritual* may concern God, God's spirit or word, or the soul upon which God acts.

RELIGION

The broadest definition of a *religion* is any system of faith, worship, beliefs, or practices that expresses the relationship between the spiritual nature of humans and the spiritual world. This relationship consists of a sense of dependence and responsibility, as well as the feelings, ideas, and practices naturally flowing from those religious beliefs. A particular religion may be a vessel for containing or channeling spiritual thoughts, feelings, imagery, and impulses. However, spirituality can exist outside the boundaries of religious institutions. This latter notion is usually what people mean when they say that they are "spiritual but not religious."

THEOLOGY

Theology is the study of religion whose object is to synthesize a philosophy of religion. In a monotheistic context, it is a set of doctrines concerning God, God's intermediaries, characteristics, and actions.

METAPHYSICS

I like to define *metaphysics* as the "science of the invisible," although this is rather idiosyncratic. A more formal definition is the science of first principles of being and knowledge, or speculative philosophy in the widest sense. When set into a religious context, it shares many features with theology.

SPIRITUAL EXPERIENCES AND THEIR TYPES

Taking into account these definitions of *consciousness, spiritual,* and *religion,* we have the necessary components with which to construct a definition of *spiritual experience.* It is an altered state of consciousness with unique spiritual characteristics. These characteristics include a sense of the state being unusual, rare, and valuable. It consists of images, thoughts, and feelings that one considers spiritual, undeniably distinct from everyday life.[2]

A *religious experience* is a type of spiritual experience occurring within the context of a religion. It partakes of imagery, vocabulary, and concepts consistent with that tradition.

A *mystical experience* is a spiritual experience that possesses certain subjective features. It may occur within or outside of a religious tradition. For the purposes of this book, I specify that it lacks imagery, concepts, and verbal content. In addition, one's sense of self merges, unites, or "becomes one" with something "other." That "other" is a spiritual thing such as God or the spiritual essence of a natural or other phenomenon, like a beautiful landscape or music.

Recognizing the unitive, or merging, characteristics of the mystical experience allows us to consider "non-mystical" spiritual states, what I call *interactive-relational* ones. The characteristics of the interactive-relational type include the maintenance of a sense of self, which allows one to distinguish and interact willfully with the contents of the experience, its images, ideas, and voices.

I make the distinction between *mystical-unitive* and *interactive-relational* types of spiritual states frequently throughout this book because much of contemporary medical research in the field of spirituality takes as its default type the mystical-unitive, rather than the interactive-relational.[3] As will become readily apparent, the prophetic state is interactive and relational, never mystical nor unitive.

Finally, a *near-death experience* is a spiritual experience occurring when one is nearly dead. It may be mystical-unitive, interactive-relational, or both, and it may or may not contain a specific religion's themes.

ETHICS AND MORALITY

In this book, I raise the importance of the practical relevance of spiritual experiences, both prophetic and psychedelic. One way we might address this issue concerns changes in behavior and attitudes, the purview of ethics and morality.

These two terms, *ethics* and *morality,* usually occur together, and I follow this convention to a large extent. Both refer to human character and behavior, especially with respect to principles of right and wrong. While it is difficult to draw a clear line between the two words, *morality* tends toward more personal and spiritual standards, whereas *ethics* refers to a social code of behavior. For example, there is a code of ethics for physicians and attorneys, but not a code of morals. Morals, in this case, would refer to the guidelines for behavior and attitude that the individual attorney or physician would use to regulate his or her decisions at the personal, rather than professional, level. We might consider ethics as an individual or communal application of morality.

3 The Path to DMT

Psychedelic Drugs, Meditation, and the
Pineal Gland

The notion of Hebrew Bible prophecy as a model for the DMT experience, and for the Western psychedelic drug experience in general, started forming in my mind several years after completing my drug studies in the mid-1990s. That research project represented the culmination of a decades-long interest in the biology of spiritual experience that began during my undergraduate training in the late 1960s. In these next two chapters, I trace the impetus for my research; its intellectual, biological, personal, and spiritual backdrops; the data that the project generated; and how those data forced me to search outside my preexisting models for more adequate ones. That search ultimately led to the Hebrew Bible and its notion of prophecy.

ALTERED STATES OF CONSCIOUSNESS: EAST MEETS WEST

During the middle of the twentieth century, two powerful mind-altering technologies burst upon the West. One came from the West itself and the other from Asia. Both provided reliable and widely accessible methods for profoundly altering human consciousness. The Western side of this coin brought forth the psychedelic drugs, especially LSD. The other produced Eastern meditation practices, particularly those of Hinduism and Buddhism.*

Psychedelic Drugs

The term *psychedelic* means "mind-manifesting" or "mind-disclosing." When it qualifies the word *drug,* it refers to a family of chemical compounds that regularly occasion a unique constellation of psychological effects. These effects include seeing visions; hearing voices and other information-bearing sounds; feeling intense emotions, both positive and negative; experiencing unusual thought processes and novel insights; and undergoing changes in the sense of self.

Several other names exist for these substances, examples of which are LSD, mescaline from peyote cactus, psilocybin from "magic" mushrooms, and DMT. The traditional medical-legal term is *hallucinogen,* although this is overly restrictive because these drugs do not routinely cause hallucinations. *Psychotomimetic* (mimicking psychosis) inordinately emphasizes serious psychopathology and ignores these drugs' reinforcing and sought-after qualities. We rarely encounter the term today. The more recent *entheogen,* meaning "generating divinity from within," also is too exclusive for general use because it implies a belief in spirituality that not everyone shares, and it refers to a particular type of experience that not everyone undergoes.

I prefer the term *psychedelic* because it casts the widest possible net for the range of effects these substances elicit. They nearly invariably reveal to the mind previously invisible processes and contents. At the same time, the term subsumes the highly complex and variable responses they bring about, beatific or horrific, insightful or confusing. While *psychedelic* has accumulated a significant amount of cultural baggage from the divisive and chaotic 1960s, it also is the most flexible

---

*In addition, fascination with the newly described near-death experience contemporaneously drew attention to yet another highly altered state of consciousness, albeit one under much less voluntary control.[1]

and inclusive term. For that reason, I have decided to use it, rather than pejorative or overly restrictive ones.*

LSD originated in the modern European pharmaceutical laboratory in the 1940s[2] and was one of the three legs of the scientific tripod upon which scientists erected the edifice of modern biological psychiatry, or human psychopharmacology, the preeminent model for understanding mental function and the treatment of psychiatric disorders. Another leg of this tripod was the nearly simultaneous synthesis of the antipsychotic medication Thorazine (chlorpromazine). The third was the discovery of the presence and LSD-like properties of the neurotransmitter serotonin.†

Eastern Meditation

Ancient East Asian religious traditions were the source of the multitude of meditation techniques that flooded the West at nearly the same time as did the psychedelic drugs. Hinduism and Buddhism had received some Western attention during the early 1900s; however, it was not until the psychedelic drugs had unleashed a massive level of public interest in altered consciousness that Eastern religious meditation practices began assuming their current level of popularity. The Beatles initiated an interest in Transcendental Meditation, a Hindu spiritual practice originating in India, after their "psychedelic" phase, and American West and East Coast academics and countercultural figures also popularized Buddhism, especially Japanese Zen Buddhism.

---

*Other drugs sometimes receive the name *psychedelic* but are not technically members of the "classical" compounds. MDMA ("ecstasy") is a methamphetamine derivative with qualitatively different psychological and pharmacological effects than those of LSD, psilocybin, and DMT. Ketamine and the closely related drug PCP, as well as *Salvia divinorum,* share subjective effects with the psychedelic drugs, but their pharmacology is distinct.

†Neurotransmitters are chemical substances that provide communication among nerve cells and between nerve cells and adjacent tissues, such as muscle or endocrine glands. For an in-depth discussion of these issues, see chapter 1 of *DMT: The Spirit Molecule.*

It did not take long for similarities between descriptions of psychedelic drug effects and those resulting from the practice of meditation to become apparent. For example, here are representative verses of an ancient Buddhist text:

There were banners of precious stones, constantly emitting shining light and producing beautiful sounds. . . . The finest jewels appeared spontaneously, raining inexhaustible quantities of gems and beautiful flowers all over the earth. There were rows of jewel trees, their branches and foliage lustrous and luxuriant.[3]

I found the psychedelic qualities of accounts of meditation such as these intriguing and puzzled over their implications. I began considering how resemblances between the effects of psychedelic drugs and meditation might reflect the action of common underlying biological mechanisms in both states. When the phenomenology of the two sets of subjective experiences resembled each other, one could propose similar alterations in brain activity. This idea contained practical applications as well. Did psychedelic drugs provide a shortcut to success in Buddhist meditation? Did Buddhist meditation represent a non-drug method for entering into psychedelic states?

PERSONAL FACTORS

While I was considering how to bridge psychedelic psychopharmacology and the effects of Buddhist meditation, I decided to learn more about meditation firsthand and explored various options before settling on Zen Buddhism. Up until then, my religious background consisted of a relatively ordinary Jewish upbringing within a Conservative Jewish* household. During the six supplemental hours per week of Jewish

---

*Conservative Judaism is one of the three major sects of contemporary Judaism. It occupies the middle ground between Orthodox traditionalism and Reform liberalism. Newer sects include Reconstructionist and Renewal.

education I received from the age of five to thirteen, we studied the Hebrew language; learned about Jewish history, culture, and festivals; and read from the Hebrew Bible. However, we learned little about God other than His historical involvement with the Jewish people over the millennia. Direct spiritual experience and the methods to attain it were not part of our curriculum. While Hebrew prayers were a large part of the Saturday Sabbath synagogue service, their recitation seemed rote and passionless. After my bar mitzvah at age thirteen, lacking any intellectual, emotional, or spiritual connection with Judaism, I drifted away from it.

In addition to Buddhism's entrance into popular culture, academic courses in Buddhist studies were just beginning to form when I was an undergraduate student. I was fortunate to be attending Stanford University at a time of unprecedented growth in the scholarly study of Buddhism. The stimulus for this growth was government funding for research attempting to explicate the role of Buddhism in the Vietnam conflict. Highly publicized politically disruptive acts, such as self-immolation by protesting Buddhist monks, baffled the U.S. Department of State and the Department of Defense. As a result, money soon began flowing to American universities to establish a Department of Buddhist Studies to help the American government understand this mysterious religion. Nancy Lethcoe, a newly minted Doctor of Philosophy in Buddhist Studies, joined the faculty at Stanford, and I took her class on Indian Buddhism in 1972.

Buddhism intellectually and emotionally stirred me as very few things had before. In addition, it represented a time-tested tradition that integrated and applied highly altered states of consciousness into one's life. To the extent that meditational and psychedelic drug states resembled each other, one could consider Buddhism as a model for how to live a more consistently "psychedelic" everyday life.

I was not alone in this belief. Countless Western men and women have begun Buddhist practice after first using psychedelic drugs.[4] Both psychedelic drugs and meditation elicit states of consciousness that point toward an enlightened state of mind: one in which time, space, and personal identity do not exist; opposites reconcile seamlessly; and death no longer holds any sting.* The memory of and longing for that glimpse of enlightenment pushes and draws them along the Buddhist path, a path seemingly unavailable in their own culture.

After learning Transcendental Meditation and visiting a number of Hindu and Buddhist centers in the United States, I began Buddhist practice within a Zen† order in my early twenties. I quickly found confirmation within that religious community of my ideas about the relationship between Buddhism and psychedelics. Among the dozens of its young members, nearly everyone had his or her first intimation of enlightenment‡ during a psychedelic drug experience, usually with LSD. These monks and laypeople then found in Zen a model for living a spiritual life that was consistent with the insights they had obtained from their psychedelic drug experiences.

The Japanese term for the Zen meditation practice I learned is *shikan taza,* which roughly means "just sitting." It involves directing attention to what is taking place both within one's mind and body as well as in the external world in as continuous and focused a manner as possible. Deceptively simple, but difficult in practice, the sustained and energetic application of this technique is capable of leading to a direct apprehension of the bases of experience, and ultimately, of the nature of phenomenal existence itself. From this basic meditation technique and resulting states of consciousness emerges all of Buddhism.

---

*As I discuss in chapter 5, the interactive and relational psychedelic-like visions resulting from meditation are not Buddhism's final goal. This became clear to me only after some years of study and practice within Zen.

†Zen is a sect of Japanese Buddhism, arriving by way of China more than nine hundred years ago. Chinese Buddhism originated with the influx of Indian teachers five hundred years earlier.

‡This glimpse of enlightenment, or *bodhicitta,* is the most important stage in Buddhist training.[5]

THE PINEAL GLAND
AND CONSCIOUSNESS

After establishing a meditation practice and finding a spiritual community with whom I could study and train, I began accumulating information and formulating ideas within an academic context regarding the relationship between biology and spirituality. In doing so, I took a slightly different approach than scientists at that time.

Academic research into the biology of meditation in the 1960s and 1970s never considered a possible role for endogenous psychedelic substances. Rather, researchers chose to examine less controversial topics, such as changes in brain waves and indicators of stress, including adrenaline metabolism and blood pressure.[6]

Scientists who were examining the relationship between endogenous psychedelic substances and non-drug altered states similarly overlooked those resulting from meditation. Instead, they focused on psychoses, in particular schizophrenia. In both the psychotic and psychedelic drug state, one hears and sees things that others do not, self- and body-image change radically, and thoughts lead to highly unconventional and unshakeable conclusions. Researchers hypothesized that drugs blocking the effects of LSD might similarly block psychotic symptoms, based on the idea that the two syndromes reflected the workings of the same biological processes. In other words, if there were an endogenous LSD-like substance causing psychosis, blocking LSD might block that endogenous substance's psychotomimetic effects. Naturally, DMT dominated researchers' interest because it was the only known endogenous psychedelic whose biological and psychological effects had been characterized at the time.

My approach instead was to consider the possibility that the body synthesized a compound with psychedelic properties that produced highly prized spiritual experiences, rather than highly maladaptive psychotic experiences. And rather than proposing that meditation influenced brain waves or stress hormones that were relatively remote from the immediate subjective state, I wondered whether a hypothetical "spirit molecule" directly occasioned the meditational experiences themselves. In the same vein, it seemed possible that this compound mediated the subjective elements of other nonpsychotic, non-drug-induced altered states such as dream sleep and the effects of fasting and prayer.

Where in the body might this spirit molecule arise? In my search for its origin I was led to the pineal gland by another Stanford mentor, Jim Fadiman. The pineal gland, a tiny organ sitting deep within the recesses of the human brain, has been for millennia an object of great interest to several systems of "esoteric physiology," including Hinduism and Judaism. Even the rationalist Descartes referred to the pineal gland as the "seat of the soul," the conduit between the human and spiritual worlds. Consistent with a role for the pineal gland in consciousness, its location in the brain is ideal for affecting visual and auditory pathways, as well as for releasing secretions into the cerebrospinal fluid that continually bathes the entire brain.* Most intriguing, I learned that the pineal gland contains the precursors and enzymes necessary for the synthesis of endogenous psychedelics such as 5-methoxy-DMT† and DMT.‡

Right after I completed my clinical and research training early in the 1980s, I was not in a position to embark directly on a human psychedelic drug study. Fortunately, at that time we understood very little about melatonin, the most well-known product of the pineal gland. Some research even alluded to it possessing significant psychoactivity. Therefore, I decided to initiate my search for a biological basis of spiritual experience with the pineal gland and launched the most thorough investigation of melatonin's effects in humans to date.

At the end of this two-year project, we discovered relatively modest physiological functions for melatonin, but no psychedelic effects, even at rather high doses. I needed to look elsewhere than melatonin

---

*See chapters 3 and 4 of *DMT: The Spirit Molecule* for an in-depth discussion of the possible role of the pineal gland in consciousness.
†5-methoxy-DMT is a close chemical cousin of DMT, endogenous, and highly psychoactive. I will discuss this compound in chapter 22.
‡We now know that DMT occurs in the mammalian pineal gland.[7]

in my search for an endogenous psychedelic substance. By this time I had established myself as a successful clinical research scientist and also had learned a great deal about previous investigators' findings regarding DMT. It seemed a good time to design and implement a study with this truly psychedelic endogenous compound.

WHAT DMT IS

DMT, or dimethyltryptamine, is the simplest "classical" psychedelic. This family of compounds also includes LSD, psilocybin, and mescaline. While the duration of their effects differs, they all occasion similar subjective effects and share nearly identical pharmacological properties. DMT is a strikingly small and simple molecule. Its molecular weight, the sum of the weights of all its individual atoms, is only slightly greater than that of glucose, or blood sugar. DMT is the product of several biological modifications of dietary tryptophan, the same amino-acid building block with which melatonin and serotonin synthesis begins. While scientists knew of DMT's presence in psychedelic plants as early as the 1940s, it was not until the mid-1950s that we learned that DMT itself was profoundly psychedelic.[8]

DMT is widespread throughout the plant kingdom. Hundreds, if not thousands, of species possess it, a unique abundance of which exist in Latin America. Many indigenous cultures in this region use DMT-containing plants for their psychedelic properties in healing, recreation, hunting, and spiritual practice.[9] The increasingly popular Amazon psychedelic tea *ayahuasca* contains DMT as its visionary ingredient.* DMT also occurs in every mammal that scientists have studied, including humans.[10]

---

*DMT is orally inactive because enzymes in the gut break it down nearly instantly. In ayahuasca there is, in addition to a DMT-containing plant, another plant possessing inhibitors of the gut's destructive enzymes. These inhibitors are called *beta-carbolines*. The beta-carbolines inhibit the function of monoamine oxidases, the enzymes that break down DMT in the stomach, blood, and liver. This combination of plants in ayahuasca provides an orally active DMT formulation.

The discovery of endogenous DMT in humans in the 1960s initiated a wave of provocative research attempting to determine an association between DMT and psychotic illnesses like schizophrenia using the psychotomimetic model. While results were inconclusive before the first wave of human research with psychedelics ended in 1970, they did confirm DMT's psychedelic properties and established that it was physically and psychologically safe when administered to healthy volunteers.

DMT possesses certain unique features among the psychedelics that make it particularly intriguing. One is that it seems essential for normal brain function. I say this because of data indicating that DMT is one of the few compounds for which the brain will exert energy to get into its confines. The *blood-brain barrier* prevents most endogenous and exogenous substances from entering the brain from the bloodstream. However, compounds the brain requires but cannot synthesize on its own receive special treatment, such as glucose for fuel and certain amino acids for protein synthesis. DMT is another such compound.[11] If DMT were necessary for brain function, it would explain this startling finding and suggest a critical role for DMT in the regulation of human consciousness.

More recently, we have learned how mammals synthesize endogenous DMT, and it appears that lung tissue is the major site for its production in rabbits[12] and humans.[13] Researchers have identified the gene responsible for the enzyme that finalizes DMT synthesis. After inserting the human gene into a virus and infecting mammalian cells with that virus, those cells begin producing DMT.[14]

Human research with DMT, and with all other psychedelic drugs, ceased with the enactment of the Controlled Substances Act of 1970 in the United States and comparable laws elsewhere.* While scientists had discovered a highly promising avenue of inquiry, it had yet to attain

---

*Psychedelics reside in the Controlled Substances Act's Schedule I. This category includes drugs that have no known medical use, are highly abusable, and are not safe even under medical supervision.

the level of maturity that comes from unrestricted study of the relevant phenomena. For example, scientists had not yet developed sensitive enough technology to determine whether differences existed in DMT levels between normal and psychotic people. We knew nearly nothing about ayahuasca. And there was no consideration of the possible role of endogenous DMT in spiritual experience.

4 The DMT World

Where Is This?

In this chapter, I will review the DMT research that I performed at the University of New Mexico in the 1990s. I will focus on the subjective effects resulting from administering this endogenous psychedelic molecule to a group of human volunteers, and note those effects that the models I had brought into my studies failed to satisfactorily explain. It was these findings that prompted me to search for an alternative model that led to the Hebrew Bible's notion of prophecy.

THE PROJECT

The DMT experiments took place in the General Clinical Research Center, a federally funded inpatient and outpatient facility of the University of New Mexico Hospital in Albuquerque. Because no human studies had occurred with these drugs in more than twenty years in the United States, the regulatory hurdles were daunting and required two years to overcome. The study itself took place from 1990 to 1995. I received grants from federal, university, and private sources, including the National Institutes of Health and the Scottish Rite Schizophrenia Research Program.

My interest in the biology of spiritual experience was a significant motivation in performing this project. At the same time, I utilized conventional psychopharmacological methods that would help explicate the biological and psychological effects of DMT. Animal research suggested that DMT modified serotonin function in the brain and elsewhere, so I measured in our human subjects multiple serotonin-related physiological variables, such as blood levels of various hormones, blood pressure and heart rate, pupil diameter, and body temperature.

Ours were not typical normal volunteers. They all had previous experience with psychedelic drugs, although not necessarily with DMT. There were several reasons for recruiting this type of research subject. I believed that informed consent was possible only in those who knew from their own experience the nature of psychedelic drug effects. I thought that experienced subjects would be better able to manage adverse psychological effects should they arise. They also would provide more articulate and nuanced descriptions of responses to the drug than would psychedelic-naïve individuals, as well as be able to compare the DMT state with that resulting from other psychedelic drugs. Many of our volunteers had experience with meditation and other spiritual practices and therefore could compare the effects of these mind-altering techniques with those of DMT.

The DMT volunteers were high functioning, healthy, psychologically sophisticated, and well educated. They hailed from the fields of medicine, psychology, media, software design, engineering, civil service, business, and education. In addition to satisfying their curiosity about DMT, altruism played a role in their participation. They believed that psychedelic drugs were potentially useful psychological or spiritual tools (or both) that deserved further research. They wished to contribute to expanding the frontiers of knowledge regarding these drugs as well as the frontiers of consciousness itself.

Recreational users of DMT vaporize and then inhale it. This is what people mean when they refer to "smoking" DMT. This was impractical on our research unit because of the repulsive smell and potential lung problems. Previous human studies had used the intramuscular method of administration. However, the one subject we gave DMT to by this route described its effects as slower and less intense than those he had felt from vaporizing it several years before he volunteered for our project. Because I wanted to replicate as closely as possible the experience of recreational DMT use, I decided to give the drug intravenously (IV). In the handful of subjects who had previously smoked DMT, they confirmed that the IV route elicited a similar time course and level of intensity of effects. During the five years of this research, I administered more than four hundred doses of DMT at varying strengths to nearly five dozen volunteers.

Each research subject received IV DMT while lying on a bed in a room in the research unit while a research nurse and I sat on either side of him or her. Sometimes a family member, friend, or invited guest(s) would join us. I prepared volunteers for DMT's effects during the preceding prolonged screening process, as well as on the morning of the session. I told them that DMT effects would begin very rapidly, within a few heartbeats, peak at two to three minutes, and end within thirty minutes. During the session we would be checking blood pressure regularly and drawing blood from an IV tube that the nurse had previously placed in one of the volunteer's forearm veins. The subject most likely would feel the mind separating from the body, and as a result, might fear that he or she had died. I advised the volunteer to hold on to the thought that this was a drug effect, that there were no known deaths from DMT, and that a resuscitation team was on stand-by for any medical emergencies.

Our method for supervising drug sessions partook of the "just sitting" meditation practice I described in the previous chapter. The nurse and I sat silently, directing attention outward toward the volunteer and the activities in the room, as well as inward toward our own responses to what was taking place in the suite. I chose this approach to provide an atmosphere in which subjects felt relatively unburdened by any expectations other than to have an individual experience and share it with us afterward. At the same time, we were able to respond to whatever needs arose in the session—providing physical and psychological support, dealing with equipment malfunctions, and so on.

In addition to informing our method of supervising sessions,

Buddhist psychological principles also helped me advise volunteers in contending with particular obstacles during their DMT experiences. For example, if someone felt unable to move through the buzzing, swirling display of colors into a deeper level of the experience, I suggested meditation techniques such as shifting attention toward other elements in the visual field.

The "just sitting" method of supervising sessions shared features with Freudian psychoanalytic "evenly-suspended attention." This is a mental technique whereby the therapist attends equally to and attempts to resonate with all aspects of his or her interactions with the patient. At the same time, the therapist is aware of his or her own psychological processes stimulated by this interaction. My own direct experience and study within a psychoanalytic framework, analogous to my firsthand knowledge of Zen Buddhism, helped inform our work in this regard as well. I had previously undertaken years of treatment as a patient in Freudian psychoanalysis and this assisted me in empathizing with, understanding, and responding to the highly regressed condition of our temporarily incapacitated, dependent, and helpless volunteers at the height of the drug effect. My academic training in psychoanalytic psychotherapy also provided valuable skills for this work. Offering brief interpretive comments in response to psychological conflicts emerging in drug sessions often facilitated a more satisfactory outcome for the volunteer.

PHYSIOLOGICAL EFFECTS

DMT's effects on serotonin-related systems were consistent with our hypotheses. We observed rapid and robust increases in blood levels of beta-endorphin, cortisol, prolactin, vasopressin, adrenocorticotrophic hormone (ACTH), and growth hormone.* There was no effect on

---

*Beta-endorphin is functionally similar to opiate narcotics and plays a role in endogenous pain and pleasure mechanisms; cortisol is a stress hormone made by the adrenal glands; prolactin regulates breast milk formation and secretion as well as sexual drive; vasopressin is similar to oxytocin, a hormone with pronounced pro-social and bonding effects; ACTH is a stress hormone that triggers the production of cortisol.

thyroid stimulating hormone, nor, interestingly, on melatonin. Heart rate, blood pressure, pupil diameter, and body temperature also increased after DMT administration.[1] Two volunteers experienced potentially dangerous blood pressure responses, one high and one low, that resolved quickly without intervention and with no lingering aftereffects.

SUBJECTIVE EFFECTS

I assessed the subjective effects of DMT in two ways. First, we developed a pencil-and-paper rating scale that volunteers filled out immediately after their sessions. I drafted a preliminary form of this instrument after interviewing nearly twenty recreational users of DMT before we began the project, to get a sense of what to expect from drug administration. We then used Buddhist psychological and clinical psychiatric principles of mental function to parse responses into several categories, such as perceptual alterations, emotional responses, and changes in thought processes.[2] This rating scale generated numerical scores for subjects' psychological responses to DMT.*

Second, I took detailed bedside notes during every drug session. Because DMT's effects were so short, forty-five minutes or less, I was able to capture every detail from the beginning to the end of volunteers' experiences, as well as from the thirty- to sixty-minute discussions that came on the heels of the acute drug effects. These records constitute about one thousand pages of notes and are the source for the narrative material I used in *DMT: The Spirit Molecule*. They also provide the subjective data I use in this book to compare the DMT and prophetic states.

Below, I will present a general description of the DMT effect. In the chapters that follow in which I compare the prophetic and DMT states, I will provide many examples of specific effects.

---

*This instrument, the Hallucinogen Rating Scale (HRS), demonstrated outstanding sensitivity to various doses of DMT. As further evidence of its utility, additional research groups have used this scale in studies of many other psychoactive drugs. As of 2013, more than forty scientific papers have documented its use.

The "Rush"

After receiving an intravenous injection of a psychedelic dose of DMT,* volunteers felt effects nearly instantly. These effects quickly became so overwhelming as to completely replace previously ongoing subjective experience. Responses to DMT were maximal at two to three minutes. Nearly every subject was unaware of the first blood pressure measurement, two minutes after the injection. This was all the more remarkable because the machine we used was rather noisy and exerted an uncomfortable squeezing of the upper arm. Subjects were usually only dimly aware of the second check at five minutes. The altered state began resolving at eight to ten minutes, and one could begin speaking relatively normally by twenty to thirty minutes. Volunteers felt back to "baseline" consciousness by thirty to forty-five minutes.

An extraordinarily powerful "rush" filled the initial thirty to sixty seconds of the experience, a rapid and intense buildup of internal pressure and a startling sense of acceleration. Visual coherence broke down, usually producing a pixilated quality in the visual field. Intensely vibrating, rapidly morphing geometric designs that exerted tremendous psychic force appeared whether eyes were open or closed. Volunteers experienced unpleasant disorientation if they opened their eyes at this point, trying to make sense of two simultaneous and overlapping but categorically different levels of ongoing experience. We soon required that subjects wear black silk eyeshades during their sessions. This also encouraged them to focus their awareness inward. At the climax of the rush, most volunteers felt a separation of their consciousness from their bodies, and they found themselves occupying an incorporeal disembodied world.

Physical Sensations

There was a sensation of physical lightness as the rush built in intensity. Within a minute, most volunteers felt that their consciousness had left

---

*We used a water-soluble form of the drug, DMT fumarate. Typical psychedelic effects began at a threshold dose of 0.2 mg/kg (milligrams per kilogram) and our high dose was 0.4 mg/kg. As there are approximately 2.2 pounds per kilogram, the maximum dose for a 150-pound, or 70-kg person, was about 28 mg.

their bodies, moving in an upward and outward direction. Additional somatic effects included shakiness, heart palpitations, feeling hot or cold, nausea, or sensing a crushing weight.

Emotions

Nearly all research subjects experienced some degree of psychological anxiety during the rush. How well one managed this initial anxiety usually determined the overall quality of the session. Volunteers who had the most positive responses were those who could "let go" of this anxiety and trust that everything was going to be all right. Those who found it difficult to right themselves if knocked off balance during the first few seconds—and were unable to quickly move through any fear, panic, or disorientation—usually found their sessions unpleasant, perhaps even terrifying. That being said, the vast majority did pass through the rush with emotional equilibrium and then described an extraordinarily ecstatic, blissful state. Not infrequently, however, volunteers reported that the DMT state was relatively free of emotion.

Auditory Effects

During the initial rush, subjects described a "wa-wa" oscillating sound or a crackling, crinkling noise similar to the crumpling of plastic wrap. At other times, the auditory effects were musical, "angelic," or "heavenly." Occasionally volunteers noticed cartoonlike "sproing" or "boing" sounds. While a volunteer may have perceived a spoken voice during later stages of the drug effect, this never happened during the initial rush. Later in the session, the location of the spoken voice was usually, but not always, inside the subject's mind, something the "inner" rather than "outer" ears heard.

Visual Effects

The initial morphing, geometric kaleidoscopic visual responses to DMT usually developed into more recognizable, albeit often fantastic, imagery, such as star fields, planets, architecture, animals, plants, machines, or some combination thereof. The intensity and saturation of the colors, their variegated hues, were far beyond anything they had ever witnessed during normal waking consciousness, dreams, or even in response to other psychedelic drugs. In the majority of cases, the visual contents of the experience morphed into "beings," which I will discuss shortly.

Cognitive Effects

Despite the overwhelming perceptual, physical, and emotional effects of DMT, volunteers reported relatively intact thinking processes. Most felt mentally alert, were aware of their "surroundings" within the altered mental state, and remembered what occurred there in remarkable detail.

Within this cognitive category resides what I refer to as a reality-appraising function. This provided volunteers the ability to assess how "real" the experience felt relative to normal waking and other states of consciousness. This function comprises several elements, including temporal continuity, stable self-image, perceptual solidity, and familiarity. It was striking how often subjects referred to the DMT state as being as real, or even more so, than everyday reality. In addition, they usually distinguished the DMT experience from dreams and other psychedelic drugs' effects. Many opined that it seemed as if DMT allowed them to perceive another world rather than that the drug generated the perception of it.

Volition, Will, and Self-Control

The strength of the DMT experience nearly universally overpowered volunteers. However, once the initial shock subsided, most subjects were able to maintain a sense of self-efficacy in the state. They could decide what to attend to, what to ignore, and how to interact with the contents of their visions.

Beings

More than half of the DMT research subjects perceived what they described as living and sentient "beings" in the DMT state with whom they interacted in various ways.* They were distinct figures possessing shape, color, movement, intelligence, and awareness of the volunteers, frequently expecting them. At other times, subjects did not directly see them, but heard them or felt their presence, or viewed their silhouetted or shadowed forms.

The beings possessed specific features, such as emotion, color, shape, movement, and intelligence. They also elicited particular effects in the volunteers, such as causing them to see images, feel emotions, or conceive thoughts. They were busy, actively working on or doing things, sometimes to the volunteer or else pursuing their own ends. The beings were powerful, often overwhelmingly so. It was their world, they were in charge, and while resistance was futile, it was possible to negotiate with them as well as modify one's reactions to them.

Relational Effects

A category of the DMT effect that I did not especially attend to when analyzing the volunteers' reports before beginning work on this present book is that of "relatedness." This property of the DMT experience pertains to the nature of the interactions between the volunteer and the DMT world, in particular the beings in that world. This element of the drug state only became clear once I had progressed rather far along in my comparison of the phenomenology of prophecy and the DMT effect. At a certain point, I realized that while a tremendous amount of overlap existed between the two sets of altered states, I sensed that they still differed in some essential manner. This difference was in the realm of relatedness. In retrospect, I believe my emphasis on eliciting the unitive-mystical state with DMT contributed to overlooking this important feature.

The beings and the volunteers interacted with each other, engaging in a relationship within all the categories I have just reviewed:

---

*In this and my previous work, I use the term "beings" to describe these objects. While some volunteers referred to them as "aliens," no one saw the typical four-foot-high, bug-eyed, gray-skinned humanoids popular in the "alien contact" literature. I prefer the term "beings" as its generic quality avoids the connotations "alien" may carry.

perceptual, physical, emotional, volitional, and cognitive. However, as my analysis of the prophetic state was maturing, it seemed that a new relational category was important in characterizing both sets of experiences for two reasons. One was that it helped organize disparate solitary phenomena using a higher-order level of abstraction. For example, the single relational property of "healing" subsumed an aggregate of emotional, somatic, and perceptual effects on the volunteer. Individually analyzing each component didn't adequately capture the essential feature of the exchange. Second, there were relational effects that didn't neatly fit into any of the other categories; for example, arguing or guarding.

Direct communication between the volunteer and beings occurred using the spoken word, telepathically mind to mind, or using visual symbols. Communication also occurred indirectly, in which case someone might overhear a conversation between beings in the DMT world about him or her. There were times when difficulties arose in understanding the medium of exchange, nearly always on the part of the volunteer. The intent of communication was most often to impart information to the research subject.

THE MESSAGE AND MEANING OF THE DMT STATE

The consistent experiences of volunteers entering into a seemingly alternate universe, external to themselves, nearly instantly manifest after receiving an injection of DMT and, at least as real as this reality, were undoubtedly profound and compelling. However, beyond its existence and qualities, what were the volunteers learning there? Here they were less able to articulate the nature of the information the DMT state contained than they were able to characterize the state itself; for example, its visual and auditory properties. When discussing this informational content, subjects generally focused on personal issues. When they did describe more universal insights, lessons, or theological, moral, and ethical themes, they used the concepts and vocabulary they possessed regarding spiritual matters. These were usually New Age, Eastern religious, nature based, or scientific.

I was surprised by the relative paucity of information that the DMT volunteers brought back and the seemingly related lack of change resulting from their participation in the study. While several factors contributed to the project's end,* the absence of more profound insights or practical effects in the context of a relatively high-risk experimental setting played important roles.

I have since met with several former volunteers and have modified my conclusions regarding the benefits of participation in the study. Some remarked that their problem-solving abilities had become more creative or that they felt a sense of greater altruism and less fear of death. They all noted that any long-term positive sequelae such as career or lifestyle changes took years to manifest. Perhaps this slow and subtle process was the result of a "ceiling effect" related to volunteers' high level of preexisting psychological health. I intentionally chose stable and successful individuals who had already established a mature relationship with their inner and outer worlds. There may not have been much room to improve on a relatively successful life. In addition, my studies were not psychotherapeutic or spiritually oriented in either concept or execution.

I also wondered how much of this long incubation period resulted from volunteers' and my difficulty recognizing and articulating the nature of the information that ultimately effected those personal changes. These cognitive factors may have influenced how quickly or deeply any benefit the DMT state conferred became evident. If volunteers had possessed a more sophisticated vocabulary and concepts appropriate for the DMT experience, would that have enriched their ability to mine more meaningful information from their sessions? Would these additional tools have made it easier for them to know what to expect, recognize and interact with what they did encounter, and communicate and integrate what they learned once returning to normal waking consciousness?

---

*See chapters 17–20 of *DMT: The Spirit Molecule*.

DMT AND ENLIGHTENMENT

I had hypothesized that if volunteers received a large enough dose of DMT, they would undergo an enlightenment-like state, in which they totally identified and merged with the undiluted essence of reality. In this condition there would be no form, feelings, concepts, sense of self, images, or physical sensations. However, those types of experiences were extraordinarily rare. Only one, perhaps two, volunteers had what we might call a "typical" enlightenment experience.*

The scarcity of enlightenment-like mystical-unitive states and the abundance of interactive-relational effects were major sources of perplexity for me. When I began my studies, I believed that Buddhism was going to provide an ideal model for the highest state of consciousness one might attain on DMT. I had proposed that DMT's effects on brain chemistry were similar to those occurring during the Zen enlightenment experience. When faced with the facts of my volunteers' reports being so different than those I expected, I felt my theoretical framework begin to totter.

WHERE IS THIS?

Soon after beginning the DMT project, I found that my preconceptions regarding drug effects impacted volunteers' comfort in sharing with me what took place during their sessions. Implicit in all of my models—psychopharmacology, Zen Buddhism, and psychoanalytic psychology—was the belief in the essential unreality of the DMT experience. It was "something else"; for example, brain chemistry changes, illusory and distracting brain-mind noise on the way toward the ultimate goal of enlightenment, or symbolic representations of unconscious wishes and conflicts. Any such approach dismissed one of the most significant features of volunteers' sessions: the DMT world's sense of reality.

Research subjects were already struggling with coming to terms with how shockingly real their experiences felt and how bizarre and

---

*Sean and Elena, discussed in chapter 16 of *DMT: The Spirit Molecule*.

unexpected they were. Any additional skepticism they sensed coming from me, despite my attempts at clinical and Zen neutrality, added to their discomfort. They gradually became more circumspect in describing all that they perceived, thought, and felt on DMT. I was losing access to the full range of the most interesting results of the project because of the constraints my theoretical models were imposing.

In response, I decided to perform a "thought experiment." I took at face value the claim of research subjects that they had indeed entered into a parallel level of reality. Adopting this stance allowed me to regain access to uncensored reports of the world my volunteers had just visited. I could postpone coming to any conclusions regarding the merits of this approach until I completed the studies. Then I could consider more thoroughly how this might possibly be the case and where to look for models that supported such conclusions. That is, if the DMT world were externally objective, what explanatory models were compatible with such a notion?

GENERATING THE DMT WORLD

When approaching the nature of the DMT experience, I began with the basics: DMT is a chemical substance that affects brain chemistry. These effects modify brain function, which in turn occasions the DMT experience. There are two ways to conceive of this "occasioning." One is that the mind-brain complex under the influence of DMT *generates* these experiences. The other is that DMT affects consciousness in such a way that it is now capable of perceiving something real and external to us that it could not perceive before.

The model that supposes that the brain on DMT generates the DMT world is what we might call the "bottom-up" approach and is the province of neurotheology. This discipline addresses how observable changes in brain function are associated with spiritual experience. For example, when a practitioner of Western or Eastern prayer or meditation enters into a state of consciousness he or she describes as spiritual, a researcher scans that person's brain and compares this scan with one taken in that same person during the normal waking state. This approach has allowed scientists to establish correspondences between spiritual experiences and alterations in the activity of particular brain areas.

The neurotheological model proposes that spiritual practices activate an innate response or reflex that manifests as a unique subjective effect. The brain generates these "spiritual" experiences when one of any number of appropriate stimuli activates this reflex. These stimuli may include prayer, fasting, sensory deprivation, or DMT injection. The material brain creates a spiritual experience. This is a bottom-up approach.

Neurotheology's answer to *why* this reflex occurs is consistent with its biological philosophy. Spiritual experiences provide evolutionary advantages to individuals, or to the groups to which they belong, who undergo them. Such states may enhance problem solving or lead to altruism. In this model, the "spiritual" in "spiritual experience" is an overlay, or epiphenomenon, that culture has placed on a biological reflex that provides greater evolutionary fitness.[3]

PERCEIVING THE DMT WORLD

I had immersed myself for five years in listening to DMT volunteers describe how real their drug experiences felt. And with the goal in mind of attaining as thorough accounts as possible when interviewing subjects after their sessions, I entertained the possibility that indeed they had entered into a parallel level of reality. Later, when considering how their reports might actually be describing real external existents, I began building an alternative "top-down" model. This posited that the brain is not the source of spiritual experience, but is instead the organ by which volunteers apprehended* a previously invisible level of existence that DMT-induced changes in brain chemistry made possible.

This model proposes that the catalysts occasioning these states change

---

*I use the terms *apprehend* and *apprehension* in their meaning of "laying hold of, or grasping, mentally." *Apprehending* shares features with *perceiving,* but I like its greater inclusiveness, which takes into account ideas, thoughts, and beliefs, and not simply sense impressions. I am not using *apprehend* in the sense of "expecting with anxious foreboding" or "to arrest or seize in the name of the law," two other common definitions.

brain function, which in turn affects consciousness. Consciousness, as our apprehending faculty, now perceives things it could not before, comparable to what occurs when we use any other technology, such as the microscope or telescope. This then leads to our next question. Where might such previously invisible levels of reality reside outside of our own minds? I began with answers that contemporary science suggested.

Modern physics hypothesizes that at least 90 percent of the universe's mass consists of "dark matter" which neither generates nor reflects light; that is, it is invisible. Other theories speculate that an infinite number of "parallel universes" exist, each taking its origin from the present moment. Perhaps DMT allowed research subjects to perceive these alternate levels of reality using the mind-brain complex's new receiving characteristics. These planes of existence might contain "beings" in the same manner that normal reality does.* The appeal of this notion is that it is scientifically testable. Once we are able to capture images of what exists in the dark matter universe, for example, we would be able to confirm with our own eyes what the DMT subjects saw with their "inner" eyes.

When considering whether this seemed to be a "truer" or "better" model than the neurotheological one, I found myself returning to Dr. Freedman's nagging question: "If so, so what?" What if DMT makes it possible to peer into previously invisible levels of reality? What good comes from knowing this? What truths and benefits do we obtain that are inaccessible through simply using the neurotheological model?

SCIENCE AND RELIGION

The deeper understanding of the natural world that science provides does not necessarily lead to either social or individual benefits. These benefits relate to how we use that new knowledge, applying ethical and moral guidelines. While it is possible that we might learn about

---

*For a more in-depth discussion of these speculations, see chapter 21 of *DMT: The Spirit Molecule.*

new ways to generate energy, travel through space, and other techno-logical advances, these are simply ways in which we'd become smarter, not wiser. Thus, while reflecting on the DMT volunteers' sessions, I decided that even a top-down "scientific" model didn't provide enough guidance regarding the information that the DMT world contained. Nor, for that matter, did it address the even more perplexing question of the ultimate bases and functions of those realms. What other models were available?

The world's great religious traditions also have occupied themselves for thousands of years with invisible worlds that humans perceive dur-ing spiritual experiences. However, unlike science, they have tried to extract meaning from those states of consciousness in order to improve our lives. In particular, they have articulated guidelines regarding opti-mal relationships between the human and invisible worlds, and within the visible world, both natural and social.

There is no doubt that religious institutions for millennia have misused the authority and power that spiritual experiences possess. At the same time, they have developed concepts and vocabularies relevant to these states that science has yet to maturely formulate. Thus, in the spirit of "enlarging the discussion" about psychedelic drug states, I decided to remove one of my feet from the edifice of the natural sci-ences and place it onto that of religion.

Biology, psychology, pharmacology, and physics were no longer my exclusive default modes when it came to explaining the "how?" "why?" "from where?" and other questions my DMT research raised. Rather, I would begin investigating them by using a spiritual mindset in addition to, not instead of, a scientific one. While taking such a position could turn out to be a slippery slope toward dogma and fun-damentalism, I was determined not to use either science or religion to necessarily disprove the other. Instead, I wanted to see how both could contribute to providing the fullest possible explanation of the DMT effect.

5 Candidate Religious Systems

With the widespread non-research use of psychedelic drugs that began in the 1960s, millions of young people have had spiritual experiences that probably would never have otherwise occurred. They encountered previously invisible realities, experienced feelings of tremendous awe and reverence, and attained what appeared to be profound insights into the nature of reality. Mainstream traditional Western religions were unprepared for this flood of spiritual experience taking place outside their confines. Some young psychedelic drug users found a home for the spiritual sensibilities that their psychedelic drug experiences awakened in evangelical or monastic Christianity, or kabbalistic Judaism. Both these streams of Western religions explicitly incorporate altered states of consciousness as important tools for one's spiritual development.

However, many more have followed the 1960s' meme of rejecting the familiar and turned instead to East Asian religions. As the passage of time has similarly afflicted Buddhism with the "familiarity breeds contempt" syndrome, a new generation is turning to Latin American shamanism as a way to understand and integrate the spiritual aspects of the psychedelic drug experience. Because I am much more familiar with Buddhism, especially Zen Buddhism, than shamanism, I will discuss the former to a much greater extent than the latter. Nevertheless, several of the issues I raise with respect to Buddhism also apply to shamanism.

Some also turned to New Age philosophies. However, I have found that these philosophies are a moving target, malleable and ever-changing, and difficult to articulate with anything near the rigor with which one can define Buddhism and Latin American shamanism. Since many New Age philosophies also borrow heavily from Eastern religious and shamanic models, my comments about these latter two disciplines are also applicable to many New Age beliefs and practices.

BUDDHISM AND PSYCHEDELICS

The concepts and images that Buddhism uses to explicate the subjective effects of meditation appeared extraordinarily relevant to the first generation of psychedelic drug-using youth. Overlapping phenomena included the "white light" of spiritual ecstasy; the non-identification of consciousness with the body; the experience of past lives; the awareness of the immediacy and vastness of cause and effect; and insight into the nature, bases, and remedies for suffering. These are compelling facets of the psychedelic drug experience that Buddhism teaches are also accessible using meditation. In addition, Buddhism possesses time-tested and well-characterized teachings and lifestyles that support and develop what one might apprehend during these experiences.

The 1964 publication of *The Psychedelic Experience: A Manual Based on the Tibetan Book of the Dead*[1] suggests how compatible Buddhism's approach to highly altered states of consciousness seemed to be with that of the psychedelic drug state. The *Tibetan Book of the Dead* is a centuries-old Buddhist meditation manual that practitioners use to help guide the consciousness of dying individuals out of the body and through subsequent post-death, non-corporeal states. The Harvard authors of the 1964 book believed that these meditation practices would help in negotiating similar nonmaterial states that one might encounter during psychedelic drug sessions. A more recent incarnation of this model is *Krishna in the Sky with Diamonds*,[2] a psychedelic handbook using the foundational Hindu text, the Bhagavad Gita, for its spiritual moorings. The name of the book alludes to the Beatles' song "Lucy in the Sky with Diamonds," whose initials are LSD.

Different schools of Buddhism take widely divergent stances regarding the "psychedelic-like" phenomena resulting from meditation. I use the term *psychedelic-like* in this context not to describe psychedelic drug use *per se,* but to refer to states of consciousness that share visual, emotional, somatic, and other features with those that such drugs may elicit. Some sects, for example the Tibetan schools, practice "psychedelic" meditation techniques to attain enlightenment, whereas others, such as Zen, do not. To a large extent, the decision to work or dispense with these types of practices seems a matter of personal preference, while the goal of enlightenment remains the same. And all branches of Buddhism agree that the enlightened state possesses no images, forms, concepts, visions, feelings, or other discernible content.

Buddhism and Invisible Worlds

The interpenetration of Buddhism and psychedelic drugs has had a determinative effect on how the West views the reality bases of the drug experience. Buddhist concepts, at least as Asian and Western teachers present them to their Western audiences, are consistent with an essentially psychobiological/Freudian model. All these disciplines posit a generative role for the mind-brain complex in explaining these phenomena. Buddhism's contribution to this notion is to posit that the things one sees and hears during meditation are not "real," but rather products of consciousness, distracting detritus that the mind-brain complex is shedding as it moves toward the formless enlightened state.

Note my qualifying the nature of the type of Buddhism that has made its way into the West and promulgated these beliefs. Nearly all popular Buddhist teachers of Westerners have been careful to purge the common belief among most Asian Buddhists, lay and monastic, that there indeed exist real, free-standing, external alternate levels of reality. To avoid alienating prospective students, they removed the "primitive" and "superstitious" elements of Buddhism that are common in the East.[3] Thus, they could demonstrate the ostensible superiority of

Buddhism relative to the "superstitious" Western popular religions with which their students were more familiar and had rejected. In the less abstract and intellectual forms of Buddhism, however, beings of various types reside in parallel levels of reality and can harm or help someone in this world. The beings and the realms they inhabit are not products of the mind. Rather, they reside in planes of existence that the mind can perceive and interact with in a meditative state.

As a result of this de-emphasis of the objective nature of invisible realities within Buddhism, academics and counter-cultural figures who consciously or unconsciously rejected the notion of externally existent spiritual verities—in particular an invisible God who communicates moral and ethical laws to humanity—found in Buddhism an excellent model for explaining the psychedelic drug effect. Such individuals could claim adherence to Buddhism, while disregarding much of what Buddhism really taught, in order to support their own preexisting biases. They could have their cake and eat it.

These developments led to several outcomes under which we are still laboring. One is the assumption that what people experience during the psychedelic drug state is fundamentally unreal rather than the perception of objective alternate realties. In addition, the formless, content-free, wordless enlightenment experience became the benchmark by which one measured the spiritual experience either within a Western or Eastern religious tradition, or within the context of the psychedelic drug effect. Researchers and practitioners alike now interpreted the "hallucinatory" elements with which one might interact and relate as lower-level way stations toward the "higher" mystical-unitive goal.

Social or Individual Salvation in Buddhism
Social consequences also resulted from young Westerners adopting Buddhism as a way to make sense of and apply psychedelic drug insights. These concern withdrawal from the larger sociocultural sphere. One cannot overestimate the impact of the assassinations of the Kennedys and of Martin Luther King, Jr., and the killing of students at Kent State and Jackson State universities, on the utopian impulse that the psychedelic

drug experience unleashed in the youth culture of the 1960s. The ferocity of the response of the "establishment" to the "counter-culture" caught the latter off-guard, forcing a radical reassessment of the relationship between drug-induced paradise and everyday reality.

Buddhist teachings regarding the constructed, and therefore illusory, nature of that reality comported with similar insights one might attain during a psychedelic drug experience. Such notions provided a solution for many who found themselves lost in this conflict between the ideal and the actual. If reality is not real, then why engage with it? Buddhism's teaching about the constructed nature of the self also provided solace. If there is no self, there is no one to feel anguish and dissonance regarding the gap between inner ideals and the outside world. Therefore, one's distress is meaningless. The best option is to deconstruct the illusory self that is responsible for that distress.

There is of course a very fine line between various types of renunciation, but those subtleties eluded many young adults who fled to Eastern religious systems in response to the suppression of civil disobedience and utopian idealism to which the psychedelic drug experience led many. The result was an embracing of a relatively unengaged approach by young psychedelicists who believed that this was what Buddhism truly advocated. In a relatively guilt-free manner, one could withdraw from a world possessing no substance with which no individual self interacts.

BUDDHISM AND THE DMT EXPERIENCE

Several factors led to extending my search beyond Buddhism for an optimal religious model for the DMT effect. One was the nature of the DMT state itself, the data of volunteers' reports, especially the rarity of classic Buddhist enlightenment experiences. This was the case even in those who practiced Buddhist and other forms of Eastern meditation and were hoping and expecting to attain this state.

Another factor had to do with how Buddhism interpreted the DMT effect. The Zen model I brought to my research posited the fundamental unreality of subjects' experiences. As I previously noted, such an approach interfered with establishing optimal rapport with volunteers when they recounted their sessions to me. In fact, subjects' stance regarding drug effects stood this notion on its head.

What I mean by this is that the highly articulated contents of the DMT experience, its sights, sounds, feelings, and physical sensations, felt more real than the highly articulated contents of everyday reality. Applying the yardstick of a unitive-mystical state was simply inapplicable. It was irrelevant, one that the interactive-relational DMT state simply swept aside. The frame of reference for the DMT volunteers instead changed to that of a parallel level of reality that was at least as fulsome as this one, rather than to a level of reality whose essential nature was empty of any contents.

LATIN AMERICAN SHAMANISM

Shamanism, particularly the variety emerging from Amazonian ayahuasca-using cultures, is gaining currency as another model through which to understand and apply psychedelic drug effects. There is considerable appeal to this movement with respect to DMT because this compound is the visionary ingredient in ayahuasca. My study of and participation in Latin American shamanism are substantially less than my experience with Buddhism. Nevertheless, since 1989 I have participated in numerous shamanic ceremonies, queried many Western and indigenous practitioners of ayahuasca shamanism, and studied the works of and corresponded with published authorities.

One of the most attractive aspects of Latin American shamanism is that it assumes the objective reality of the contents one apprehends in the altered states of consciousness into which their practices, including the use of psychedelic substances, lead. It thus comports with the DMT volunteers' experiences and their interpretation of them better than either a psychobiological or Buddhist model. As a corollary, shamanism has developed many tools for integrating and applying the contents of these states to normal waking consciousness.[4]

However, other factors temper my enthusiasm for the Latin

American shamanic model. For example, the ethics and morality of indigenous Amazonian shamans and their Western students are problematic. Violent, often murderous, competition for power, prestige, money, and sex is commonplace.[5] Western and Eastern religious organizations certainly have their share of money-, weapons-, and sex-related scandals. Nonetheless, one would hope that any new religious model for the psychedelic drug experience would be an advance, not a regression, in these critically important areas.

CAVEATS COMMON TO BUDDHISM AND LATIN AMERICAN SHAMANISM

Both of these non-Western systems have built into them characteristics that indicate their being less than optimal religious models for the spiritual properties of the Western psychedelic drug experience. One is theological. Neither Buddhism nor indigenous shamanism are theocentric, positing God as the creator and sustainer of the natural and spiritual worlds. Buddhism, at least ostensibly, teaches that belief in an external God is not conducive to the inner work that one must engage in to attain the enlightened state. And shamanism emphasizes a multitude of invisible spiritual forces instead of God. I believe that in order for the psychedelic drug experience to exert the greatest possible influence on Western religious sensibilities, it is advantageous to present and interpret that experience in a manner consistent with religious notions already existing within those religions. The bedrock of all three major Western religions is the belief in God. Therefore, maintaining and building upon that belief seems more likely to be accepted than what might result from discarding it and substituting non-monotheistic beliefs.

The situation is more complex in Buddhism, at least for the school in which I trained. Both during ritual and everyday activities, we routinely prayed to the Buddha, *bodhisattvas*,* and deceased teachers

---

*Spiritual beings with particular characteristics such as love, compassion, courage, energy, and so on. One may invoke their aid by prayer and other rituals.

within our lineage. We bowed to their photographs and statues. And our teacher taught that Buddhism is not atheistic after all, but that one must search for references to God in textual allusions. After some years the notion began pressing on me that if I were to bow and pray to something or someone, I preferred that it be the highest and most sublime "thing," rather than a dead human or one of many spiritual beings. And if Buddhism needed to cloak its belief in God, there seemed to be an intellectual dishonesty underlying that decision.

In a similar nontheist manner, shamanism emphasizes evoking and controlling invisible spiritual forces of nature for healing, revenge, attracting a spouse, warfare, seeking lost items, and so forth. I again found myself chafing under a model that prayed to spirits instead of their creator and sustainer: God. While Christian elements such as belief in God and Jesus are making increasing headway into Latin American shamanism, this is a relatively new phenomenon and is not intrinsic to it.[6]

Neither Latin American shamanism nor Buddhism will be able to claim much theological allegiance from Westerners who either believe in, or refuse to disbelieve in, God. Western atheistic students of Buddhism or shamanism may prefer interacting with the illusory nature of reality or a panoply of nature spirits than with their conflict-laden notion of God. However, the seeming lack of a recognizable God in both models is an obstacle to either of them providing a large-scale religious model for the contemporary Western psychedelic drug experience.

There are additional issues related to both Latin American shamanism's and Buddhism's "exoticism." In neither history, culture, nor psychology are contemporary Westerners creatures of the jungle or other non-literate indigenous cultures, at least not within the last several thousand years. Neither is the West an Asian society with its emphasis on communality rather than individuality. I have therefore wondered if the fullness of the spiritual experience a Western practitioner might have within either of these traditions may not be as great as it could be if more of those traditions' elements were congruent with Western personal and cultural backgrounds. In other words, the Buddhist notion of "emptiness" may mean something quite different to someone steeped in generations of Asian culture and religion than to someone born and raised in a Western milieu. Their experience of emptiness would partake of the accumulated experiences of millions of people over millennia with a depth and breadth not possible in a relative newcomer to the concept.

Buddhism's novelty is no longer as great as it was when it first appeared in the West, particularly as a model for the contemporary Western psychedelic drug effect. I see examples of this in students of Buddhism with an interest in psychedelic drugs now turning to shamanism with the hope that they may find a spiritual home there. However, it is unlikely that the current fascination with shamanism will prove much more enduring. Once we gain familiarity with either of these novel exotic systems, we will find the same personal and institutional foibles pervade them as any other.

Therefore, as I reviewed the elements of the DMT experience and those of a more ideal religious system by which to understand and apply those effects, certain requisite features became clear.

1. That system needed to posit the existence of free-standing, external levels of reality.
2. The contents with which one interacts and the information one brings back should stand at the summit, not the periphery, of that model's foundational spiritual experience.
3. The framework ought to possess psychological, cultural, theological, moral, and ethical resonance with the Western mind.

PART II

The Hebrew Bible:
Basic Notions

6 Introduction to the Hebrew Bible

What It Is and How to Study It

Drink water from your own cistern, and flowing water from your own spring.

PROVERBS 5:15

After completing the DMT project, I began to read and then study the Hebrew Bible. This text drew my attention for personal and professional reasons, both of which related to ending my association with the Zen Buddhist community I had studied and practiced with for more than two decades.* My growing dissatisfaction with Zen as a spiritual path played a role, as did the organization's reaction to an article I had written about the relationship between Zen practice and psychedelic drug use.[1] However, most relevant for the purposes of this book is how my DMT data were not comporting with the Buddhist model I had brought to bear on my research. The silver lining to an otherwise difficult set of circumstances was that I now felt freer to explore other systems of religious thought for understanding the results of my project.

In this chapter, I begin making the case that the Hebrew Bible's notion of prophecy provides a viable alternative model to contemporary religious and scientific ones for understanding and applying the spiritual

---

*For details, see chapter 20 of *DMT: The Spirit Molecule*.

elements of the psychedelic drug experience. While it may be unclear at first why I am providing as much detail as this chapter contains, I hope that as we progress through this material, my decision becomes clearer. One of my goals for this book is to raise interest in the Hebrew Bible as a spiritual reference for such a model. This will be easier to attain if I make it easier to enter into its world. Because so many secular, educated Westerners have only a smattering of knowledge of the text, I believe a relatively thorough introduction like this one ultimately may prove useful.

A CHANCE ENCOUNTER

It was in a somewhat unsettled state that I found myself one day in 1998 browsing through the bookshelves of Phoenix Rising, a locally owned bookstore in Port Townsend, Washington, where I was then living and working. My Zen community and I had just parted ways, and other personal circumstances were just as vexing. I wistfully walked by row after row of books on Buddhism and Hinduism, realizing that Eastern religions and I had just about exhausted each other. I stopped in front of their almost embarrassingly modest "Judaism" section, curious as to what the West might offer. A slight, thin book with a bright turquoise cover stood out: *The Kabbalah of Envy,* by Nilton Bonder. I noticed with surprise and some irony that the publisher was Shambhala, an imprint specializing in Buddhism. Overcoming some instinctual and inchoate anxiety, I began flipping through its pages and read this passage:

> Do not seek revenge. How to define "revenge"? Imagine that one person says to another, "Lend me your sickle," and the other denies the request. The next day, the latter says, "Lend me your chisel,"* and the former replies that he will not lend the chisel, as the sickle was not lent to him. Such behavior is called revenge.[2]

---

*Less valuable and prone to damage than a sickle.

Do not bear a grudge. How to define a "grudge"? Imagine that one person says to another, "Lend me your chisel," and the latter refuses. The next day, the latter says, "Lend me your sickle," and the first replies, "Here it is. I am not like you, who would not lend me your chisel." Such behavior is how grudges begin.[3]

This discussion occurs in the Talmud, a collection of legal, ethical, and moral teachings that the rabbis committed to writing in Israel and Babylonia during the first several centuries of the common era.[4] The passage puzzled me. What significance did the ancient Jewish sages attribute to an argument over tools between two farmers? I was determined to understand how they distinguished between revenge and a grudge, and why it mattered. After some reflection, I realized that this was a unique way to view our spiritual nature; that is, through social relationship and interaction. In the case of the two farmers, the rabbis were demonstrating an understanding of anger that was highly sophisticated while at the same time highly practical. The perspective was vast but the arena was intimate.

Bonder's analyses of the causes and effects of anger demonstrated that they derive from, and extend to, a much larger arena than that of two people arguing over tools. If we are revengeful or bear a grudge, how does this impact our relationship with others and with ourselves? Our dealings with the market? How do grudges and revenge determine the relationships between a government and its people? Nations and other nations? Our relationship with the natural world? With spiritual realities? Relationship, not transcendence or union, is the realm in which this type of spirituality manifests. In addition to sensing that this model opened a new door on my own spiritual path, I also felt a faint intimation that its emphasis on relationship and interactions might provide a more resonant platform upon which to build an understanding of the DMT effect. The DMT effect was, after all, interactive and relational, not unitive and transcendent. I decided to explore Bonder's sources, and this led me to the Hebrew Bible.

THE HEBREW BIBLE'S MODEL

The previous chapter ended with my concluding that the psychological, biophysical, Buddhist, or shamanic models I had brought to my research, or studied soon thereafter, did not satisfactorily account for all aspects of the DMT experience. They rejected the possibility that the contents of the DMT experience were objectively real, did not sufficiently attend to the highly interactive nature of the state, suffered from ethical shortcomings, or lacked cultural compatibility.

As I worked my way through the Hebrew Bible, the notion of prophecy began to press upon me. While its detailed characteristics were still vague, it clearly was a form of spiritual experience replete with voices, visions, extreme emotional and physical effects, and novel insights. In these respects, it resonated with the DMT volunteers' reports. Even more compelling was that prophecy was interactive and relational. It was an exchange between humans and a usually invisible level of reality, one that is external, free-standing, and absolutely objective, at least as real as everyday life. Angels with characteristics much like the DMT beings populated that world, as did God, who created and sustained that world as well as this one. Those beings and God interacted with humans and with each other in much the same way as the research subjects described their own interactions with beings, and beings' interactions with each other, in the DMT state.

In addition, I felt myself "strangely at home" reading the Hebrew Bible. While the details were abundantly unclear to me, the text's figures and the narratives involving them stirred a powerful sense of familiarity. Who among us is not at least subliminally aware of Adam and Eve's expulsion from the Garden of Eden, Noah and his family escaping the devastation of the flood in the ark, Abraham nearly sacrificing his son Isaac, the twelve tribes of Israel and their enslavement in Egypt, and the revelation of the Ten Commandments at Mount Sinai to Moses and the Hebrews? How many of our children are named after biblical figures: Aaron, Sarah, Rebecca, Rachel, Moses, the angel Gabriel? Similarly, the contents of the prophetic message resonated with me at an instinctual level: the Golden Rule, the messiah, creation from nothing, and the phrase "beating swords into plowshares."

WHAT IS THE HEBREW BIBLE?

Once I began to form a notion of Hebrew biblical prophecy, the text's power, popularity, and longevity started making sense. Its thousands of years of worldwide influence are the result of it being a product of prophecy. It is a prophetic text. It articulates and thus potentially evokes a particular type of spiritual experience: prophecy. The spirit of prophecy infuses the imagery and message of the Hebrew Bible. To the extent that spiritual experience is rewarding and inspiring, so is a text that captures and evokes its various manifestations.

The Hebrew Bible (the Christian "Old Testament") is the only Bible for Jews, who number approximately 6 million people, or 0.2 percent of the world's population. In addition, the Hebrew Bible is the foundational scripture for more than half of the world's population. Two billion Christians conjoin it with their "New Testament," and Muslims, numbering another 1.5 billion people, regularly refer to the Hebrew Bible in their holy book, the Qur'an.

The adjective *old* qualifying *testament,* as in "Old Testament," conjures up notions such as outdated, archaic, obsolete, or no longer applicable. A more accurate term is *Hebrew Bible,* and I will use it here as do nearly all present-day scholars. The word *Hebrew* in this context refers to the Hebrew Bible's language. It also refers to the people out of whose history and culture the text emerged. The Hebrew people are a collection of closely related Semitic* tribes who, after a time, began referring to themselves as the "children," "nation," or "people" of Israel. The term *Jew* is a relatively late formulation, and first appears in the biblical Book of Esther as "Judean," referring to the inhabitants of the land of Judea.†

---

*A Middle Eastern language family, as well as the people who share both that language family and geographical proximity.

†Judea in turn is the name of the Southern Kingdom of Israel. The Northern Kingdom was Samaria, or "Israel," the home of ten of the twelve tribes of Israel whose exile by the Assyrians in 722 BCE resulted in the "ten lost tribes of Israel."

There are twenty-four books in the Hebrew Bible divided into three sections. These three are Torah, Prophets, and Writings. Often the Hebrew Bible is referred to as the Tanakh,* the acronym of the Hebrew words for these three sections. The Torah consists of the Hebrew Bible's first five books†: Genesis, Exodus, Leviticus, Numbers, and Deuteronomy. The Torah begins with God creating "the heavens and the earth" and ends with the death of Moses just before Joshua his heir leads the Hebrews into Canaan. This latter episode took place at the end of a forty-year sojourn in the wilderness following the Hebrews' exodus from centuries of Egyptian bondage. In addition to countless other narratives, the Torah describes Abraham's initial prophetic encounter with God. Because Abraham is the first patriarch of Judaism, this spiritual experience marks the birth of the "Abrahamitic" religions: Judaism, Christianity, and Islam.

The next section of the Hebrew Bible is Prophets. It records the annals of the Hebrew nation, including the reigns of David and his son Solomon, after it settled Canaan and ends with the construction of a new temple, the Second Temple, in Jerusalem. This Second Temple was the crowning achievement of the Judeans who returned from a seventy-year exile in Babylonia. That exile began with the Babylonians razing the First Temple, or Solomon's Temple, and the remainder of Jerusalem in 586 BCE. The books of the canonical prophets Isaiah, Jeremiah, Ezekiel, and the twelve minor prophets‡ reside in this section. The last part of the Hebrew Bible is Writings. These books consist of a mix of history, poetry, and wisdom and include, among others, Job, Psalms, Proverbs, Song of Songs, Ecclesiastes, and Daniel.

AUTHORSHIP AND LANGUAGE

The present canon of the Hebrew Bible is the product of a compiling and editing process that took place from the fifth century BCE to the

---

*Or Tanach. Both the "ch" (or "kh") is pronounced as a guttural throat clearing like the Scottish word *loch*.

†The ancient Greek translation of the Hebrew Bible refers to the Torah as the *Pentateuch*, meaning "five cases" or "five rolls."

‡"Minor" refers to the length of the individual prophet's book, not his importance.

second century CE. The text's language is nearly entirely Hebrew, except for a fraction in Aramaic, which is a closely related language that uses the same alphabet. Biblical Hebrew is a remarkable language. By using approximately two hundred three-letter roots, it is possible to generate an enormous lexicon by changing vowels or by adding a prefix and/or suffix to the root. For example, certain modifications of the three-letter root for the verb "take" may result in one word meaning "by my having caused you to be taken."

The original text of the Hebrew Bible contained no vowels or punctuation. This leads to a highly dynamic and malleable interpretation of the text. The resulting ambiguity has been a major factor in contributing to the enormous number of commentaries that generations of scholars have produced on the text. Consider the vowel-free three-letter English root *t-l-l*. Depending on the associated vowels, the word might be "tell," "tall," "till," "toll," or "tally," and the same word—toll, till, or tally—may be either a noun or a verb. A standardized version of the Hebrew Bible containing vowels and punctuation did not exist until the tenth century CE; this is the Masoretic Text. Other religions or sects rely on different independent translations of the original Hebrew, such as the Aramaic, Greek, Samaritan, German, Latin, and so on.

Learning biblical Hebrew, while not practical for many of us, is the most direct first step in attaining a deeper understanding of the Hebrew Bible. I began relearning this language so I could translate for myself what the original text was saying.* It is, at the same time, possible to reach a quite sophisticated level of comprehension using high quality English translations and commentaries.

STUDYING THE HEBREW BIBLE

Despite its great popularity, penetrating beyond a superficial understanding of the Hebrew Bible requires extraordinary effort. Much of

---

*In this project I found great assistance in two Hebrew biblical dictionaries: Davidson, *The Analytical Hebrew and Chaldee Lexicon*; and Brown, Driver, and Briggs, *A Hebrew and English Lexicon of the Old Testament*.

this difficulty lies in understanding what it is actually saying; that is, the text requires guidance to interpret. However, a significant contribution to many people's problems understanding the Hebrew Bible derives from powerful and unexamined emotional and intellectual reactions to it. These responses may be to what the text says or to how people have used it throughout history.

The first chapter of the first book of the Hebrew Bible is Genesis's narrative detailing the creation of the heavens, the earth, and all their contents, including humans. It immediately forced upon me several questions: What *is* this book? Is it "true" or a "metaphor"? Or both? And does it matter? These questions were identical to those that my DMT volunteers' reports confronted me with. Were their experiences "real" or did they represent "something else"? And did it matter?

I knew that just as in the case with the DMT reports, how I viewed the contents of the Hebrew Bible did matter. I would make little progress in learning what it said and meant if I treated its contents as simply metaphoric. Having learned the hard way from my drug research, I decided to engage in the same thought experiment I had performed during the DMT study. I suspended disbelief and decided that the world of the Hebrew Bible, for all I knew, was as real as this one. I then could follow the various consequences of accepting the text at face value.

Intellectual Issues and the Medieval Jewish Philosophers

My primary guides in conducting this thought experiment have been the medieval Jewish philosophers, who lived from the ninth to fourteenth centuries CE. These men were all observant Jews, and nearly all were rabbis. They also were men of letters: theologians, physicians, mathematicians, astronomers, astrologers,* and statesmen. The medieval Jewish philosophers assumed the real, objective existence of the biblical world and its spiritual and material constituents. They then articulated its nature and rules in such a way as to maintain a coherent

---

*Astrology possessed a higher rank and reputability in medieval times than it does today. It was an applied science consisting of an amalgam of early astronomy with psychology, medicine, and history.

and self-consistent whole whenever possible. Only rarely did they resort to an allegorical interpretation of the text, and even then, they never lost sight of the text's plain or literal meaning.

I include the Dutch philosopher Baruch Spinoza (also known as Benedict de Spinoza) in this group, although he differs in several respects from the classical commentators. While he was born into a Jewish home and underwent rigorous religious training as a youth, in his adult years he was neither observant nor a rabbi.* In addition, he lived several hundred years after any of the other writers to which I refer. However, his unique perspective on religion and science marked the formal end to a particular "medieval" style of thinking.[5] How he did this is of great interest because his work continues to exert an effect on our approach to biblical, scientific, and religious issues.

The preeminent medieval Jewish Bible commentators hailed from Babylonia, France, Spain, and Egypt. The earliest is Saadiah[†] ben Joseph, or simply Saadiah, who was active in the 900s. He was the head of one of the two main Baghdad Jewish academies that the exiled Judean community had founded in Babylonia after the destruction of Jerusalem and the First Temple. He adjudicated cases originating in communities throughout all of Europe and the Middle East. While he authored a Hebrew Bible commentary, his primary contribution has been *The Book of Beliefs and Opinions,*[6] the first attempt to systematize a philosophy of the Hebrew Bible.

The southern French rabbi and commentator Solomon ben Isaac, better known as Rashi, lived from 1040 to 1104. His three daughters are the subjects of recent popular novels.[7] Rashi wrote exhaustive and hugely popular commentaries on the Hebrew Bible and the Talmud. The latter provided the first real entrée into this titanic, previously impenetrable corpus of rabbinic writings. While he frequently adduced material from the Talmud and other rabbinic texts instead of focusing on the plain meaning of the Hebrew Bible's verses, Rashi's thoroughness

---

*In fact, the Jewish community excommunicated Spinoza twice for heresy, the first time while he was in his twenties.

[†] Often spelled "Saadia."

and popularity influenced my decision to make his commentary the first one I read from cover to cover.[8]

The other commentators I have learned from originated from Spain, but at some point they all left their homeland, as religious persecution by local Muslims and Christians was so unrelenting.

Abraham ibn Ezra (1089–1167) is the least well known, and fittingly, the one about whom the most legends have sprung up. One tale relates that he was killed by a pack of black dogs that surrounded him on a road in the English countryside. His wit and brilliant grammatical mind shine through his writings, and he takes no prisoners when disagreeing with someone else's views, no matter how esteemed his opponent. Despite astrology's banned status within Judaism, ibn Ezra supported himself with a busy astrological practice as well as from writing biblical commentaries, his most renowned being that of the Torah.[9] He also wrote a very useful summary of methods of Hebrew Bible interpretation and a guide to religious observance.[10] I have especially appreciated his spiritual approach to language, as for example, when he remarks about words, that "in them, soul and body appear to unite."*

Moses ben Nachman is better known as either Ramban or Nachmanides. He lived from 1194 to 1270 and was the Jewish representative in a famous weeks-long "disputation" in front of the king of Spain in 1263.[11] Leader of Barcelona and greater Spanish Jewry, he had a fierce intellect and convincingly defeated his Christian opponent. While the king acknowledged his victory, Nachmanides had to flee for his life and died soon after arriving in Jerusalem. He is the first classical biblical commentator to explicitly refer to the Kabbalah.[12] Most traditional Jews consider Rashi, ibn Ezra, and Nachmanides to be the elite troika of the Torah commentators.

Two other Spaniards did not write Bible commentaries but instead left behind more systematic philosophical treatises, which have been essential to my understanding of the Hebrew Bible and its notion of prophecy. Judah Halevi (1085–1140) was a poet, physician, and perhaps

---

*Or "spirit and form"—his commentary on Isa. 38:19.

ibn Ezra's father-in-law. His major philosophical work is *The Kuzari*.[13] This book consists of a fictional conversation between a rabbi and the king of the Khazars, an ancient Balkan people. In the king's dream an angel informed him that his thoughts were pleasing to God but not how he put them into practice. Seeking a better way to lead his life, he interviewed a philosopher, a Christian, a Muslim, and a Jew. He decided to study with his rabbinic mentor, who instructed him in Jewish beliefs, history, and the Hebrew language.

Moses ben Maimon (1135–1204) is referred to as Maimonides, or Rambam, and lived most of his adult life in the old section of Cairo. There he was the vizier's personal physician and the leader of the local and much of the international Jewish community. His *Guide of the Perplexed** is an erudite and sophisticated attempt to bridge the world of the Hebrew Bible with that of the Aristotelian science of his day.[14] Maimonides possessed a unerringly focused mind and allegedly a photographic memory. In addition to writing the benchmark summary of Talmudic law, he also mastered medicine and other secular disciplines: mathematics, natural science, philosophy, philology, and astronomy. Thus, he was able to accurately identify and respond to objections from both science and fundamentalist Judaism to his attempt to bridge faith and reason.

Emotional Issues

With effort I found I could overcome many of the intellectual obstacles that the Hebrew Bible presents by studying the works of the medieval Jewish commentators. However, as I alluded to in my account of finding Bonder's book in the Port Townsend bookshop, there are disconcerting emotional reactions to the Hebrew Bible as well. These may interfere even more with one's ability to learn from it than do the cognitive stumbling blocks. There were times I recoiled from certain elements in the text, or my knowing how others have misused those notions, and had to ask myself: Is the Hebrew Bible an evil book? It certainly contains apparent examples of misogyny, homophobia, and calls to genocide.

---

*Sometimes *Guide for the Perplexed*.

Several ways of dealing with these emotional responses have assisted me with overcoming these obstacles.

Gaining an intellectual understanding that a medieval Jewish philosopher provides regarding a word or turn of phrase sometimes shed light on a viscerally difficult passage. For example, we read that God commanded Adam and Eve to be fruitful and multiply (Gen. 1:28). I immediately wondered if our adherence to this command is why the human race is overrunning and wiping out the rest of the planet. What kind of God would command something like that? However, ibn Ezra uses his understanding of Hebrew grammar to suggest that the statement is a prediction, rather than a command. And as I will describe later, predictions often are conditional. We can change our behavior to modify the conditions that would otherwise lead to a particular outcome. At other times, the commentators' historical perspective may help in contending with repellant laws. For example, they inform us that especially harsh punishments for seemingly mild infractions never took place; for example, in the case of a woman arousing her husband's jealousy (Num. 5:11–31).

Admittedly, certain admonitions defy anything but a literal interpretation, such as killing men who engage in a homosexual act (Lev. 18:22). In these cases, after exhausting several attempts to accept these statements' reasoning and seeking an explanation from the medieval commentators, I set aside my struggle against them in the interest of progressing through the text. Perhaps something later on might shed light on such laws. In the meantime, I personally would not accept their validity.

Another approach to overcoming emotional resistances to studying the Hebrew Bible addresses the feelings directly. This is something one might do when facing any situation that stirs up painful emotions. Rather than simply responding by rejecting the text that arouses those feelings, we can investigate them, trace their origins, and if possible, work through them by noting their lack of relevance to our present adult lives. I found this especially useful when reading about God's "punishing" and "angry" characteristics, in which case I noted how such descriptions triggered feelings about punishing and angry people from my childhood. While realizing I needed to understand what these terms actually meant, I also gained some solace by recognizing that no one was punishing me or was angry with me at the moment.

THE HEBREW BIBLE
AFFECTS OUR CONSCIOUSNESS

I made an unexpected discovery once my intellectual and emotional resistances to studying the Hebrew Bible began moderating. Sustained and intense involvement with the text resulted in an altered state of consciousness. Attending to any object with prolonged and energetic focus is, after all, a type of meditation practice. One effect of "meditating" on the text was that it became easier to understand. I was more relaxed and I could associate more readily to what it was saying. This then fed back onto the altered state because the prophetic nature of the Hebrew Bible itself reflects the altered state of prophecy. Lessening my resistance to the text allowed it to exert its unique effects on my own consciousness. Identification with what I was reading increased, and I either understood, or could now defer outright rejection of, elements of the Hebrew Bible that I previously found impenetrable.

This is comparable to the effects I noticed when I first began reading Buddhist scripture. The text reflects a state of mind, a particular type of spiritual experience; in this case, the unitive enlightenment experience. The Hebrew Bible similarly articulates and evokes intimations of the interactive-relational prophetic state.

I found something similar occurring with prolonged immersion in the medieval Jewish philosophers' writings. In the early stages of my investigations, I found their work more accessible than the Hebrew Bible itself, and I quickly learned to trust their purity of intent and intellectual rigor when shifting between the Hebrew Bible and their attempts to clarify its meaning. After their intellectual tools became part of my own repertoire, I felt more secure in navigating the text without turning to them as often.

Reading out loud at a normal conversational volume has also been effective in eliciting a mild altered state when reading the Hebrew Bible and its commentaries. Doing this in Hebrew for the Bible itself is especially powerful, particularly in combination with a growing comprehension of the language. Besides the effects on consciousness, reading the text out loud also helps in comprehending it, providing a more lifelike quality to its record of the sights, sounds, ideas, and feelings it is documenting. It is like listening to someone tell a story while following a written version at the same time, rather than simply reading it silently.

OUR CONSCIOUSNESS AFFECTS
OUR RELATIONSHIP WITH THE HEBREW BIBLE

Using meditation to facilitate "letting go" into the Hebrew Bible is not dissimilar to what I found helped volunteers enter into the DMT state. In both cases, one willfully surrenders control to something that we believe is fundamentally safe and good. A preexisting meditative state, alert but not grasping, helps reduce much of what occurs as we transition into either new world: physical discomfort, anxiety, excitement, fear, and a confusing jumble of thoughts. Awareness of breathing and posture makes prolonged focus less difficult, and training our attention to ignore distracting thoughts and perceptions can be very helpful. Once our reactions to the text lessen, it is better able to propel as well as guide our consciousness through its world. And especially in the beginning of one's study, the medieval Jewish commentators assume the role of supervising one's study sessions much as a trusted figure guides one's psychedelic sessions. They ease our anxiety and explain what's taking place.

Finally, judiciously entering into a "prophecy-like" state with the pharmacological assistance that psychedelic drugs provide may allow a greater understanding of the text. Such would occur because of the resonance existing between the two states of consciousness: the one out of which the text emerged and that of the person now reading it. I discuss this suggestion in my concluding chapters, where I offer practical applications that result from the proposal that the prophetic and DMT states share common features and underlying mechanisms. I wish to introduce the idea here because it concerns the relationship of our consciousness to comprehending the Hebrew Bible.

EXCURSUS: ANOTHER LOOK AT
ADAM AND EVE IN THE GARDEN OF EDEN

One of the earliest tales in the Hebrew Bible presents us with an opportunity to demonstrate how a mature investigation of a scriptural narrative provides a fresh perspective on it. This concerns Adam and Eve in the Garden of Eden in chapters 2 and 3 in Genesis. Many secularly educated Westerners mock the notion of a God who expelled Adam and Eve from the paradisiacal garden for eating "the fruit of the tree of knowledge." This "proves" that the Hebrew Bible's God is petty, jealous, and vindictive. He wants humans to remain ignorant, and such a God deserves our disparagement. While this conclusion seemed simple-minded to me before studying the narrative more closely, I didn't know how else to interpret it. I admit to bracing myself and preparing to mount all manner of objections to God's behavior when I began studying this narrative. However, Maimonides' explanation provided me with an entirely new level of understanding of the tale and encouraged me to continue my studies using his and other commentators' aid.

The text explicitly states that the tree is not "of knowledge" but "of the knowledge of good and evil." According to Maimonides, before eating the tree's fruit Adam and Eve knew only truth and falsity, objective reality, things as they are. After learning about good and evil, a subjective judgment rather than objective truth, their natures changed. They now inhabited the world of opinions, value judgments, and relativity. This change made it impossible for them to live in a world solely of objective truth. They no longer met the criteria, so to speak, for living in the Garden. It was cause and effect; like, for example, becoming too tall to sit on a particular piece of furniture. In the case of Adam and Eve, we see this as "punishment," but that is only what we call a particular case of cause and effect. We wouldn't consider the inability to sit on the aforementioned piece of furniture to be "punishment."

7 God

Some would deny any legitimate use of the word God because it has been misused so much. Certainly it is the most burdened of all human words. Precisely for that reason it is the most imperishable and unavoidable.

MARTIN BUBER, *I AND THOU*, 123.

One of the greatest stumbling blocks to any effort to plumb the Hebrew Bible is its notion of God. However, any discussion of a prophetic model for the psychedelic drug experience cannot ignore this topic because God plays a necessary role in every element of prophecy. According to the Hebrew Bible, God created and sustains the natural world, including our mind-brain complex through which we experience prophecy. God created and sustains the spiritual world, which one apprehends in the prophetic state. Finally, God is the source, goal, explicator, and final arbiter of prophecy. It is because of this critical role for God in prophecy that I lay out in such detail the material this chapter contains.

I also wish to add a dimension to the understanding of the Hebrew Bible's notion of God that may be unfamiliar to those who already possess some degree of belief in, and love and knowledge of, God. This additional dimension consists of the metaphysics of the medieval Jewish philosophers, a system that uses the tools and concepts of science to extract certain highly sophisticated principles about God.

These principles provide a significantly vaster view of God than a literal interpretation of scripture might otherwise provide.

Consistent with the worldview of the Hebrew Bible, I will be discussing God as a "real thing," albeit a spiritual one, and not as an archaeological, psychological, cultural, or biological epiphenomenon. While the latter perspectives lend valuable insights into certain aspects of the concept of God, this chapter assumes the Bible's default position: God exists *as* God and is not the product of some other underlying process.

The material in this chapter is rather dense, and I will not add to its density by excessively excerpting biblical passages. In chapters 17 and 18, Message and Meaning I and II, I will quote more extensively from the Hebrew Bible in support of particular notions regarding God's nature and activities, ones that I first introduce here.

While this chapter does not contain many excerpts from the Hebrew Bible, it nevertheless is where I begin to systematically introduce textual verses in support of many of this book's themes. Therefore this is a good place to comment on my English translations of Hebrew biblical verses.*

My references are Hebrew to English translations of the Hebrew Bible published by Judaica Press (New York, NY), ArtScroll/Mesorah (Brooklyn, NY), and the Jewish Publication Society (Philadelphia, PA). ArtScroll/Mesorah[1] and the Jewish Publication Society[2] have each issued a single-volume Hebrew Bible that contains all of its twenty-four books. In addition, all three publishers have published multiple single-book volumes; e.g., Joshua, Song of Songs, and Ezekiel. More or less subtle differences exist in the Hebrew to English translations among this vast number of books, usually reflecting the theological biases of the publisher. When deciding the exact words to choose in presenting the English translations that appear here, I use my own understanding of biblical Hebrew while also considering the rationale each of the various editions uses in its decision making. As a result, my translations may also slightly differ from those that appear in any of the Jewish versions of the Hebrew Bible.

---

*I have already noted how the versification of the text differs between Jewish and non-Jewish translations.

A NOTE ON GOD'S PRONOUN

In earlier versions of this chapter, I experimented with changing God's third-person pronoun—what in English includes the words *he, him, she, her,* and *it*—from the traditional but sometimes problematic *He* and *Him* to the non-gendered *It.* I did this to forestall negative reactions to the male gender connotations that a default masculine pronoun for God may elicit. At first, this change from male-gendered to non-gendered made sense grammatically. There is no non-gendered third-person pronoun *it* in the Hebrew language. Instead, there is only *he* and *him,* and *she* and *her,* depending on the gender of the noun. For example, *day* in Hebrew is a masculine noun. Any reference to *day* uses masculine forms of verbs, adjectives, and third-person pronouns. Thus, with respect to *day,* the Hebrew pronoun is the same word that one may translate as *it* or *he.* When translating the Hebrew into English, one naturally uses *it,* not *he* when referring to day. When speaking of a day's brightness, we say *its brightness,* not *his brightness.*

I similarly tried using *It* as a non-gendered third-person pronoun for God despite the fact that only the masculine third-person pronoun occurs in the Hebrew Bible when referring to God. In addition to quelling objections by gender-sensitive readers, *It* also would sidestep the awkward *He/She* and *Him/Her* alternative to *He* and *Him.* Capitalizing *It* also provided the dignity that any pronoun of God calls for. I went so far as to change all English translations of biblical verses accordingly. However, further reflection led me to revert back to *He* and *Him* in nearly all instances.

While the God of the Hebrew Bible possesses no physical gender, all biblical references to God are in the masculine form. For example, the word for the second-person pronoun *you* differs in Hebrew depending on the subject's gender. In all cases of God it is the masculine form of *You.* I also found only male adjectives describing God. And the text only uses masculine images for God, such as "king" but never "queen."

Nevertheless, there are instances in which *He* and *Him* simply feel too restrictive. Thus, I use *It* when discussing certain of God's attributes or actions, if doing so provides a more expansive appreciation for what the text is attempting to say. For example, the use of *He* when God speaks to humans, rather than *It* speaking, feels appropriate. However, *It* feels more appropriate when discussing something less "humanlike," such as God's omnipresence. Thus, translating the Hebrew verse as "It is everywhere" has the effect of enlarging the notion of presence beyond what "He is everywhere" might otherwise convey.

HOW I "FOUND" GOD

My childhood education within the Conservative Jewish tradition did not explicitly address God's spiritual attributes nor cultivate a personal relationship with Him. And while later studying and practicing within a Zen Buddhist setting, I rarely considered God. However, once I began to study the Hebrew Bible and the medieval Jewish commentators, I could no longer set aside the question of God's existence. In addition, as God's importance in prophecy became increasingly clear, it led me to look more carefully at my bedside DMT notes for volunteers' references to God or "God-like" phenomena. I noted that while these were not especially frequent, neither were they especially rare.

I therefore saw the value of learning what the Hebrew Bible and its expositors taught about God because this information would help me determine how resonant were prophetic descriptions of It with those of the DMT volunteers. If the two sets of descriptions were similar, this would provide additional evidence in support of my hypothesis that the prophetic and DMT states resembled each other.

Early in my studies, I had to confront the most fundamental questions concerning God. Does God exist? Is God real? I knew that learning about God would be easier if I accepted Its reality. I decided if I couldn't flatly deny that God exists, I was free to engage in another thought experiment. If God were real, then what would It be? What would It be like, and what would It do? By what means would It act?

Reflecting on Buddhist teachings, I saw that the closest thing to

God in Buddhism is cause and effect. Cause and effect are the bases of this reality. Things are what they are now because of what came before, and the present determines what will take place in the future. Cause and effect underlie and perpetuate all of existence. In the notion of cause and effect, I sensed a concept of God I could accept using these Buddhist ideas, ones with which I was more familiar at the time than those of the Hebrew Bible. Using cause and effect as a toehold, it was possible to posit God's existence. Several avenues of thought drew me to this conclusion.

I had always wondered about the Buddhist proposition that cause and effect were eternal. The process had never been, and would never be, nonexistent. But Buddhism also taught that everything arises, exists, and finally passes away. What would "predate" cause and effect? And what would "exist" after it? Even more perplexing was considering what had created cause and effect in the first place and what sustains it. Positing God's existence, Its reality, provided tentative answers to these questions. It is God who created and sustains cause and effect. God predates cause and effect and will exist after their extinction. These ideas are, in fact, one way to look at the theological notion of God's creating this world "from nothing." Our minds cannot grasp existence without cause and effect. It doesn't "exist" and is therefore "no-thing."

Buddhism also teaches that cause and effect are impersonal. However, they did not seem entirely that way. If while hiking I stub my toe when feeling angry at someone, why does that happen? Unconscious psychological process might be at work, but those processes simply describe how cause and effect affect this particular sphere. They explain *how* things that already exist operate, their mechanisms, but not *why* they got that way in the first place. Why not get rich as an immediate consequence of feeling anger? Or fly? There appeared to be a system at work, one that seemed to discourage anger; in this case, by setting up a sequence of events leading to physical pain. This was another access point in my approach to God. I could grasp the notion of a God who established the laws of the moral universe as well as the physical one. Those moral laws reflected God's desire, as it were, for how we live our lives.

NAMES OF GOD

The Hebrew Bible uses several names for God and chooses them carefully, as they refer to God's different characteristics. The two most common are *YHVH* and *Elohim*. These represent two polar notions of God and provide a useful foundation for investigating God's nature at greater depth.

I raise the issue of God's names as another example of how it may be helpful for someone who has experienced "God" in a psychedelic drug state to avail him- or herself of the Hebrew Bible's concepts and vocabulary concerning prophecy. Most of us habitually assign a number of unexamined and general qualities to "God" when we think about It. Learning about God's various aspects, which Its names convey, may help someone become more discerning in their work with certain God or God-like phenomena they encounter in the psychedelic drug state.

YHVH

This is the Hebrew Bible's unique name for God. God tells Moses and Isaiah respectively about YHVH: *This is My name eternally, and this is how to remember Me* (Exod. 3:15), and: *I am YHVH; that is My name* (Isa. 42:8). It appears thousands of times in the text. It consists of four letters, thus the Greek term *Tetragrammaton*, which means "four letters." This is how the word YHVH looks when written in Hebrew script, read from right to left:

יהוה

where י is *yud* (*y*), ה is *hei* (*h*), and ו is *vav* (*v*, or silent if it carries the sound of an associated vowel). It is likely that the root of YHVH is *H-V-H*, which means "to be."

Traditional Judaism never pronounces this name, and it rarely appears with vowels in the vowelized Hebrew Bible. Non-Jewish religions have added vowels and pronounce the name *Yahweh, Yehovah*, or *Jehovah*. A common Jewish convention refers to YHVH as "the name," or in Hebrew, *HaShem*. When reading from the Hebrew prayer book, the spoken pronunciation is *Adonai*, which means "my Lord." The most common translation of YHVH found in English translations of the Hebrew Bible is "the Lord." In this book, I will use the written term *YHVH*.

YHVH is the aspect of God that usually speaks with or appears to one experiencing prophecy. YHVH also receives the elaborate sacrificial service that the Hebrew Bible details. This fact prompted the medieval Jewish commentators to suggest that YHVH represents God's attribute of mercy. YHVH "bends" the laws of cause and effect by "accepting" prayer or sacrifice, and thus mitigates the detriment or magnifies the benefit to which a strict application of cause and effect would otherwise lead.

Elohim

The other name of God the Hebrew Bible uses thousands of times is the third word that appears in the first paragraph of Genesis: *Elohim*. This is God in Its attribute of creator and sustainer of the heavens and the earth. The most common English translation of Elohim is "God." *Elohim* and *YHVH* refer to the same God, as we note when Elohim tells Moses: *I am YHVH* (Exod. 6:2).

Elohim derives from *El,* a word signifying strength, another name for God (Gen. 31:13). Unlike *YHVH,* the Hebrew Bible uses the word *elohim* for things other than God; for example, idols, other nations' "gods," angels, spirits of the dead, judges, and powerful individuals. Except in some unusual circumstances, I translate the word as "God."

Here is how the word *elohim* appears in Hebrew:

אלהים

From right to left the letters are *aleph* (silent, or taking the sound of the associated vowel), *lamed* (*l*), *hei* (*h*), *yud* (*y,* or taking the associated vowel's sound), and *mem* (*m*).

Elohim refers to God's power and efficacy in the world. It is the complement of YHVH. While YHVH is merciful, we recognize

Elohim by His manifesting strict justice, immutable laws, inexorable cause and effect. The twelfth-century Spaniard Judah Halevi suggests that *Elohim* is the impersonal name of philosophers' and scientists' God, whose existence we can infer by examining the natural world, whereas *YHVH* represents God's name relative to His will and purpose as reflected in the "idiosyncratic" features of existence, why things are one way and not another.

WHAT GOD IS NOT: ANTHROPOMORPHISMS AND HOMONYMOUS TERMS

Despite the Hebrew Bible referring to God possessing certain characteristics, the medieval Jewish philosophers uniformly agree that God is not a material object nor does It reside in one, such as a star or statue. However, when speaking about God, we're limited by language and need to start somewhere. This is where *anthropomorphisms* come into play. Anthropomorphisms are human qualities that we apply to something nonhuman that help us understand certain ideas by using familiar images; in this case, physical expressions for nonphysical attributes. When the Bible states that God's "outstretched arm" freed the Hebrews from Egypt (Exod. 6:6), it does not mean that God possesses arms, but that It has unlimited power to act in the world. Similarly, referring to God's "eyes" means that It is aware of what is happening in the world, not that It possesses physical organs of sight with a retina, lens, and so on.

Anthropopathisms are the psychological counterparts of this analogizing process. God is not like a human, who gets jealous or is merciful; rather, these are words that the Hebrew Bible uses to describe the operation of a particular facet of cause and effect. Expressions that suggest God "loves" or "is angry" refer to what we might imagine are the psychological preconditions or correlates that result in particular outcomes using a human frame of reference.

We might believe God is "angry" when witnessing the catastrophic destruction of an earthquake. However, that earthquake is the result of an incomprehensibly complex web of moral and natural cause and effect that God created and sustains, rather than the result of God's "anger." The moral element might be greed that led to mining resources in a dangerous terrain, and the natural element is the resultant strain on the earth's crust causing the seismic event. Thus, we see how God set up cause and effect in such a way that encourages some and discourages other attitudes and behavior. Maimonides summarizes this idea by teaching that the Hebrew Bible expresses itself in terms that the majority of people can understand. Since most of us only have a clear apprehension of things that are similar to us, the text attributes to God physical and psychological attributes in order to convey certain ideas.

Another factor in this discussion concerning "what God is" involves the larger idea of what the medieval Jewish commentators refer to as homonymous terms. This notion extends the analogizing process to an even more fundamental level. For example, what does it mean when we say that God "exists"? God has never not been in existence and will never not exist. These are properties that we cannot fathom. However, when positing God's existence in the context of the universe as we experience it, the medieval Jewish philosophers state that God exists, rather than saying It does not exist. In this case, "exists" only approximates the true situation.

Similarly, we say that God is "wise," but God's wisdom and ours differ qualitatively. How can we relate to a wisdom that takes into account every possible future outcome, everything transpiring in the present, and all events from the past? Nevertheless, calling God "wise" is better and more accurate than saying that God is "ignorant." Both *exist* and *wise* are examples of homonymous terms.

Technically, a homonym is a word that is spelled and pronounced like another word but is different in meaning, like a dog's bark and tree bark. Therefore, "homonym" is not a perfect rendition of the medieval Jewish philosophers' notion. Friedländer in his translation of *Guide of the Perplexed* refers to "homonymous" expressions or terms; that is, the words are "like homonyms." Pine in his translation renders the idea as "amphibolous," which emphasizes the ambiguity of the terms involved. In the example of God "existing," rigorously applying the idea of a homonym would mean that God doesn't really exist because the words have totally different meanings. But what the medieval Jewish philosophers wish to impart is the notion that these terms are "nearly" unrelated because of how God's existence differs from how we normally conceive of existence.

While on the subject of homonymity, let me briefly digress into a related issue. This concerns what God doesn't do. God does not do the impossible; for example, causing the sum of the angles of a triangle in two-dimensional space to be other than 180 degrees. Doing the impossible makes no sense, it's "non-sense." If God could "do" the "impossible," we would have to view both terms as homonymous, unlike how we currently understand them.

INTERMEDIARIES AND ANGELS

How can an incorporeal God affect the corporeal world? The medieval Jewish philosophers answered this question with the notion of *intermediaries.* This is a concept they borrowed and modified from contemporary "neoplatonized Aristotelianism."[3] Aristotle inferred the existence of God as the "first cause," who then created "separate intelligences," what the medieval Jewish philosophers refer to as "angels." These are intermediaries between an incorporeal God and a physical world.

Medieval neoplatonized Aristotelianism held that different angels, or separate intelligences, regulate the functions, and are aware of the contents, of their respective "spheres" of the universe. These spheres contain celestial bodies such as constellations, stars, planets, and the moon. "Higher" spheres contain "lower" spheres and influence their contents and activities by means of the synonymous terms: *emanation, efflux,* or *overflow.* Emanation is a "natural" process; that is, it occurs by virtue of the attributes of the emanating thing. It is a function of its existence. Just as the sun's nature results in it radiating light, so does the nature of God and Its intermediaries result in emanation of their influence.

The first level of overflow, or emanation, takes place between God and Its closest intermediary, and the last level occurs between the moon's sphere and the earth, the "sublunar" sphere. This last sphere is the domain of the *Active Intellect,* an externally existent storehouse of all natural, historical, and moral information and laws affecting earthly life. While some medieval Jewish philosophers posit that God's influence directly emanates upon earthly existence, most suggest that this influence is indirect, through the aegis of the Active Intellect.

I found myself attracted to this notion of intermediaries, as I sensed it could help me with several aspects of the DMT state I was having trouble interpreting. One area concerned the beings. I was eager to see how the medieval Jewish philosophers' metaphysical understanding of intermediaries might shed light on their nature, location, and function.

The beings as intermediaries also put into perspective one of the elements I found troubling in shamanism. Their placement in medieval metaphysics *between* us and God, rather than *in place of* God, provided a conceptual foundation from which I could respond to what seemed to be shamanism's misguided preoccupation with spiritual forces. This distinction, as I was to learn later, is one of the ways to avoid worshiping God's creations rather than God Himself; that is, idolatry. The medieval Jewish philosophical notion of intermediaries also brought additional clarity to my discomfort with Buddhist views of the beings as simply products of our minds. While we perceive them in our minds, their existence is external to us.

Finally, I liked how the idea of intermediaries added a spiritual level to physical phenomena, seeing them as invisible Godly influences regulating and organizing processes that otherwise seem inexplicable. While we may understand mechanisms underlying natural responses, say healing an infection, spiritual intermediaries are their nonphysical proximate cause. Healing occurs through physiological actions that we objectively may characterize and understand. However, according to the medievalists, these processes reflect the activity of an invisible but inferred healing force that regulates the observable biological processes. In the case of healing, for example, this angel is Raphael, the English translation of the Hebrew being "El (or God) heals." This idea increased my appreciation and understanding of God's nature. Why is there such a thing as healing? Because God's attributes of being "good," "powerful," and "wise" manifest by means of emanation via intermediates to direct the healing process.

LEARNING ABOUT GOD'S NATURE

We can learn about God's attributes in two ways: by studying nature and through prophetic experience. Through reason, experiments, and deduction science indirectly demonstrates God's wisdom and power, while prophecy may transmit that information more directly and in terms more readily understood by the majority of people. For example, both prophecy and science have arrived at the same "findings" of "creation from nothing" regarding the birth of the universe, one through revelation and the other through experimentation.

THEODICY

Theodicy means "justification of God," as in someone justifying his or her behavior that appears to be illegal or immoral. In this case, it refers to the problem of reconciling the notion of a loving, powerful, omniscient, and fair God with an obviously unfair world. If impartial "reward and punishment" are the norm, why do evildoers prosper and good people suffer?

The classic treatment of theodicy lies in the Book of Job, and I will provide several excerpts from it and other books in chapter 18, Message and Meaning II. The medieval Jewish philosophers have also strenuously exerted themselves in extracting satisfactory answers from the text. Ultimately, our authors see in theodicy the limits of human reasoning and not God's limits. For example, Spinoza refutes the idea that there is any evil from God's perspective, even though there may be from ours. And Maimonides points out that God did not create the universe solely for humans.

Nevertheless, the medieval Jewish philosophers offer possible explanations, most of which propose that suffering takes place to bring about an ultimately greater good; for example, pain resulting from curative surgery. Or we actually suffer less than that which might result from a strict application of cause and effect. An individual's suffering may allow the species to survive. Undeserved suffering may even serve to increase one's love of God, as in Job's case. The other face of theodicy is the success of the wicked, those who lie, cheat, steal, defame, hurt, and so on. One possible solution to this puzzle is that wicked people live a long life in order to give birth to a good child. Or they may have more time to repent. Certain evildoers may end up being necessary to combat an even greater evil.

The notion of theodicy may seem rather removed from the DMT state. However, the reality of undeserved suffering as well as the success of wicked people are topics that may occupy a significant part of anyone's psychedelic experience. Thus, the Hebrew Bible may help us work through elements of a psychedelic drug session using terms and concepts that otherwise would be unavailable.

8 Prophet and Prophecy
The Biblical Record

In this book, I define *prophecy* as any spiritual experience that the Hebrew Bible recounts. Prediction may occur, but isn't an essential criterion. In addition to varying from its popular meaning as foretelling, my definition also varies somewhat from how most medieval Jewish philosophers use the term. They primarily assign the experience to the canonical prophets, whereas my definition takes into account anyone undergoing contact with the spiritual world. Canonical prophets are those whose names grace biblical books, such as Isaiah, Jeremiah, Ezekiel, Daniel, and Amos. They preached publically, and the words they and their heirs spoke constitute much of the prophetic message, which I detail in part III. However, many other people in the Hebrew Bible beheld and communicated with God and angels but did not preach. These are the non-canonical prophets.

Hebrew biblical prophecy stands on three pillars: the individual experiencing prophecy, the spiritual world that person encounters, and the process by which communication takes place. The text explicitly details the first two of these three, while it simply assumes the existence of the third—that humans and the spiritual world interact. The medieval Jewish philosophers, on the other hand, occupy themselves with this third pillar, assuming the task of detailing the mechanisms through which prophecy takes place.

I have already presented a general overview of the Hebrew Bible's notion of God, especially as the medieval Jewish philosophers have explicated it. In chapter 19, The Metaphysics of Prophecy, and chapter 20, The Metaphysics of DMT, I will discuss biological and metaphysical mechanisms for prophecy in the context of developing my theoneurological model. In this chapter, I will explain how the Hebrew Bible describes the person of the prophet, the experience of prophecy itself, and various conditions that may increase the likelihood of attaining the state.

This material also provides a Western religious context for the DMT experience. To the extent that prophecy and the DMT state share features, the Hebrew Bible may provide valuable guidelines for those wishing to optimize the spiritual potential of their work with psychedelic substances. By learning about the way the text views the nature of prophecy, and who attains it and how, people may use this information to make their psychedelic experiences more "prophetic."

NAMES FOR SOMEONE EXPERIENCING PROPHECY

The Hebrew Bible uses several different words for the person of the prophet, each of which sheds light on important nuances and elements of its notion of prophecy.

Navi

A common expression in the text for a prophet is *navi,* whose three-letter Hebrew root is *N-V-A.* Words with the same root in related ancient Near Eastern languages mean "to utter in a low voice or sound." In biblical Hebrew, definitions of the root include "announce," "acquaint," "inform," "make intelligent," "call," "proclaim," "name," "speak," and "interpret." Other possible three-letter Hebrew roots from which the word *navi* may have emerged refer to "bubbling forth," or "to be high or elevated" in the sense of ranking high in esteem or being capable of accessing spiritual information.

We gain insight into how the Hebrew Bible understands the

function of a prophet in his or her role as *navi* when reading an exchange between Moses and God. During the vision of the burning bush (Exod. 3–4), God commissions Moses to lead the enslaved Hebrew nation out of Egypt. However, Moses doesn't feel his communication skills are adequate to the task. To solve this, God assigns Moses's older brother, Aaron, to be his spokesman (Exod. 7:1). God speaks to Moses, Moses tells Aaron what God said, and Aaron relays this information to Pharaoh, the Egyptian king. God refers to Moses in this capacity as being Pharaoh's *elohim* and to Aaron as Moses's *navi*. God speaks to a *navi*, who speaks on His behalf to one's audience.

The first translation of the Hebrew Bible was Greek and appeared around 250 BCE. It translates *navi* as *prophētēs*. This word means one who speaks (*phanai*) before (*pro*) something happens; that is, one who predicts. The Greek's emphasis on foretelling as essential to the definition of a prophet is probably due to their emphasizing divine inspiration's role in prediction, a process they referred to as *divination*. Thus, the popular definition of prophecy resulted from a Greek interpretation of spirituality that affected the translation of a Hebrew word whose basic meaning only peripherally subsumes foretelling. This is an example of how "all translations are commentaries," whether we realize it or not.

Chozeh

Another frequent term for prophet in the Hebrew Bible is *chozeh*.*
Its three-letter Hebrew root is *Ch-Z-H*, which means "see," "gaze at," "behold," "apprehend," "perceive," and "intuitively experience." The word first appears in reference to a prophet in the case of Nathan, King David's court prophet, who is "the navi, David's chozeh" (2 Sam. 24:11).

Chozeh may be the Hebrew Bible's most poetic expression for a prophet. Adding an alliterative touch, the Hebrew word for "window," especially those in Jerusalem's First Temple, derives from the same root. The *chozeh*, as it were, possesses a window to spiritual worlds.

---

*Where the "ch" sound is a guttural throat-clearing.

Interestingly, the Hebrew Bible calls astrologers, whom it generally disparages, "*chozim*** of the stars" (Isa. 47:13). Perhaps this points to the inspired nature of at least some types of astrology.

Ro'eh

The most common translation in English-language Hebrew Bibles for the term *ro'eh* is "seer." The Hebrew three-letter root *R-A-H* means "see," "observe," "look at or out for," "view," and "perceive." Thus, *ro'eh* seems to emphasize a particular aspect of a prophet's experience, the visual element. Another Hebrew word that sounds exactly the same but whose spelling is slightly different means "shepherd." This may refer to the role of the prophet in guiding the community.

Samuel was the first of a particular type of prophet, one who played a major role in the political life of ancient Israel. He anointed the nation's first king, Saul, and then Saul's usurper, David. Perhaps as an indication of his liminal status, the Hebrew Bible calls him both a *ro'eh* (1 Chron. 9:22) and a *navi* (2 Chron. 35:18). This historical footnote indicates how Samuel ushered in a new type of prophet: *He who is called the navi today was formerly called the ro'eh* (1 Sam. 9:9).

We can therefore roughly differentiate the Hebrew Bible's terms for prophet from one another. The *navi* announces, communicates, or interprets; the *chozeh* is a visionary; while the *ro'eh* sees and discerns.

The prophet's intimate relationship with God is clear from additional terms such as *man of God* (Jer. 35:4; Deut. 33:1; 2 Chron. 8:14), while God Himself calls the prophets "My servants" (2 Kings 17:13). The Hebrew Bible refers to the Second Temple prophets Haggai (Hag. 1:13) and Malachi (Mal. 3:1) as "messengers," presumably God's. It is worth noting that the Hebrew word for messenger also means "angel." As I indicated in the last chapter, the medieval Jewish philosophers describe how an angel is an intermediary allowing a non-corporeal God to interact with a physical world, a similar role to that of a prophet.

While other terms for prophet appear in the text, they emphasize

---

*Plural of *chozeh*.

his or her social status, rather than a particular type of prophetic experience. For example, Ezekiel is a "sentinel" (Ezek. 3:17), and for the royalty the prophet is a "madman" (2 Kings 9:11).

WORDS FOR PROPHECY

Most often the text refers to prophecy itself, the experience of prophecy, simply as a "word," as in "the word of God came to the prophet" (Jer. 1:4). This emphasizes the verbal, if not necessarily auditory, qualities of prophecy. When more specialized terms appear, they derive from the same three-letter roots as do the terms for *prophet*.

With respect to *Ch-Z-H*-related words, the Hebrew Bible describes a prophetic "vision" (e.g., Obad. 1:1). The three-letter root *R-A-H* may refer to the notion of "semblance" of something in addition to its more usual sense of a vision. In the former case, Ezekiel describes the "semblance of the appearance" of spinning wheels in his vision (Ezek. 1:16). In the latter case, God makes Itself known to a prophet in a "vision" (Num. 12:6), and Samuel hears God's voice in a "vision" (1 Sam. 3:15). Surprisingly, only rarely do we find expressions for prophecy that use the three-letter root of *navi* (2 Chron. 9:29).

A NOTE ON THE BUDDHA AND ENLIGHTENMENT

In the spirit of continuing to make salient comparisons between the Hebrew Bible's model of prophecy and those that are currently popular for understanding the spiritual properties of the psychedelic drug experience, I will briefly compare what we have so far discussed about prophecy with notions in Buddhism.

The three most common terms for one who attains enlightenment in Buddhism are *arhat, tathagata,* and *buddha.* All refer to personal characteristics or accomplishments, and none refers to mediating between the spiritual and the human spheres. For example, *arhat* refers to one who is either "worthy" or who "vanquishes affliction." *Tathagata* refers to one who is "thus come and thus gone," signifying a certain disengagement from the human condition. *Buddha* is someone who is "awakened."

Similarly, the Buddhist terms for enlightenment—*nirvana, samadhi,* and *anuttara-samyak-sambodhi*—refer to its characteristically unitive, conceptless, and formless attributes. *Nirvana* is a state free of suffering, of perfect peace, and extinguishing of selfhood. *Samadhi* occurs when there is no differentiation between subject and object. *Anuttara-samyak-sambodhi* is an "unsurpassed, correct enlightenment" or "awakening." None of these terms posits the apprehension of an external, free-standing level of reality, especially one allowing converse with an external God with whom one interacts at an immediate and intimate level.

CHARACTERISTICS OF THE PROPHET

One may possess certain traits at birth or a status by inheritance that makes attaining prophecy more likely. The former include one's intellectual and imaginative powers, while the latter may provide authority for mounting a pulpit. In addition, one may seek prophecy through training, desire, and physical or mental aids. However, no matter what one's social rank, genetics, or training, the Hebrew Bible consistently states that the final arbiter in the process is God. Without God's will, one cannot attain prophecy.

In the Hebrew Bible, those who experience prophecy come from the entire spectrum of humanity. They usually are male but sometimes female.[1] There are occasional references to a prophet being the descendent of another prophet (1 Kings 16:1; Zech. 1:1). However, a genetic "predisposition" is no guarantee, as neither Moses's nor Samuel's sons were prophets.

We glean little about physical requirements from the text. Saul, Israel's first king who experiences several episodes of prophecy, is the "tallest and most handsome man in Israel" (1 Sam. 9:2), and the prophet Daniel belongs to a group of Hebrew youths: *in whom there was no blemish, who were good-looking . . . and who have the stamina to stand in the King's palace* (Dan. 1:4–5). At the same time, we read about God's assuaging Samuel's anxiety about the future prophet David's plain appearance: *YHVH looks into the heart . . . and not his appearance or tall stature* (1 Sam. 16:7). Age doesn't seem to matter either. Moses was eighty and his brother, Aaron, eighty-three when God first appeared to them with their prophetic missions (Exod. 7:7), while the text describes Samuel as a "youth" at the time of his initial theophany (1 Sam. 2:11).

Social status varies widely. Sarah, Abraham's wife, is unable to conceive for many years. As was customary, she encourages her husband to bear children with her maidservant, Hagar the Egyptian. As tensions rise, Sarah expels Hagar to the wilderness, and angels appear to the shamed foreign slave and advise her in various ways (Gen. 16:7–12). Samson's mother is seemingly so insignificant that we never learn her name, but she too encounters God's angel twice (Judg. 13:3–10). On the other side of the social spectrum is Solomon, David's favorite son and the most powerful king in Israel's history (1 Kings 3:12). Intermediate between these two extremes are the figures in the Book of Judges, a large number of ad hoc leaders in pre-monarchical ancient Israel. When a national crisis develops, God bestows prophecy upon these mostly unremarkable men and women to help lead the people both morally and militarily.

TRAINING, DISCIPLESHIP, AND GUILDS

The Hebrew Bible describes what appear to be prophetic schools where the attendees are called the "children of prophets" (2 Kings 4:1), thus alluding to the existence of formal training opportunities. Reference to large communities of prophets in Jerusalem similarly indicates the presence of professional prophetic collectives (1 Kings 18:4).

Joshua attended Moses for nearly forty years, thus seemingly becoming qualified to take the prophetic reins from his teacher after his death (Num. 27:18). Elisha, Elijah's disciple, similarly asks for prophetic transmission before his teacher dies, and receives it (2 Kings 2:9, 15). However, discipleship is no guarantee of attaining prophecy. When Jeremiah's longtime and faithful attendant Baruch complains about not experiencing prophecy, God tells Jeremiah to ask him rhetorically: *Do you seek great things for yourself?* (Jer. 45:5).

TRANSFER OF PROPHECY

The Hebrew Bible narrates occasions of the transfer of prophecy from an established prophet to someone with no previous experience with the state. Moses transfers some of his "splendor" to seventy elders in the wilderness, who then prophesy (Num. 11:25). Elisha was a fierce and powerful prophet, whom many feared to even gaze upon. He "opens the eyes" of his attendant, thus causing him to see an army of fiery beings (2 Kings 6:17).

HOW TO MAKE PROPHECY MORE LIKELY

Usually prophecy comes upon the recipient through God's aegis, rather than from engaging in a particular practice or from external non-Godly influences. However, examples do appear of specific methods, techniques, or external conditions that may contribute to initiating a prophetic state.

Sensory Stimulation or Deprivation
The general fervor of large gatherings may conduce to prophetic experience, as in the case of an unknown individual who began to prophesy "in the midst of the assembly" (2 Chron. 20:14). And a band of prophets engaging in group ecstasy has this effect on Saul (1 Sam. 10:5–6, 10). Delicious food may stimulate prophecy. Isaac requests a meal of his favorite delicacies before predicting his sons' futures (Gen. 27:4). Music also may have this effect. Elisha requests a song: *And it came to pass that as the musician played, the hand of YHVH came upon [Elisha]* (2 Kings 3:15). Several of David's colleagues prophesy with harps, lyres, and cymbals (1 Chron. 25:1).

On the other hand, reducing sensory experience may help one attain prophecy. A Nazirite abstains from wine and liquor during his periods of ascetic dedication to God (Num. 6:2–3), presumably to enhance his closeness to the deity. Both Moses (Exod. 24:18; 34:28; Deut. 9:9, 11, 18, 25) and Elijah (1 Kings 19:8) fast for prolonged periods on Mount Sinai, where each receives his theophany. Daniel mourns for three weeks before a vision finally appears to him (Dan. 10:2). Sexual abstinence may enhance sensitivity to prophecy. God tells the Hebrews to avoid marital relations for three days in anticipation of the revelation at Mount Sinai (Exod. 19:15). On the other hand, God commands Hosea—an eighth-century BCE Northern Kingdom prophet—to marry the prostitute Gomer (Hosea 1:2). And many prophets had families, including Isaiah (Isa. 7:3; 8:3) and Moses (Exod. 2:21; 18:3–4).

Proximity to death also catalyzes prophecy. Elijah, Elisha's teacher and a formidable presence whom King Ahav and Queen Jezebel continually seek to kill, lies down to die before an angel rouses him (1 Kings 19:4–5). Hagar, Sarah's expelled maidservant, and her son are dying of thirst before an angel appears to her (Gen. 21:15–17). Jacob's prophetic blessings of his twelve sons occur on his deathbed (Gen. 49:33), and Joseph prefaces his prediction of the exodus from Egypt with: *I am about to die* (Gen. 50:24).

Physical Postures

The Hebrew Bible describes many episodes of someone "falling upon the face," indicating a prostrate physical position, face down on the ground. It is often difficult to determine what this really represents. It may be physical weakness attendant to the onset of the prophetic state. It may indicate respect for God, who appears in prophecy. Or it may reflect submission or despair.

However, there are instances in which "falling upon the face" seems to directly lead to prophecy. The glory of God appears immediately after Moses and Aaron fall upon their faces in the wilderness (Num. 20:6). Ezekiel, after receiving his initial vision, falls upon his face at which point: *I heard a voice speaking* (Ezek. 1:28). And Balaam, the pagan prophet, also experiences his prophetic encounters "while fallen" (Num. 24:4).

Other changes in physical posture may catalyze prophecy. Before Elijah performs the miracle of ending a severe drought: *he bent to the ground and set his face between his knees* (1 Kings 18:42). And Ezekiel remains immobile on his right side for forty days (Ezek. 4:6).

"Raising the eyes" is an expression that we often find in the Hebrew Bible, in which case it refers to seeing something that had been previously invisible. Daniel notes: *I raised my eyes and saw one man, his loins girded with fine gold, his body like crystal, his face like the appearance of lightning, his eyes like flaming torches* (Dan. 10:5–6). In addition, David: *raised his eyes and saw the angel of YHVH standing between the earth and the heavens* (1 Chron. 21:16). I have wondered if the expression refers to a technique similar to the yogic practice of gazing intently upward that may occasion an altered state of consciousness.

Ritual, Prayer, and Silence

Particular rituals may lead to prophecy. God tells Abraham to conduct an elaborate animal sacrifice, which culminates in his vision (Gen. 15:9–21). Prayer also is effective. God responds to Jeremiah after he offers a prayer of thanksgiving and praise (Jer. 32:17–25). An angel explicitly tells Daniel why he has appeared to him: *I have come because of your words* (Dan. 10:12). David advises more silent contemplation: *Be mute before YHVH and wait with longing for Him* (Ps. 37:7).

Samuel's initial prophetic experience demonstrates how one might use prayer to convert a whispering intimation of God into a wide-open dialog. Lying in his room at night on the grounds of the Tabernacle, he's uncertain whether he is hearing God's voice or that of his mentor, the High Priest Eli. Eli suggests Samuel respond to that voice the next time he hears it by saying: *Speak, YHVH, for your servant is listening* (1 Sam. 3:9), and this leads to his theophany. Isaiah similarly teaches: *Seek YHVH when He can be found; call upon Him when He is near* (Isa. 55:6). In other words, the inkling of inspiration, the intimation of God's nearness, indicates that prophecy is more accessible than usual.

A passage in Daniel suggests that study also is an effective preparation for receiving prophecy. Attempting to understand what Jeremiah meant when he said the exile in Babylonia would last seventy years, Daniel: *consulted the books concerning the number of years about which the word of YHVH had come to the prophet Jeremiah, to complete the seventy years from the ruins of Jerusalem* (Dan. 9:2). Thereafter: *the man Gabriel, whom I had previously seen in the vision, was sent forth in flight and reached me* (Dan. 9:21).

SPECIAL PLACES

The Hebrew Bible alludes to particular places being more conducive to attaining prophecy than others. Jacob declares after his nocturnal vision: *How awesome is this place. This is none other than the abode of God and this is the gate of the heavens* (Gen. 28:17). Another stimulus appears to be proximity to water, as both Daniel (Dan. 10:4) and Ezekiel (Ezek. 1:1) describe their visions' onset along the banks of a river. And Mount Sinai clearly holds special prophecy-eliciting properties, as Moses, Elijah, and the entire Hebrew nation apprehend God there.

EXOGENOUS PSYCHEDELIC
SUBSTANCES IN THE HEBREW BIBLE?

Some authors propose that biblical figures experienced prophecy as a consequence of using psychedelic plants or plant products. One possible candidate is marijuana, an alleged ingredient of the sacred incense (Exod. 30:23).[2] Priests burned this incense on an altar in the holiest room of either the traveling temple that was the Tabernacle of the wilderness or the Temple in Jerusalem itself.

The Israeli psychologist Benny Shanon has suggested that the burning bush mediating Moses's theophany (Exod. 3:2) was a type of DMT-containing acacia, whose vaporized fumes he inhaled.[3] Or perhaps a similarly psychedelic, LSD-like compound existed in the manna that sustained the massive Hebrew camp during their forty-year sojourn through the desert.[4]

The lack of explicit reference to mind-altering substances in the

Hebrew Bible other than wine or liquor suggests that these hypotheses are unlikely to hold up under scrutiny. Besides, they are unnecessary. Even if one could definitively establish specific examples of the use of exogenous agents, the existence of endogenous psychedelics makes moot their discovery. We know that every human body is capable of making DMT, and we know the psychedelic nature of its effects. While we do not yet know if endogenous DMT rises in conditions of non-drug-induced altered states, I believe this scenario is significantly more likely to be the case than discovering that Hebrew biblical figures experienced prophecy through the agency of exogenous substances.

Be that as it may, I cannot resist weighing in with the only example I see in the Hebrew Bible that suggests an exogenous mind-altering agent. In doing so, however, I am not proposing that any specific substance is responsible. God explains how once a year the High Priest may enter the holiest section of the Tabernacle without dying. God then adds: *For in a cloud I will appear upon the Ark-cover* (Lev. 16:2). The Spanish commentator ibn Ezra suggests that this means that the High Priest entered the sanctuary burning the cloud-forming incense (Exod. 30:34–36). While commentators have suggested several possible effects of this cloud of incense, such as shielding the priest from the lethality of direct apprehension of God, none has suggested that these effects allowed the priest to behold God; that is, experience prophecy. Such a novel interpretation, which I believe is grammatically sound, would translate the verse from Leviticus as: "Through the agency of the cloud I will appear upon the Ark-cover."

THE URIM AND THUMMIM

The High Priest of the Hebrew nation wore eight special garments and vestments when performing his ritual functions. One of these items was the breastplate that lay on the outside surface of the outermost layer of clothing. A folded compartment behind the breastplate contained the enigmatic *Urim* and *Thummim*,* which we encounter during the

---

*Pronounced *ooreem* and *toomeem,* with the accent on the second syllable of each word.

first year of the Hebrews' forty-year desert sojourn (Exod. 28:30). Most medieval Jewish commentators believe that when the Hebrew Bible says that royalty and clerics "inquired of God" (Num. 27:21), they were using the Urim and Thummim. The "answers" they provided occupied the same rank as dreams and prophecy (1 Sam. 28:6). These "prophetic instruments" were particularly useful for giving relatively simple answers to relatively simple questions—usually military in nature—such as which tribe should go first in a campaign (Judg. 1:1).[5] By the fifth century BCE, during the construction of the Second Temple, they were no longer in use (Ezra 2:63; Neh. 7:65).

PART III

The Prophetic State: Comparison with the DMT Experience

9 Overview

One of the theses of this book is that similarities between the DMT state and Hebrew Bible prophecy reflect similar underlying mechanisms. We therefore first need to determine how close the resemblances are between the two sets of experiences. In part III, which makes up the largest part of this book, I will present a thorough description of the prophetic experience, comparing and contrasting it with reports from my DMT volunteers. DMT excerpts that originally appeared in my book *DMT: The Spirit Molecule* are cited as (*DMT,* pg), whereas those appearing here for the first time have no citation.

MATERIALS AND METHODS

When writing a scientific paper, authors divide the manuscript into several sections. One of these is "materials and methods." *Materials* are who or what constitute the source of the experimental data. Are research subjects humans or rats? If rats, what strain? If humans, what are their gender and age? *Materials* also include the variables you are measuring, such as blood hormone levels or the accuracy with which an animal runs through a maze. *Methods* are how the authors collect and analyze the data that they gathered. How did they measure those hormone levels or the accuracy of maze running? In addition, *methods* refer to the statistical treatment of the data, which indicates whether the results are due to chance or the experimental intervention itself.

Materials

Prophetic figures and DMT volunteers are the "subjects" of this study. The data they provide are their accounts of the prophetic and DMT states. These two sets of individuals and their narratives are not entirely comparable. In the case of the DMT research, I was present in the room in our General Clinical Research Center with the volunteers. I knew many of these men and women quite well, especially the first set of subjects. We shared culture, psychology, and understanding of the context of their drug sessions. I closely observed, supervised, and monitored their sessions, and carefully interviewed them immediately after the drug effects had worn off.

The "clinical data" I will use for articulating the prophetic state of consciousness, on the other hand, are reports from the Hebrew Bible of men and women who lived thousands of years ago in the ancient Near East: present-day Israel, Egypt, Syria, Jordan, Lebanon, and Iraq. The altered state they entered was not the result of "drug administration" but "prophecy" coming upon them. They possessed vastly different psychology, language, culture, and worldview than the research subjects; that is, vastly different sets and settings.* I never met nor spoke with them at any time before, during, or after their prophetic experiences.

Nevertheless, I believe that the prophetic figures and the DMT volunteers have more in common than not. The Hebrew Bible paints those whose prophetic experiences it records as being similarly flesh-and-blood individuals with their own lives, and their own fears and hopes for themselves, their families, and their larger community. As did the DMT volunteers, they also wrestle with how to understand and articulate what has happened to them by virtue of having entered into these other worlds.

---

*"Set" refers to the individual in whom the experience is occurring. It includes the biology, psychology, state of mind, expectations, previous such experiences, and so on. "Setting" refers to the environment in which the experience takes place, such as indoors or outdoors, and recreational or research, as well as the set of those in the immediate environment.

Methods

When setting out to compare the prophetic and DMT states, I quickly realized I could employ tools I already had developed from my DMT research. These were the categories of subjective experience I used in constructing the Hallucinogen Rating Scale, which quantified phenomenological elements of the drug effect. These categories, what we called "clinical clusters," are more or less separable functions of consciousness we constructed using Buddhist psychological and clinical psychiatric models.[1]

These clinical clusters are:

1. *Somatic effects**: Sensations of the body's position in or movement through space, weight, temperature, and visceral sensations such as nausea or cramping. An example of an item from the DMT questionnaire in this category: "feel heart beating."
2. *Affect:* The quality or quantity of emotions. An example: "awe."
3. *Perception:* Comprising the five external senses: taste, touch, smell, hearing, and vision. An example: "visual field overlaid with kaleidoscopic patterns."
4. *Cognition:* Effects on thinking processes or thought content, including new ideas or insights. An example: "change in rate of thinking." It also contains one's appraisal of the state; that is, how real or unreal it seemed.
5. *Volition:* The ability to willfully interact with one's own self and with the outside world, a sense of efficacy or lack thereof with respect to the body and mind. For example: "in control."†

I began "binning" Hebrew Bible verses that referred to any spiritual—that is, prophetic—experience it records into these categories. When Jeremiah, for example, complains of abdominal pain

---

*I call this category *somaesthesia* in our scientific papers.
†We also developed an *Intensity* category, which to a large extent reflects to what degree changes occur within the other five. It also assesses an overall, integrated impression of the strength of the drug effect. I do not believe this category is as relevant to our purposes as it was in the DMT work and will not include it in treating the prophetic state.

during his prophetic state, I placed that verse into the somatic cat-egory. In the case of Ezekiel's vision containing rapidly moving and brightly colored angelic beings, I binned that verse into the perceptual category.*

BEINGS

The appearance and behavior of beings in the Hebrew Bible, as well as their relationship with those apprehending them, share many features with those we find in the DMT state. In the chapters that follow, I compare the characteristics of the two sets of beings using the categories I have just discussed. For example, prophetic and DMT beings look and sound a certain way; possess and effect particular emotional qualities; and demonstrate will, intellect, and awareness. Just as compelling, if not more so, are the interactions that take place between the beings and those who perceive them. This property was so striking that it led me to develop an additional category with which to compare the DMT and prophetic states: "relatedness."

RELATEDNESS

In the course of binning scriptural examples of the prophetic state into the aforementioned five mental clusters, I began sensing that I was ignoring a major property of the state. On further reflection, I noted that the missing factor also existed in the DMT experience, but I hadn't felt its absence as sharply when analyzing those results, perhaps due to my original preoccupation with the unitive-mystical Zen enlightenment experience. This category is that of *relatedness* and concerns the nature of the interactions between the beings and those perceiving them. Examples include healing, harming, guarding, and most important, communicating information.

---

*Note that I have not subjected the biblical data to the same statistical analyses that we performed with the data from the DMT study. Such a project would be of great interest.

Relatedness provided a new metric by which I could now compare and contrast the DMT and prophetic states. As will become clear, it has helped me generate additional evidence supporting my contention that the Hebrew Bible's interactive-relational model of prophecy is a more suitable model for the DMT experience than is Buddhism's unitive-mystical one.

COMPARING MESSAGES

In the prophetic experiences of the canonical prophets, the phenomenology of their visions almost always is less important than the information they convey. We see this in how often someone introduces the prophetic experience simply by stating that he or she "received the word of God" and describes no associated visual or other perceptual features. In contrast, the DMT experience was generally message-poor and phenomenology-rich. This finding required that I switch my frame of reference when constructing message categories for the two states.

What I mean by this is that the DMT experience was my frame of reference when I compared the two states' phenomenology. I binned prophetic excerpts into my well-established DMT categories of perception, cognition, and others. However, when comparing the two sets of experiences' message content, the more highly developed, complex, and sophisticated prophetic message forced me to reverse this process. I first developed message categories through analyzing the prophetic message and then binned DMT excerpts into them. For example, the Hebrew Bible's Golden Rule suggests that we love our fellow as we love ourselves and is therefore an "ethical" message. If one of the DMT research subjects described having come to a realization of something akin to the Golden Rule during his or her session, I binned that comment into the same "ethical" category into which I placed the Golden Rule.

It is because of this different frame of reference that I will vary how I present the prophetic and DMT excerpts when comparing their messages. Instead of beginning with examples of specific phenomenological categories from my DMT volunteers and following with biblical ones,

I will explicate the biblical message categories first, provide scriptural examples, and then present corresponding excerpts from the DMT volunteers.

THE APPROACH OF THE MEDIEVAL JEWISH PHILOSOPHERS

I was surprised by the medieval Jewish commentators' relative lack of assiduousness in articulating a unique state of prophetic consciousness. At the same time, I was gratified because this provided an opportunity for me to approach prophecy in an innovative manner. Most of our authors define prophecy simply as apprehending God or His angels.[2] This approach to characterizing the prophetic state contrasts with the greater emphasis we find in handbooks for practitioners of kabbalistic meditation, who needed guidelines for gauging their progress toward union with God.* Those benchmarks consist of specific alterations in consciousness, which kabbalistic authors analyzed in much finer detail than did the medieval commentators.[3]

Maimonides does list some features of the prophetic state; for example, feelings of energy and inspiration, and whether the experience occurs while awake or asleep. However, his primary contribution to the phenomenology of prophecy consists of constructing a prophetic hierarchy.[4] He draws on certain elements of prophetic experience to establish one's prophetic rank, instead of using those elements to establish a more value-free purely descriptive catalog. He takes this stance in part because of his desire to maintain—especially in the face of his controversial scientific approach to prophecy—Moses's rank as the greatest of all the Hebrew prophets. This is critical for his own project because he must maintain the inviolability of Mosaic law within normative Judaism, whose leader he was at the time.

As an example of these contrasting approaches, Maimonides points to the floridly psychedelic nature of Ezekiel's visions as evidence that

---

*A goal we incidentally never find in the Hebrew Bible.

his level of prophecy was lower than Moses's, in whom the medium is nearly entirely verbal. My analysis of Ezekiel's prophetic experiences refers to their possessing certain visual, somatic, emotional, and auditory properties that overlap with those of the DMT state. Maimonides also suggests that Abraham's dread during his nighttime vision (Gen. 15:12) reflects a lower level of prophecy than Moses's, because the latter usually did not experience fear when communicating with God. By contrast, I refer to Abraham's dread as an emotional feature of his prophetic experience, comparable to that which sometimes swept over the DMT volunteers.

10 The Body

When I began organizing the chapters that follow, in which I compare the prophetic and DMT states, I was uncertain how to arrange them. Then I remembered one of the prayers from my Zen community's morning liturgy, the Heart Sutra.[1] Midway through this short scripture is a list of the five *skandhas,* the mental functions that work together in creating subjective experience. The order in which they appear in the translation my Zen community used was: form (somatic effects), feeling (emotions), perception, consciousness (cognition), and volition. I decided to follow this order, and as my work progressed, there seemed an inherent intelligence in how the Buddhist scripture sequenced these categories. While they exist along a certain hierarchy of "gross" to "subtle," they also comported nicely with respect to the volume of examples that my present investigation yielded. The perceptual category, in the middle of the list, contains the most excerpts from the Hebrew Bible and my DMT notes, whereas the other four quantitatively bookend perceptual effects in a symmetric manner.

Alterations in the subjective experience of the body occur in the DMT and prophetic states. We find in both physical shakiness; a sense of something touching the body; changes in feelings of physical strength; fluctuations in body temperature; and gastrointestinal, cardiac, and respiratory symptoms. The beings that one perceives in either state may effect these experiences; for example, touching someone or strengthening him or her.

TUMULTUOUS ONSET

Various somatic sensations occur as one transitions between the normal waking state and the prophetic or DMT one.

🐾 DMT

Kevin was a thirty-nine-year-old mathematician when he entered the DMT study. He was married to Brenda,* another volunteer. He described the onset of the DMT effect: *I feel a tremendous rush in my chest . . . waves coursing through my body* (*DMT,* 261).

🐾 PROPHECY

The Hebrew word for *rush* actually appears in the Hebrew Bible when it describes the onset of the prophetic state. Samuel the prophet anoints Saul as Israel's first king after God chooses him, despite both God and Samuel warning the people that monarchies inevitably lead to a nation's ruin. Nevertheless, they insist, clamoring for a king so that they would be like their neighbors. Saul is a tragic character, a weak-willed ruler whose inability to follow God's dictates results in his losing the crown to David. In one of his earliest prophetic experiences, Saul encounters a "band of prophets" approaching him. At that moment: *the spirit of God rushed upon him, and he prophesied in their midst* (1 Sam. 10:10).

We also read about a wind or whirlwind—swirling, tumultuous, and rushing—appearing at prophecy's onset. It is noteworthy that in both the examples that follow, we read about "the" whirlwind with the definite article "the," as if it were a known phenomenon within the culture of prophecy.

Elijah lived in the ninth-century BCE Northern Kingdom and is one of the two men in the Hebrew Bible who do not die; rather, God "takes him."† Elijah performed miracles, including raising a dead child

---

*In *DMT: The Spirit Molecule* her name was Sarah, also the name of a biblical figure. In order to avoid confusion, I have changed her name here to Brenda.
†The other is Enoch (Gen. 5:24).

back to life. The text introduces Elijah's handing over his prophetic mantle to his disciple Elisha as he is about to leave this level of existence: *And it came to pass, in YHVH's taking, in the whirlwind, Elijah up to heaven . . .* (2 Kings 2:1).

The biblical figure Job loses his wealth, his children, and his health as a result of a wager between God and "the Satan"* over whether Job will maintain his love of God even in such dire circumstances. While Job rails against God, he never loses his belief in Him, and as a reward receives the answer he is seeking: a direct encounter with God. The first words in the account of his theophany are: *And YHVH answered Job from the whirlwind* (Job 38:1).

WEIGHT

I have been unable to find explicit references to feeling physical heaviness or lightness in the Hebrew Bible, thus limiting it to the DMT effect.

✺ DMT

As a prelude to consciousness leaving the body, volunteers often reported feelings of physical lightness, as Leo noted: *My body felt cool and light* (*DMT,* 344).

On the other hand, some volunteers described a crushing weight, for example, Ken. He was among our youngest volunteers, twenty-three years old, a student at a school of alternative medicine in Albuquerque. Once he got his bearings in the DMT state, he said: *There were two crocodiles, on my chest, crushing me* (*DMT,* 252).

MOVEMENT THROUGH SPACE

The DMT volunteers often reported that their consciousness left their physical body and their unencumbered "DMT body" swiftly moved

---

*The Hebrew Bible mentions "a Satan" or "the Satan" in a few rare instances: here and in 1 Chronicles, 1 Kings, and Zechariah. In each case, it refers to an accusing, adversarial, or enticing being.

through space. Movement felt upward or outward (or both) and might include the sense of flying. Those in the prophetic state describe similar sensations of movement.

🦎 DMT

Sean was a thirty-eight-year-old family physician who received more DMT in more protocols than anyone else during the Albuquerque project. He described this sensation: *I felt myself lifting off the bed three or four feet* (*DMT,* 243).

Philip was forty-six years old when he received the very first dose of DMT in our research. He was a long-time friend and a psychotherapist. After one of his sessions, he told us: *I was flying within a vastness* (*DMT,* 15).

The beings also moved the research subject through space. Cassandra was twenty-two years old, and in the course of her participation, experienced significant relief from some post-traumatic stress symptoms. She said: *Something took my hand and yanked me* (*DMT,* 169).

🦎 PROPHECY

A powerful wind announces the beginning of Ezekiel's prophetic experience. It also carries him: *and then a wind lifted me and took me* (Ezek. 3:14).

Similar to what we find in the DMT state, biblical beings also effect movement through space, as Ezekiel reports: *Then [the angel] put forth the form of a hand and took me by a lock of my head* (Ezek. 8:3).

SHAKINESS

This symptom appeared more commonly at the end of the DMT experience, while in prophecy it seems to occur at various points throughout.

🏍 DMT

William* was one of our oldest volunteers, fifty years old. He was retired military and was using the G.I. Bill to train in clinical counseling. As one of his sessions ended, he commented: *I feel shaky. . . . There are little tremors going through my body* (*DMT*, 198).

🏍 PROPHECY

We will read many excerpts from the Book of Daniel in the chapters that follow. Many of us have heard of him surviving imprisonment in the king of Babylonia's lion's den, where the king's attendants cast him for refusing to bow to the monarch. Daniel's visions and psychosomatic reactions to prophecy are some of the most remarkable in the Hebrew Bible. He lived in the sixth century BCE, where his natural talents and those of his two friends resulted in their selection for high-level government training. During one especially grueling and confusing set of visions, he remarks: *in the vision, my joints shuddered* (Dan. 10:16).

Habakkuk is one of the twelve minor prophets of the Hebrew Bible. He lived in seventh-century BCE Judah, the Southern Kingdom of Israel. He describes how, when he entered a prophetic state: *I heard, and my inward parts trembled; my lips quivered at the sound . . . and I quaked in my place* (Hab. 3:16).

TEMPERATURE

A feeling of inner heat or cold occurred in some of our DMT volunteers. I found accounts suggestive of only heat in the Hebrew Bible.

🏍 DMT

Ida was thirty-nine years old, the mother of three, and one of the few volunteers who dropped out after a low screening dose of DMT.†

---

*"Jeremiah" in *DMT: The Spirit Molecule*.

†All volunteers received a low dose of DMT before the high, fully psychedelic one. This was in order for them to learn about the experimental setting and for us to be alert to any unusual sensitivity to the drug, especially with respect to blood pressure elevation.

Among other unpleasant sensations, she noted: *My head got real hot* (*DMT,* 250).

Heather was a twenty-seven-year-old midwife, one of our most psychedelic drug-experienced volunteers, and the domestic partner of Dmitri, another research subject. She reported the opposite temperature effect: *I felt I was freezing, like not just freezing, but turning into ice.**

A being may effect a change in temperature, as in Sean's case: *Then she [touched my right forehead] and warmed it up* (*DMT,* 244).

✌ PROPHECY

The Book of Isaiah recounts events from the second half of the eighth century BCE in Jerusalem and from sixth-century Babylonia after the exile to that country. The historical Isaiah was a contemporary of the prophets Amos, Hosea, and Micah. His wife was a prophet, and they had two sons. The first part of the book deals with Isaiah's rebuke of the Hebrew nation, especially the corrupt monarchy; the second deals with redemption and employs soaring messianic themes and language. In Isaiah's initial call to prophecy, we read about how a being mediates a temperature-related effect: *One of the seraphim† flew to me, and in his hand was a glowing coal. He had taken it with tongs from atop the altar. He touched it to my mouth* (Isa. 6:6–7).

In addition to the subjective sense of heat in the DMT volunteers, we sometimes saw localized hives appear in response to the drug, where heat, redness, and itching occurred over the affected area.‡ The biblical verse describing Moses's face after he experiences prophecy points toward a similar effect: *The skin of his face sent forth light beams when He spoke to him* (Exod. 34:29).

---

*Any unreferenced DMT excerpts are from my research notes that did not get included in *DMT: The Spirit Molecule*.

†A Hebrew word for a fiery angel whose three-letter Hebrew root *S-R-F* means "to burn" or "to flame." *Seraphim* is the plural of *seraph*.

‡For example, Ben (*DMT,* 198).

GASTROINTESTINAL
SYMPTOMS

DMT volunteers rarely reported nausea.* In the prophetic state, abdominal pain may appear.

✂ DMT

Nils was one of the first two DMT volunteers, thirty-six years old at the time. He lived in a remote area of Texas and was the proverbial jack-of-all-trades. He received a dose of DMT, 0.6 mg/kg, that we believed was too disorienting for subsequent use. As the drug effect began, he exclaimed: *I am going to vomit!* (*DMT,* 9).

✂ PROPHECY

Jeremiah is one of the three major canonical prophets, along with Isaiah and Ezekiel. He lived in late seventh- and early sixth-century BCE Jerusalem. During his mission, he predicts and witnesses the fall of the capital city and the razing of the First Temple by the Babylonian legions. Jeremiah is the paradigmatic suffering prophet whom God compels to preach to unbelieving, mocking crowds and royalty, who imprison him and threaten him with death. Here he complains of abdominal symptoms attending his prophetic encounter: *My bowels, my bowels! I writhe in pain* (Jer. 4:19).

CARDIAC AND RESPIRATORY
SYMPTOMS

Those in either the DMT or prophetic state may experience difficulty breathing or feel their heart pounding.

---

*This is in contrast to the nausea, vomiting, and diarrhea that may occur after ayahuasca consumption. These symptoms most likely result from the beta-carbolines in the brew rather than the DMT itself.

DMT

Ida: *It was hard to breathe* (*DMT,* 250).

Kevin: *My heart is hammering* (*DMT,* 261).

PROPHECY

Daniel: *. . . nor is breath left in me* (Dan. 10:17).

Jeremiah: *The walls of my heart! My heart is tumultuous within me* (Jer. 4:19).

STRENGTH

Physical weakness occurs in both states. A sensation of greater strength may result from the prophetic experience but not the DMT one.

DMT

Ida: *I couldn't have moved if you'd asked me to* (*DMT,* 250).

In Ken's case, the crocodiles pinned him firmly: *I couldn't move* (*DMT,* 252).

PROPHECY

Daniel often weakens when prophecy affects him: *No strength remained in me, . . . and I could retain no strength* (Dan. 10:8).

When prophecy overcomes Saul: *[He] rushed and fell his full length to the ground* (1 Sam. 28:20).

In contrast to the DMT effect, increased strength sometimes occurs in prophecy. Micah is one of the twelve minor prophets, a contemporary of Isaiah, preaching in the last half of the eighth century BCE in Judah. He notes: *But I am truly full of strength from the spirit of YHVH* (Mic. 3:8).

At other times, the "strengthening" is simply the return to one's previous state after resolution of the weakness attendant to the initial encounter. Daniel recounts, after fainting: *Then he, the likeness of a human being, touched me again and strengthened me* (Dan. 10:18).

PHYSICAL STRUGGLE

While rare in either syndrome, one may experience assault by beings, with or without the ability to fight back.

🦎 DMT

Ken described a terrifying vision: *Two crocodiles . . . on my chest . . . crushing me, raping me anally* (DMT, 252).

🦎 PROPHECY

Jacob is a key figure in the Hebrew Bible. He is the son of Rebecca and Isaac and the grandson of Sarah and Abraham. Jacob had four wives with whom he had altogether a daughter and twelve sons. The latter's descendants became the twelve tribes of Israel. After serving his father-in-law for fourteen years in exchange for his wives, he flees with his family, only to confront his brother, Esau, and his four-hundred-man legion on the way back home to his parents. Awaiting what he thinks might be his last stand, he experiences this nocturnal event: *Jacob was left alone, and a man wrestled with him until the break of dawn* (Gen. 32:25).

TRANSITION TO NORMAL CONSCIOUSNESS

Certain symptoms accompany the return to normal waking consciousness from both the prophetic and DMT states. Those with respect to the DMT experience were more striking.

🦎 DMT

Volunteers commented on their consciousness reentering their body "downward," corresponding to how they felt it move upward and outward at the onset of the drug effects.

Sean described: *Finally I felt myself tumbling gently and sliding backward away from this Light, sliding down a ramp* (DMT, 245).

⚘ PROPHECY

While consciousness "descends" at the end of the DMT experience, prophetic experience "ascends" from the individual at its termination. From the point of view of the prophet, this would feel like a relative descent "from" prophecy.

God tells Abraham that he, at one hundred years old, and his ninety-year-old wife, Sarah, will soon have a child: *When He had finished talking with him, God ascended from upon Abraham* (Gen. 17:22).

Ezekiel notes: *The vision which I had seen rose up from me* (Ezek. 11:24).

RETURNING TO THE BODY

A characteristic of both states, more common with DMT because of its nearly universal dissociative effects, is the physical sense of being "reincarnated."

⚘ DMT

Leo gradually recognized elements of his own body: *I felt my breathing, my face, my fingers* (*DMT,* 345).

⚘ PROPHECY

Ezekiel's vision in the Valley of the Bones may be analogous, although he is not describing his own body's reanimation but that of others: *The bones drew near, bone to matching bone. Then I looked, and behold, sinews were upon them, and flesh had come up, and skin had been drawn over them* (Ezek. 37:7–8).

SUMMARY

This chapter is the first to make a head-to-head comparison between the DMT and prophetic experiences. Minor differences exist with respect to somatic effects, such as physical heaviness or lightness in the DMT state only, heat in prophecy versus heat and cold in response to

DMT, and both strength and weakness in the prophetic state but weakness alone after DMT. Much more striking is the presence of substantial similarities. In both states, there is a tumultuous onset, effects on physical strength, movement through space, shakiness, alterations in temperature sensation, gastrointestinal and respiratory-cardiac symptoms, a sense of physical struggle, and a noticeable physical element to transitioning back into normal consciousness.

11 Emotions

Varied and powerful emotions characterize both the prophetic and DMT states. While some differences exist between the two, there are many more areas of overlap.

AWE, FEAR, AND REVERENCE

These three terms encompass a broad spectrum of related feelings. Supporting the notion of their kindred nature, the same three-letter Hebrew root *Y-R-A* forms the basis for all three of these words when they appear in English translations of the Hebrew Bible. While the context determines the exact meaning, in cases of doubt, my default definition is "awe" because it appears most inclusive. My dictionary defines *awe* as "reverential fear" or "dread mingled with veneration." *Fear* and *reverence* each captures only one end of a particular spectrum, whereas *awe* integrates them both into a more all-encompassing term.

✎ DMT

Andrea was a mother, wife, and software developer. Thirty-three years old when she volunteered for the study, she was facing some difficult life decisions. During the first several moments of the DMT effect, she screamed: *No! No! No!* She later explained: *I was afraid. I was totally unprepared and startled and scared (DMT, 255).*

Brenda was a forty-two-year-old science writer, a mother of three, and married to Kevin, another volunteer. Regarding her first several DMT sessions, she remarked: *The colors were aggressive, terrifying; I felt as if they would consume me. . . . I was terrified* (*DMT,* 212).

Ken said, in response to his crocodilian rape vision: *It's the most scared I've ever been in my life* (*DMT,* 152).

Sean, who in addition to his medical training received his undergraduate degree in religious studies, was perhaps more attuned to the nuances of the various emotional qualities of the state: *It was the awe and fear of God* (*DMT,* 243).

PROPHECY

The Book of Job consists nearly entirely of dialogue, most of which occurs between Job and his four friends, one of whom describes: *When thoughts are filled with nocturnal visions . . . fear came upon me* (Job 4:13–14).

Fear and awe may mingle in prophecy, too. As Jacob flees the wrath of his brother, Esau, after stealing the latter's blessing from their father Isaac, he dreams a prophetic dream and upon awakening: *became frightened and said, "How awesome is this place"* (Gen. 28:17).

During Ezekiel's initiatory vision he beholds an intricate mélange of wheels, globes, and angels. The prophet describes the wheel-like *Ofanim**: *And there was height to them and awe to them* (Ezek. 1:18).

Daniel describes one of the creatures in his vision of four beasts: *I was watching in night visions, and behold, a fourth beast excessively terrifying, awesome, and strong* (Dan. 7:7).

We read about the "witch"† of Endor, whom King Saul commissions to raise the ghost of the prophet Samuel. Saul is unable to prophesy and needs advice from his late teacher. When the diviner raises Samuel's spirit, her reaction is similar to Andrea's: *The woman saw Samuel, and she screamed in a loud voice* (1 Sam. 28:12).‡

---

*"Round things."

†More accurately "diviner."

‡Interestingly she saw Samuel but did not hear him, while Saul heard but did not see him. This may be an example of a less than entirely successful "transfer" of prophecy from one to the other, a phenomenon I discussed in chapter 8, Prophet and Prophecy.

David succeeds Saul as the second king of Israel. One of his goals is to house the ark containing the stone tablets upon which God had inscribed the Ten Commandments. He comes to its temporary housing to pay obeisance: *But [he] could not go before it to seek God, for he was terrified of the sword of the angel of YHVH* (1 Chron. 21:30).

Samson is a Hebrew warrior whose uncut hair provides him extraordinary strength, the secret of which his mistress Delilah tricks him into divulging. She cuts off his hair in order to deliver him to her comrades, enemies of Israel, and they put him to death. An angel predicts his prophetic stature to his parents even before his mother becomes pregnant. His soon-to-be mother describes the angel to her husband: *His appearance was like the appearance of an angel of God, very awesome* (Judg. 13:6).

SAFETY, REASSURANCE, AND PEACE

At the other end of the spectrum, someone in the DMT or prophetic state may feel great security and comfort.

DMT

Chris was thirty-five years old when he joined the research project, married, a computer salesman, and a part-time actor. He described how well he felt during the experience: *Probably the most reassuring thing of my life* (DMT, 191).

Rex was a journeyman carpenter and forty years old when he volunteered. During our preliminary studies with psilocybin, he asked me to look at a lesion on his shin, an ominous mole that a dermatologist immediately diagnosed as melanoma. While this precluded any further participation in our research, we stayed in touch until his tragic death several years later. Rex and Brenda provided two of the most detailed accounts of the otherworldly nature of the DMT state.[1] During one session, a being helped guide him through the novel terrain: *When I was with her I had a deep feeling of relaxation and tranquility* (DMT, 209).

Carlos was one of our few non-Anglo volunteers, a Hispanic-

Amerindian who owned a software business and also led an urban shamanism group. He was forty-four years old when he joined the DMT
study. He commented on the beings' (unsuccessful) attempt to soothe him:
They wanted to try and reduce my anxiety so we could relate (*DMT,* 190).

✂ PROPHECY

In addition to the physical weakness and confusion Daniel often feels,
he's frequently frightened, too. His angelic guide calms him by saying:
Fear not. . . . Peace to you (Dan. 10:19).

Gideon is one of the judges of Israel who periodically assume leadership of the Hebrew tribes' loose confederation during times of national
crisis before the establishment of the monarchy. He lived in the twelfth-
century BCE Northern Kingdom. Gideon's encounter with an angel
causes him to fear for his life. God reassures him: *Peace be to you; fear
not; you shall not die* (Judg. 6:23).

After Moses gains God's pardon for the Hebrews' making the
Golden Calf, he asks God to reveal Himself to him. God begins His
response with: *My presence will go and provide you rest* (Exod. 33:14).

EUPHORIA, JOY, AND HAPPINESS

These feelings are rare in the prophetic state but relatively common in
the DMT one, especially after resolution of any distress associated with
the tumultuous onset.

✂ DMT

After passing through the anxiety of the DMT rush, intensely powerful positive feelings usually followed. Cleo was a forty-year-old therapist
and masseuse who was legally blind. She underwent an experience with
more mystical-unitive properties than most of our volunteers. Here she
commented on the emotional quality of her session: *The euphoria goes
on to eternity* (*DMT,* 230).

Leo also noted: *The ecstasy was so great that my body could not
contain it* (*DMT,* 344).

The beings themselves may express their own happiness. Brenda noted: *They were glad to see me* (*DMT,* 214).

She also described something that one never encounters in the prophetic record: beings eliciting laughter. She reported: *I "flew" on and saw clowns performing. They were like toys, or animated clowns. . . . I laughed out loud watching those clowns* (*DMT,* 213).

✒ PROPHECY

The Book of Psalms contains 150 poems to God or about God (or both). David composed many of them, while others also contributed to the collection. On Maimonides' scale of prophetic excellence, David's level of prophecy ranks at the lowest rung; that is, experiencing an impulse to do or teach something great to a large number of people. Therefore it is of interest to note that in Psalms we find the greatest number of references to feeling joyful in a relationship with God. In other words, joy is not necessarily a sign of high prophetic attainment. Correspondingly, I have rarely found a canonical or other high-ranking prophet describe joy as an explicit element of their experience.

As an example of David's joy, he writes: *I have set YHVH before me always. . . . For this reason my heart rejoices and my soul is elated* (Ps. 16:8–9).

Prayer for David is also joyful: *My heart and my flesh sing joyfully to the living God* (Ps. 84:2).

This excerpt from Jeremiah, generally the most melancholic of the canonical prophets, is one of the few I could locate in which it appears his actual prophetic state is joyful. When asking God to explain why his comrades treat him so poorly, even threatening to kill him, he notes how God's reply affects him: *Your words come and I eat them, for me Your word was the joy and gladness of my heart* (Jer. 15:16).

GRIEF, SORROW, AND DESPAIR

These feelings are rare in the DMT state but relatively common in the prophetic one. This allows us the opportunity to distinguish between the intrinsic emotional properties of the two states and the emotional responses to each state's message. Much of the prophetic message, at least with respect to the canonical prophets, concerns the destruction and exile of the Israelite nation because of their errant beliefs and behavior. The DMT experiences our volunteers underwent usually conveyed much less dire information.

✒ DMT

Cassandra's comment followed a session in which she felt a tremendous unburdening of emotional trauma. Even in this case, it's not clear she was feeling sorrow when crying: *These aren't sad tears, they are tears of enlightenment* (*DMT,* 172).

While Leo didn't describe the end of his DMT session as grievous or despairing, it is not difficult to read between the lines: *I was dimly aware of an encroaching darkness. Were there flames, smoke, dust, battling troops, enormous suffering?* (*DMT,* 345).

✒ PROPHECY

Responding to God's forecast of the tragic fate of the kings of Judah, Jeremiah laments: *For the wound of the daughter of my people, I am wounded; I am blackened, desolation has grasped me* (Jer. 8:21).

Isaiah is disconsolate after learning of Jerusalem's imminent downfall: *Leave me alone; I will weep bitterly. Do not insist on comforting me for the calamity of my people* (Isa. 22:4–5).

LOVE AND COMPASSION

Similar to the experience of joy, descriptions of feeling love in the prophetic state are relatively rare compared to the DMT one.

✒ DMT

Volunteers felt a sense of love suffuse the DMT experience and even shared that love with the beings.

One of the first things Philip said as he emerged from the DMT world: *I love. I love* (*DMT,* 14).

Rex described his reaction to seeing a beehivelike futuristic world: *I decided it must be a wonderful thing to live in a loving and sensual environment such as that* (*DMT,* 210).

Elena, a thirty-nine-year-old psychotherapist, was married to another volunteer, Karl. She commented after a particularly eventful high-dose session: *The great power sought to fill all possibilities. It was "amoral," but it was love, and it just was* (*DMT,* 240).

Cassandra attributed, at least in part, her emotional healing to the beings: *I was loved by the entities or whatever they are* (*DMT,* 173).

A webpage designer and yoga practitioner, Dmitri was twenty-six years old when he joined our study, and also was Heather's partner. He described his encounter with the beings: *I was filled with feelings of love for them* (*DMT,* 197).

✺ PROPHECY

Most biblical verses that address love refer to instructions for how to relate to God. For example, a verse in the Hebrew Bible that occurs in the holiest prayer of the Jewish liturgy, the Shema,* advises: *You shall love YHVH, your God, with all your heart, with all your soul, and with all your might* (Deut. 6:5).

One of the only cases I could find of a being loving someone in the prophetic state itself occurs in Daniel, when an angel tells him: *Fear not, greatly beloved† man* (Dan. 10:19).

ANGER, HATRED, AND BITTERNESS

These feelings occurred rarely in the DMT state, and when they did, it was in response to certain phenomenological properties of the state itself; for example, physical discomfort. In the prophetic state, on the

---

*This is the first Hebrew word of the verse and means "Listen!"

†Even here, the Hebrew word more accurately means "delighted in" or "desired" rather than "beloved."

other hand, these emotions relate to the prophetic message one receives.

✒ DMT

Carlos said about the physical shakiness he felt at the end of nearly every drug session: *I hate this part* (*DMT,* 228).

Ida referred to her altered body image: *I hated it* (*DMT,* 250).

✒ PROPHECY

God tells Ezekiel to speak to the recalcitrant Israelite exiles and immediately afterward we read: *Then a wind lifted me and took me, and I went in bitterness in the anger of my spirit* (Ezek. 3:14).

Here, God charges Ezekiel with specific feelings: *Now you, son of man, groan with breaking loins and with bitterness, groan in their sight* (Ezek. 21:11).

Jeremiah describes how God's foretelling Israel's destruction affects him: *Therefore, I am full of the fury of YHVH; I am weary of containing it* (Jer. 6:11).

HUMILIATION

Humiliation is a rare phenomenon and seems to occur only in relation to a being.

✒ DMT

Don, a waiter at a high-end local restaurant and a poet, was thirty-six years old when he began the DMT study. He described a "bubble" that communicated with him in the DMT state, derogating him: *We're not going to be mean, but you're a putz.*

✒ PROPHECY

The king of Babylonia expresses a similar reduction in self-esteem when Daniel interprets a dream for him in which: *a voice fell from heaven [and said to him], . . . "We are driving you from mankind, and your dwelling will be with the beasts of the field"* (Dan. 4:28–29).

ISOLATION

In the Hebrew Bible, this feeling is related to the social and psychological consequences of the prophetic message, whereas in the DMT state, it is more an intrinsic property of the experience.

🦎 DMT

Brenda described: *I felt abandoned. I'm completely and totally lost. I have never been so alone* (*DMT,* 212).

Roland was a long-standing member of a local pagan community. Forty-three years old at the time of his participation, he was a successful commercial pharmacist. He noted the isolated emotional quality of his session: *It was like I was a mountain being mined by machines.*

🦎 PROPHECY

Micah is one of the twelve minor prophets. A contemporary of Isaiah, he lived in the late eighth century BCE. His message focused on how God was to bring about the fall of Judah because of the ruling class' injustice and obsession with court intrigue. He laments: *Woe is to me, for I am as the last of the figs, like the gleanings* of the vintage* (Micah 7:1).

Jeremiah also bemoans his isolation when he says to God: *Because of Your hand I sat in seclusion* (Jer. 15:17).

AMOUNT OF EMOTIONS

These examples represent either an abundance of feelings or a lack of them.

🦎 DMT

Stan was a local government administrator, in his early forties while participating in the project. He noted: *The emotions are intense* (*DMT,* 160).

---

*Leftover grapes on the vine after the harvest.

In contrast, Carlos said: *There were no more emotions, because emotions work only up to a certain point* (*DMT,* 230).

✍ PROPHECY

Jeremiah quantifies his grief: *My eyes drip tears day and night and do not stop* (Jer. 14:17).

Here, the prophetic state precludes normal grief. After Ezekiel's wife dies, God tells him: *You will not lament, nor weep, nor will you shed your tear* (Ezek. 24:16).

SUMMARY

Similar to what we found for physical symptoms in the prophetic and DMT states, emotional effects also are quite common in both and demonstrate convincing overlap between them. We frequently read about awe, fear, and reverence as well as peace, safety, and a sense of reassurance. Love, euphoria, laughter, joy, and ecstasy are less common or do not occur at all in prophecy compared to the DMT state. However, lower-level prophetic inspiration, such as occurs in the Psalms, may elicit these feelings more frequently. Unpleasant emotions occur in both syndromes. The DMT state itself may be dysphoric; in particular, the physical and psychic concomitants of the rush. When sadness, anger, grief, or a sense of isolation occurs in the prophetic state, it usually is in response to a distressing message.

12 Perception

The preceding two chapters addressed physical and emotional aspects of the DMT and prophetic states. They have begun accommodating us to the notion that the two sets of experiences resemble each other to an impressive degree. Now I will consider perceptual properties: taste, touch, sight, sound, and smell. This chapter is by far the largest of this section and brings nearly overwhelmingly convincing evidence that the two experiences share profound phenomenological similarities.

Auditory effects are common in the DMT and prophetic states, while visual ones are even more prevalent and make up the greatest quantity of material in this chapter. Tactile sensations occur, but not frequently, and effects in the spheres of smell and taste are rare or non-existent. The role of the beings with respect to perceptual effects is quite significant in both conditions.

TASTE

✍ DMT
Nils described a metallic, slightly bitter taste (*DMT,* 8–9).

✍ PROPHECY
The prophetic literature contains occasional references to taste. However, these may be metaphoric, in the sense of partaking of something at an intimate level.

Ezekiel describes the taste of a scroll that God gives him to eat: *I ate it, and it was in my mouth as sweet as honey* (Ezek. 3:3).

The psalmist states: *Taste and see that YHVH is good* (Ps. 34:9).

TACTILE EFFECTS

Tactile sensations are of something physical impinging on or occurring just below the skin's surface.

🦎 DMT

Chris noted "many hands" in his DMT session: *feeling my eyes and face* (*DMT,* 191).

Rex described an unusual tactile effect: *I felt wet stuff hitting me all over my body* (*DMT,* 210).

Ben, a twenty-nine-year-old former military policeman, experienced a cactus-like being perform the following procedure on him: *I felt like something was inserted into my left forearm, right here, about three inches below this . . . tattoo* (*DMT,* 199).

🦎 PROPHECY

Job's friend describes the onset of a nocturnal vision: *A spirit brushed my face* (Job 4:15).

In Jeremiah's case, God touches the prophet: *And YHVH stretched out His hand and touched my mouth* (Jer. 1:9).

The Hebrew Bible also describes an example of "marking" like in Ben's case. Cain is the firstborn of Adam and Eve. He and his younger brother Abel offer sacrifices to God. Cain offers crops while his brother offers sheep. God chooses Abel's offering, and soon thereafter Cain kills Abel. Cain pleads for lenience from God, knowing that because he murdered his brother, his own life now hangs in the balance. God agrees and: *placed a mark upon Cain, so that none that meet him might kill him* (Gen. 4:15).

AUDITORY EFFECTS

A Sound

At the onset of both the prophetic and DMT experiences, particular sounds accompany the transition from the normal waking state into the fully developed altered one.

🦎 DMT

Willow was a thirty-nine-year-old married social worker. She noted a sound as the drug effects took hold: *kind of like wings beating, off to the side.*

Vladan was forty-two years old when he began in our study. A filmmaker, he participated in several protocols and received more psilocybin than any other volunteer in our early trials with this drug. He described the onset of the DMT state: *There was a sense of whispering voices, more like maybe wind through the leaves, but not a rustling sound . . . like hearing another world.*

Dmitri described the increasing intensity and overpowering nature of the sound that accompanied the transition into a non-corporeal state: *Then there was this loud intense hum. . . . It began engulfing me. I let go into it and then . . . WHAM!* (DMT, 196).

All volunteers received code names—DMT-1, DMT-2, and so forth—to preserve anonymity and confidentiality. Karl was DMT-1, although not the first volunteer to receive the drug in our study. He was forty-two years old, a metalwork artist, and married to Elena, another one of our volunteers. He commented: *I heard a giggling sound—the elves laughing or talking at high-speed volume, chattering, twittering* (DMT, 188).

🦎 PROPHECY

Ezekiel describes the sound that the beings in his initial vision generate: *Then I heard the sound of their wings like the sound of great waters . . . as they moved, the sound of a multitude like the sound of a camp* (Ezek. 1:24).

I described Ezekiel's vision of the Valley of the Bones in chapter 10, on somatic effects. As the dry bones reanimate: *there was a noise while I prophesied, and behold, a rattling* (Ezek. 37:7).

God's glory is a complex and fascinating notion, occupying a transitional stage between God and His angels. I will discuss at some length glory's features in chapter 16, Kavod. Its perceptual attributes figure prominently, so I will provide a few examples here, too. Many descriptions emphasize its visual properties, but there also are auditory ones, as Ezekiel notes: *The glory of the God of Israel was coming from the east. Its sound was like the sound of a multitude of waters* (Ezek. 43:2).

The *shofar* is a hollowed-out ram's horn that emits a piercing blast when one blows through it. The shofar plays a significant role in certain Jewish holidays. We first learn about it at the commencement of the revelation at Mount Sinai, an event that is replete with prophetic phenomena, forty-nine days after Moses leads the Hebrew nation out of their enslaved state in Egypt. According to the Hebrew Bible, more than 603,000 adult males witness the revelation, and rabbinic estimates of the entire camp set the number at over 2 million. This is a group prophetic experience taking place on an unimaginable scale. The text describes the auditory environment as the revelation begins: *The sound of the shofar grew continually much stronger* (Exod. 19:19).

Moses reminds the Hebrew nation of what they said regarding this increasingly powerful noise: *If we continue to hear the sound of YHVH our God any longer, we will die* (Deut. 5:22).

Music and Singing
These types of auditory phenomena evince a more melodic quality, rather than being simply "noise" or "a sound."

✐ DMT
A forty-five-year-old, married African-American activist, Marsha described this auditory effect: *There was calliope music in the background* (DMT, 164).

Willow: *There was a sound like music, like a score* (DMT, 224).

🍃 PROPHECY

Hearing music is rare in prophecy. In fact, I could find only one example that even alludes to it. Crying is not musical, but keening does suggest some form of melody. Jeremiah mourns the fall of Jerusalem, empathizing with its inhabitants: *For a sound* like a travailing woman I heard, in pain as a woman bearing her first child* (Jer. 4:31).

Spoken Voice

Exchange of verbal information serves an important function in both the DMT and prophetic states. However, it is not entirely clear whether what people "hear" is a spoken voice or telepathic communication, mind to mind or voice to ear.

Sometimes the speaker of a voice is visible, and other times the speaker is not. Maimonides suggests that the former case represents a higher level of prophecy than the latter. We see examples of both in the DMT and prophetic experiences. In addition, the curious phenomenon of overhearing a voice, sometimes discussing the listener, also occurs in both states.

🍃 DMT

Vladan could not see who was speaking: *I heard voices but couldn't locate them; there was a male voice and a female voice that were real distinct.*

On the other hand, Roland located but could not see: *a normal male voice. It was about four inches away from my right ear.*

Leo clearly perceived the beings speaking to him: *Welcoming, curious, they almost sang, "Now do you see?"* (*DMT,* 344).

🍃 PROPHECY

Daniel cannot see who's speaking, but hears: *a human voice in the middle of the [river] Ulai* (Dan. 8:16).

Ezekiel describes an angel: *It called in my ear with a loud voice* (Ezek. 9:1).

---

*The Hebrew word *kol* (pronounced "coal") could mean either "voice" or "sound."

Ezekiel also notes the phenomenon of overhearing: *As for the Ofanim, they were called "the Galgal"* in my ear* (Ezek. 10:13).

Isaiah notes the formidable power of angels' voices: *The doorposts moved two cubits† at the sound of the[ir] calling* (Isa. 6:4).

Someone experiencing prophecy may identify the spatial location of God's voice, but not see God actually speaking to him or her. In Moses's case: *he heard the voice speaking to him from atop the cover that was upon the Ark of the Testimony, from between the two Cheruvim‡* (Num. 7:89).

Silence
Let's end the discussion of sound with silence, the ostensible lack of sound.

✍ DMT
I refer to Leo's description of the auditory effects of his DMT experience in the Prologue. Looking more closely at those effects, they appear ambiguous and might be interpreted as fulsome or empty, or somehow both. Here, I will adduce them in exemplifying a "type" of silence of the DMT state: *I heard absolutely nothing, but my mind was completely full of some sort of sound, like the aftereffects of a large ringing bell* (*DMT*, 344).

✍ PROPHECY
Similarly complicating the notion of prophetic silence, we read about one of Job's friends encountering a spirit: *I heard silence and a voice* (Job 4:16).

VISION

The DMT effect and prophecy are extraordinarily visual. These features are the most numerous and detailed of any perceptual category,

---

*Like Ofanim, but perhaps more spherical than wheel-like.

†Approximately three feet.

‡Sometimes spelled *Cherubim*. It is the plural of *cheruv* (or *cherub*), an angelic figure.

and for that matter, of any category of the syndromes' phenomenology. I will begin with darkness and proceed to colors and their characteristics. Then I detail second-order properties of the visual components, such as their movement and recursiveness. I conclude by describing the images themselves, ranging from simple to more complex.

Darkness

✦ DMT

Rex: *It looked like it was in a field of black space* (*DMT,* 208).

✦ PROPHECY

At the onset of Abraham's vision: *a great darkness fell upon him* (Gen. 15:12). In the vision itself, the text qualifies the nature of the darkness: *and it was dense darkness* (Gen. 15:17).

Deep Space

This phenomenon occurred only in the DMT state and contains both darkness and the first glimmerings of light, either from stars or the earth.

✦ DMT

Willow: *I saw deep space, white with stars. I thought I could see the light below, the world's light* (*DMT,* 225).

Cleo described her first high-dose session: *I went out, into the universe—being, dancing with, a star system* (*DMT,* 237).

View from High above Earth

Those in either the prophetic or DMT state refer to viewing things from great height.

✦ DMT

Philip: *Then I was above a strange landscape, like Earth, but very unearthly* (*DMT,* 182).

✒ PROPHECY

Ezekiel finds himself high above earth, but not in deep space: *A wind lifted me up between the earth and the heavens* (Ezek. 8:3).

Clouds or a Cloud

We find accounts of a cloud or clouds, sometimes smoke or clouds of smoke, in both sets of altered states. In the Hebrew Bible, such images often occur in the context of God's glory. Prophetic clouds frequently are fiery and occupy relatively well-demarcated space. They fill parts or all of the movable Tabernacle or Jerusalem Temple, and pillars of smoke or fire travel with the Hebrews in the wilderness. Clouds also are relevant to the notion of "emerging," a process by which an identifiable image appears or takes shape out of a relatively amorphous visual matrix.

✒ DMT

Sean: *There were bright yellow clouds I was floating through.*

As an example of emerging, Philip described a humanoid figure: *coming out of the clouds.*

✒ PROPHECY

In the beginning of Ezekiel's vision in Babylonia, by the Kevar River, he sees: *a great cloud with flashing fire and a brilliance surrounding it* (Ezek. 1:4).

After dividing certain sacrificial items in half, Abraham's vision begins with: *a smoky furnace and a torch of fire that passed between the pieces* (Gen. 15:17).

Moses receives the Ten Commandments on the top of Mount Sinai, where: *the mountain was burning with the fire up to the heart of the heavens, darkness, cloud, and thick cloud* (Deut. 4:11).

Daniel witnesses the emerging phenomenon: *I was watching in night visions, and behold, with the clouds of heaven one like a man came* (Dan. 7:13).

Flashes, Sparks, and Fire: The Equivalence of Imagery

The Hebrew Bible constantly refers to fire and fiery images, either by themselves or associated with clouds or smoke. While DMT volunteers rarely used the word "fire" to describe what they saw, images in the DMT state do flash, shoot off sparks, and are "fiery." Many of the colors they described are common to fire: red, yellow, and orange.

It seems that the DMT volunteers and those experiencing biblical prophecy may be calling by different names visual images that appear to be quite similar. This finding led me to the idea of "equivalence of imagery." The same image receives a label consistent with that person's psychological and cultural repertoire. This repertoire comprises the raw materials with which one constructs a notion of and labels for what he or she sees. The research subjects and people in a prophetic state both see flaming red, yellow, and orange light that moves rapidly, glows, and shoots off sparks. Whereas DMT volunteers see much less fire in their lives than did nomadic and agricultural tribes from the ancient Near East, our biblical figures never saw neon lights and Day-Glo paint. Thus, the prophets see "fire" while the research volunteers described more modern-day facsimiles.

✒ DMT

Mike was a married, thirty-year-old psychology graduate student, who during a session glimpsed: *a large orangish sphere, flaming, flashing, sparkling, but not on fire.*

Leo described an example of the "emerging" phenomenon from a fiery background: *Out of the raging colossal waterfall of flaming color expanding into my visual field . . . they stepped, or rather, emerged* (DMT, 344).

✒ PROPHECY

David describes his vision: *From out of the brilliance that is before [God] burned fiery coals* (2 Sam. 22:13).

Similarly, Ezekiel notes: *There was a brilliance to the fire, and from the fire went forth lightning* (Ezek. 1:13).

Daniel sees: *[God's] throne's fiery flames, its wheels blazing fire* (Dan. 7:9).

Beings themselves may be fiery. Ezekiel describes the Chayot he sees in his initial vision: *Their appearance was like fiery coals, burning like the appearance of torches* (Ezek. 1:13).

A being emerges from fire at the onset of Moses's initial theophany at the burning bush: *An angel of YHVH appeared to him in a flame of fire from within the thorn bush* (Exod. 3:2).

Ezekiel also reports: *a great cloud with flashing fire and a brilliance surrounding it, and from its midst came a semblance of Chashmal* from the midst of the fire* (Ezek. 1:4).

Color

🦎 DMT

Allan[†] was a thirty-four-year-old architect turned software designer. He noted specific colors: *There's the blue yellow core of meaning and semantics* (*DMT,* 179).

Chris: *There were the same colors—red, golden yellows* (*DMT,* 191).

Several volunteers remarked on the preternatural intensity and clarity of the colors. Philip described a planet over which he hovered: *like a super-bright Day-Glo poster but much more complex* (*DMT,* 182).

🦎 PROPHECY

Blue appears often in prophecy. In addition, the frequent occurrence of fire suggests yellow, red, and orange.

Moses and the elders of Israel share this vision on Mount Sinai: *Under [God's] feet was that which was like paved work of sapphire[‡] brick, and it was like the essence of the heavens in purity* (Exod. 24:10).

After describing the complex array of beings in his vision, Ezekiel

---

*Possibly a type of angelic being.

[†] Eli in *DMT: The Spirit Molecule.*

[‡] A deep, pure blue gemstone or the color of that stone.

observes: *Above the expanse that was over their heads was like the appearance of sapphire stone* (Ezek. 1:26).

Movement and Recursiveness

The final visual characteristics I wish to describe before moving on to the forms of the visual images themselves concern how the visual constituents of the DMT and prophetic states comport themselves in space. We have already encountered the phenomenon of emerging from an amorphous background like clouds or fire. In addition, there may be movement within the visions. Finally, there is recursiveness, the endless repetition of an image.

MOVEMENT

✌ DMT

Philip reported seeing: *trailing flags, exquisite rainbow colors; they were dripping colors.*

Forty-six-year-old Robert* specialized in cutting-edge consciousness alteration using non-drug methods such as brainwave entrainment. He described bursting into a: *Day-Glo-colored space . . . throbbing and pulsing electrically* (*DMT*, 182).

✌ PROPHECY

Deborah was one of the judges who ruled and prophesied among the loosely confederated tribes that settled Canaan after Moses's death and before the monarchy began with Saul. In her prophetic song, she recounts: *The heavens flowed . . . and mountains melted* (Judg. 5:4–5).

In front of God's throne, Daniel sees: *a stream of fire was flowing* (Dan. 7:10).

After Adam and Eve leave the Garden of Eden, God wished to prevent either their or their descendants' re-entry. In order to do this: *He stationed at the east of the Garden of Eden the Cherubim and the flaming blade of the turning sword* (Gen. 3:24).

---

*"Aaron" in *DMT: The Spirit Molecule*.

Whole beings may also move through space. For example, Daniel describes: *the man Gabriel, whom I saw in the beginning vision, was lifted in flight approaching me* (Dan. 9:21).

Ezekiel's vision of the "chariot" is one of the most complex and confounding in the entire Hebrew Bible. Some believe this is because of his relatively poorly developed prophetic capacity to recognize and communicate what he sees. Here, he describes the movement of the four-faced or four-sided angelic beings: *They did not turn as they moved; each went in the direction of its faces* (Ezek. 1:9); *when they went, they would go toward their four sides, and they did not turn when they went* (Ezek. 1:17); *for whatever place the head inclined, they went after it* (Ezek. 10:11).

Ezekiel also comments on the flashing rapidity of the beings' movement: *The Chayot ran and returned like the appearance of the lightning* (Ezek. 1:14).

RECURSIVENESS

This is a phenomenon in which patterns or images endlessly repeat themselves, as when two mirrors face each other and reflect an object extending outward to the visual horizon.

∂ DMT

Marsha saw: *one merry-go-round after another after another* (*DMT*, 164).

And Chris observed: *thousands of things flew out of these blue hands* (*DMT*, 192).

∂ PROPHECY

Daniel reports: *A thousand thousands were serving [God] and a myriad myriads were standing before Him* (Dan. 7:10).

In Jacob's prophetic dream he sees: *A ladder was set earthward and its top reached heavenward, and behold, angels of God ascending and descending on it* (Gen. 28:12).

Formed Images

Now that we have characterized the static and dynamic components of the visual phenomena that the prophetic and DMT states share, we can move on to the specific images the visions contain. These encompass a vast range from quite simple to indescribably complex.

ROUND THINGS: HOLES, TUNNELS, TUBES, SPIRALS, AND BALLS

🦎 DMT

Willow: *First I saw a tunnel or channel of light off to the right. . . . It got bigger farther away, like a funnel* (DMT, 224).

Philip: *The visuals were dropping back into tubes, like protozoa, like the inside of a cell, seeing the DNA twirling and spiraling* (DMT, 177).

Cal was a forty-year-old video and audio engineer. His wife, Shanti, also was in the study. He observed: *There seemed to be an incubator, shaped like a rectangle, with a sphere inside it.*

🦎 PROPHECY

An angel transports Ezekiel to Jerusalem: *He brought me to the door of the courtyard. I looked, and behold, a hole in the wall* (Ezek. 8:7).

Zechariah is one of the twelve minor prophets. His mission took place during the early Second Temple period in Jerusalem in the sixth century BCE. During one of his visions he sees: *an entirely gold candelabrum with its bowl on top of it, and its seven lamps upon it; seven tubes for the lamps on its top* (Zech. 4:2).

TREES

🦎 DMT

Ben: *They looked like saguaro cactus,* very Peruvian in color. They were flexible, fluid, geometrical cacti. Not solid* (DMT, 198).

Karl described a tree with being-like qualities: *There was a female presence that showed me a sentient tree, in full leaf.*

---

*A very large, treelike cactus of the Sonoran Desert possessing mostly upright, cylindrical "arms."

PROPHECY

In Zechariah's vision of the golden candelabrum, he also observes: *two olive trees above it; one at the right of the bowl, and one on its left* (Zech. 4:3).

The king of Babylonia relates his prophetic dream to Daniel: *A tree grew and became strong; its height reached to the heavens; it was visible to the end of the entire earth* (Dan. 4:7).

Functional Items

This subcategory encompasses a broad array of images, their unifying quality being their utility.

FURNITURE

DMT

Robert: *Rising in front of "me" was a podium-like table* (*DMT,* 182).

Tyrone was a thirty-seven-year-old psychiatric resident. He described his vision of a futuristic apartment: *There was life in the furniture, like it was molded out of something alive, an animal, a living being* (*DMT,* 181).

PROPHECY

Isaiah reports: *I beheld my Lord seated on a high and lofty throne* (Isa. 6:1).

Daniel: *I watched as thrones were set up . . . and the Ancient of Days** *sat, . . . His throne fiery flames* (Dan. 7:9).

WEAPONS

DMT

An African female warrior confronted Kevin: *She is black, carries a spear, a shield, and appears to have a mask on* (*DMT,* 261).

When describing treelike beings, Rex noted: *one of them carrying a trident-like thing.*

---

*A name for God.

PROPHECY

David: *raised his eyes and saw the angel of YHVH standing between the earth and the heavens with his sword drawn in his hand* (1 Chron. 21:16).

Joshua, too, beholds: *a man standing opposite him and his sword drawn in his hand* (Josh. 5:13).

Balaam is an enigmatic character in the Hebrew Bible. Some ancient Hebrew sages consider his prophetic stature equal to that of Moses. A local Canaanite king hires him to curse the Hebrew camp on its way to Canaan, and a disaster befalls the camp soon thereafter. On the road to the king, Balaam's riding donkey sees the angel before he does. Finally, he himself sees: *the angel of YHVH standing on the road with his sword drawn in his hand* (Num. 22:31).

Architecture

DMT

Sean: *I watched a low-lying city on a flat plane on the far horizon* (*DMT,* 243).

Marsha found herself "in a beautiful domed structure, a virtual Taj Mahal" (*DMT,* 163).

PROPHECY

Architecture plays a significant role in the Hebrew Bible, beginning with the construction of the Tabernacle, a portable sanctuary that accompanies the Hebrews during their forty-year sojourn in the wilderness. God shows Moses in a vision all the details of the Tabernacle and its contents: *They shall make a sanctuary for Me . . . like everything that I show you, the form of the Tabernacle and the form of all its utensils* (Exod. 25:8–9).

Ezekiel, like Sean, also describes a city: *In visions of God [the angel] brought me to the land of Israel and set me down on a very high mountain, and on it was like a built city to the south* (Ezek. 40:2).

Repositories of Information

The beings usually convey the prophetic and DMT states' message verbally. Occasionally, other elements of the experience play this role; for example, visual symbols or script.

🖎 DMT

Vladan: *It was like a fantasy alphabet, a cross between runes and Russian or Arabic writing. It felt like there was some information in it, like it was data. It wasn't just random* (DMT, 178).

Allan: *Then it breaks into a ruffled reality. When I looked around, it seemed like the meaning or symbols were there. Some kind of core of reality where all meaning is stored* (DMT, 179).

🖎 PROPHECY

The king of Babylonia experiences a vision of writing that only Daniel can decipher: *The fingers of a man's hand came forth and wrote on the plaster of the wall of the king's palace* (Dan. 5:5).

Ezekiel: *In [a hand] was a scroll of a book. And it spread it out before me; it was inscribed within and without* (Ezek. 2:9–10).

Beings

Sometimes one sees only a part or parts of beings.

Eyes
🖎 DMT

Cleo: *There were some eyes, looking at me, friendly* (DMT, 237).

🖎 PROPHECY

Daniel describes the fourth beast of his apocalyptic vision: *There were eyes like human eyes in this horn* (Dan. 7:8).

Ezekiel adds a detail to his description of the creatures of the chariot: *And their whole body, their back, their hands, and their wings, and the Ofanim were full of eyes all around* (Ezek. 10:12).

HANDS AND WINGS

🪰 DMT

Chris: *There was a set of many hands* (*DMT,* 191).

Willow commented on the beings that lined the tunnel she passed through: *They had wings and tails and stuff* (*DMT,* 224).

🪰 PROPHECY

Ezekiel: *Then I saw, and behold, a hand was outstretched to me* (Ezek. 2:9).

Zechariah describes flying women: *They had wings like a stork's wings* (Zech. 5:9).

Hands and wings often associate with each other in prophetic visions. Ezekiel describes the Chayot: *Each one had four faces and each one had four wings for every one, and there was the form of human hands beneath their wings* (Ezek. 10:21).

A MOUTH

🪰 PROPHECY

Daniel describes the fourth beast's little horn possessing: *a mouth speaking haughty words* (Dan. 7:7–8).

OUTLINED FIGURES

Once whole figures begin to appear, they may first appear as silhouettes.

🪰 DMT

Rex: *There were serpentine colors surrounding them, producing an outline of their shape* (*DMT,* 204).

🪰 PROPHECY

The vision of a friend of Job may possess this particular property: *He stood, but I could make nothing of his appearance; an image was before my eyes* (Job 4:16).

STATUARY

❦ DMT

Tyrone described: *a massive granitic, Egyptian-like woman figure.*

❦ PROPHECY

The king of Babylonia dreams of: *a huge statue, which was immense, and whose brightness was extraordinary . . . and its appearance was fearsome* (Dan. 2:31).

ANIMALS

Insects

❦ DMT

Rex: *When I was first going under there were these insect creatures all around me* (*DMT,* 206).

❦ PROPHECY

Thus my Lord YHVH showed me, and behold, He was forming locusts (Amos 7:1).

Birds

❦ DMT

Gerald, a forty-two-year-old acupuncturist, reported: *The presence was almost birdlike, a predator, like a hawk or eagle.*

❦ PROPHECY

In describing the multiple faces of the creatures in his vision, Ezekiel reports: *the fourth, the face of an eagle* (Ezek. 10:14).

Reptiles

❦ DMT

Ken: *There were two crocodiles* (*DMT,* 252).

✒ PROPHECY

The Hebrew Bible mentions Leviathan, a massive reptilian sea crea-ture, in Isaiah (27:1) and Job (40:25–32). However, it doesn't seem to appear as a visual image in the prophetic state itself. Rather, the notion of Leviathan plays a role in parables conveying certain moral teachings or geopolitical predictions.

Mammals

✒ PROPHECY

The prophet Elijah and his disciple Elisha: *were walking and talking, and behold, a chariot of fire and horses of fire* (2 Kings 2:11).

The second of the four beasts in Daniel's vision is mammalian: *its appearance like a bear* (Dan. 7:5).

HUMANS

✒ DMT

Volunteers rarely saw something clearly human; more often, the figures were humanoid, and I will discuss these below in the section entitled "Bizarre Figures."

Marsha noted: *There were all these dolls in 1890s outfits, life-sized, men and women. The women were in corsets. They had big breasts and big butts and teeny skinny waists. . . . The men had top hats, riding on two-seater bicycles. The women had red circles painted on their cheeks* (*DMT,* 164).

✒ PROPHECY

Many times, we read simply about a "man" appearing in pro-phetic visions. For example, after a three-week fast, Daniel sees: *one man clothed in linen, his loins girded with fine gold. His body was like tarshish,** *his face like the appearance of lightning, his eyes like flaming torches, and his arms and legs the color of burnished copper* (Dan. 10:5–6).

---

*A "shining white" substance.

GOD

No DMT research subject reported seeing God. And the Hebrew Bible doesn't explicate God's appearance except in the isolated example from Daniel below. The general absence of "seeing" an image of God supports the medieval Jewish philosophers' contention that while God's angels or glory may appear in visions, God Itself is not visible.

✍ PROPHECY

Michaiah was a prophet in the Northern Kingdom who preached during the ninth century BCE. His outspoken criticism of the royal court earned him their perpetual animosity. This is as detailed a description he provides for God's appearance: *I saw YHVH seated on His throne* (1 Kings 22:19).

Habakkuk describes what he sees of God: *A glow was like light; rays from His hand* (Hab. 3:4).

Here is Daniel's strikingly anthropomorphic description of God, not in His aspect of YHVH or of Elohim, but in one that only occurs in Daniel's book, the "Ancient of Days": *His garment white as snow, and the hair of His head like clean wool* (Dan. 7:9).

BIZARRE FIGURES

Let's end this section on visual imagery with some of the most psychedelic contents of the DMT and prophetic states. I already have included many biblical verses from Ezekiel and Daniel that describe the fantastical beings they encounter. In Daniel's case, they include whole animals and their parts, humanoid figures, and statuary. Ezekiel's enigmatic Chayot, Ofanim, Galgalim, Chashmal, and Cheruvim seem to straddle the worlds of the animate and inanimate. Similarly, the DMT volunteers also described strange creatures, some of which were also chimerical: human-animal, animal-animal, and human-machine.

The notion of equivalence of imagery that I discussed in the section on fire and colors above is relevant here as well when comparing the volunteers' visions of machines to some of the bizarre figures in the prophetic literature. Consistent with this notion is that the Talmud refers to Ezekiel's vision of the creatures as "the vision of the chariot," a term more appropriate for a machine than for living beings. It may represent the apprehension of an intermediate stage between inert matter and life, like Tyrone's vision of living furniture.

Equivalence of imagery suggests that the text uses language consistent with its psycho-social-historical matrix in order to articulate the character of highly novel images. Similarly, our present-day DMT volunteers wrapped language around the images that drew from their own conceptual and symbolic repertoire. For example, Ezekiel sees wheels and spheres, whereas Marsha saw merry-go-rounds.

✒ DMT

William described a being: *One big eye, one small eye. . . . It had a slit for a mouth on one side of his face, below his big eye. He had a head that was the whole body, almost like a peak. It almost had a smile. I couldn't see how it moved; if it had legs, they were very short. It was dark gray.*

Willow observed humanlike creatures: *There were large beings in the tunnel, on the right side, next to me. There were gremlins, small, faces mostly (DMT, 224).*

William also described a humanlike creature when he found himself in: *a high-tech nursery with a single Gumby,* three feet tall, attending me (DMT, 193).*

Volunteers occasionally reported seeing human-animal or human-machine hybrids. Chris noted: *There were rays coming out of their bodies and then back to their bodies. They were reptilian and humanoid (DMT, 191).*

Lucas was one of our older volunteers, fifty-six years old. He lived off the grid and wrote about counter-cultural themes. Just before his blood pressure dropped to dangerously low levels, he reported seeing: *androidlike creatures that looked like a cross between crash dummies and*

---

*Gumby is a figure that first appeared in 1950s children's television. The show's producers molded green clay over a wire, humanlike figure and bent it into various postures, using stop-motion photography to give the impression of movement.

the Empire troops from Star Wars, except that they were living beings, not robots (*DMT,* 189).

Before we instituted the practice of placing eyeshades on our volunteers, Sean observed beings on the wall of our study room: *"They" were trying to get out of the wall/hall. They were bright blue, shiny, silvery. The legs were moving real quickly. They weren't alive, more like robots, androids.*

More explicitly machinelike objects also appeared; for example, in Brenda's case: *I saw some equipment or something, sticks with teardrops coming out of them. It looked like machinery* (*DMT,* 216).

William's description is the most detailed of a machine, and he alluded to its lifelike qualities: *Amazing instruments. Machine-type things. . . . There was one big machine in the center, with round conduits, almost writhing—not like a snake, more in a technical manner. The conduits were not open at the end. They were solid blue-gray tubes, made of plastic?* (*DMT,* 194).

✒ PROPHECY

I have already presented some of the biblical verses that follow. However, I believe it's useful to provide more extensive excerpts in this section to better capture the complexity of what prophetic figures behold in these states.

The first of the four beasts in Daniel's vision is a human-bird-mammal hybrid: *like a lion with eagle's wings. . . . It stood upon two feet like a man, and it was given a human heart* (Dan. 7:4).

The third beast is an amalgam of two animals: *like a leopard with four birds' wings on its back* (Dan. 7:6).

And the fourth, quite difficult to categorize:

> *It had immense iron teeth, it was devouring and crumbling, and trampling the rest with its feet. . . . It had ten horns. As I was gazing at the horns, behold, another horn, a small one, came up among them, and three of the previous horns were uprooted before it. There were eyes like human eyes in this horn, and a mouth speaking haughty words.* (Dan. 7:7–8)

Ezekiel's Ofanim appear to possess mechanical features:

> *The appearance of the Ofanim and their nature were like the color of tarshish . . . and their appearance and their works were as if there would be a wheel within a wheel.* (Ezek. 1:16)

And finally, Ezekiel's Chayot, the living things:

> *They had the likeness of a man. Each had four faces for each, and each one of them had four wings. Their legs were a straight leg, and the sole of their feet was like the sole of a rounded foot, and they glittered like burnished bronze. There were human hands under their wings on their four sides. Their faces and wings were [such for the] four of them. Their wings were joined to one another. . . . As for the likeness of their faces: there was a human face, and a lion's face to the right for the four of them, and an ox's face to the left for the four of them, and an eagle's face for the four of them. And as for their faces, their wings extended upward; for each [face] two [wings] were joined to each other, and two [wings] covered their bodies. As for the likeness of the Chayot, their appearance was like fiery coals, burning like the appearance of torches. It [the fire] spread about among the Chayot. There was a brilliance to the fire, and from the fire went forth lightning. The Chayot ran to and fro like the appearance of a flash.* (Ezek. 1:5–14)

Clairvoyance

DMT volunteers never reported seeing things remotely, while such experiences occasionally occur in prophetic visions.

PROPHECY

God wishes for Ezekiel to see the idol worship occurring in the Temple in Jerusalem before its destruction. It is as if Ezekiel's disembodied consciousness is doing the observing far from his physical body's location: *So I entered and saw, and behold, every form of creeping thing and abominable animal and every idol of the Family of Israel, carved into the wall, all around. And seventy men of the elders of the Family of Israel . . . standing before them* (Ezek. 8:9–11).

God similarly wants Ezekiel to identify the men who have led the people astray: *A wind lifted me up and brought me to the east gate of the House of YHVH . . . and behold, at the entrance of the gate, twenty-five men; in their midst I saw the leaders of the people* (Ezek. 11:1).

SYNESTHESIA

Synesthesia is a blending or crossover of sensory modalities; for example, sounds assume visual form. Less common is the experience of visual percepts becoming auditory ones.

ᴥ DMT

When the noise of a vacuum cleaner, in reality, imposed itself on one of Sean's sessions, he observed: *The [sound of the] vacuum cleaner became an image in my mind of a big copying machine spitting out foamy paper.*

In Cleo's visions she heard colors and felt them physically: *The colors were words. I heard what the colors were saying to me. . . . I not only heard what I was seeing, but also felt it in my cells* (*DMT,* 238).

ᴥ PROPHECY

In the more typical sound-to-vision metamorphosis, we read about the Sinai revelation: *And all the people could see the sounds* (Exod. 20:15).

Moses enlarges upon this: *YHVH spoke to you from the midst of the fire; you were hearing the sound of words, but you were not seeing a likeness, only a sound* (Deut. 4:12).

SUMMARY

The sheer quantity of information in this chapter may feel overwhelming. If so, I hope that overwhelming has been in the service of impressing upon you the striking degree of overlap, in quality and quantity, of the perceptual properties of the prophetic and DMT experiences. The length of this chapter is evidence of these properties' preeminent role in bridging the phenomenology of the two states.

Effects on smell are absent in the prophetic and DMT experiences, those on taste are rare, and there are occasional tactile ones. With respect to auditory phenomena, both states include rustling, roaring, beating, and fluttering sounds that may build in intensity and threaten to overwhelm those perceiving them. A spoken voice, with or without a visually identifiable speaker, is common to the DMT effect and prophecy. The voice may directly or indirectly address the listener, or he or she may simply be overhearing it. Music in the DMT experience rarely occurred, and we never truly encounter it in prophecy.

In the visual realm, we find even more features common to the DMT and prophetic states. These include darkness, vast visual perspectives, clouds, fire or fiery colors, intensely saturated and melting or flowing colors, and the recursiveness of images. When examining the actual forms that the experiences contain, common to both are round objects, vegetation, functional items such as furniture and weapons, architecture, and information-containing symbols. Regarding the beings in both altered states, one apprehends parts of beings, such as eyes, hands, and wings; statuary; and more or less living creatures partaking of nonhuman, humanoid, and human features. Some of these figures are quite bizarre: chimeras of animals and other animals, animals and humans, and animate objects with inanimate or machinelike objects.

The visual components of the two syndromes have different elements as well. One may find oneself in deep, star-filled space after receiving DMT but not during prophecy. Reptiles do not appear in the prophetic state, while they did in the DMT one; the opposite holds true for mammals. Interestingly, clearly human figures occur only rarely in the DMT experience, whereas they are more common in the prophetic. The palette of colors in the DMT state at first may appear greater than that of prophecy; however, the frequent presence of fire in prophecy may actually represent those fiery colors that the DMT subjects often report. This last finding raises the issue of functional equivalence of certain features of the two states, where different psychological and cultural factors influence what people apprehend and how they describe it.

13 Cognition

Two aspects of cognitive function, or "thinking," figure in this comparison of the prophetic and DMT states: thought processes and thought content. Thought processes involve *how* we think—fast or slow, clear or muddled. Thought content involves *what* we think—ideas or verbal information. The latter category constitutes the message the altered state contains. In this chapter I will focus primarily on thought processes. The meaning and the message of prophecy and the DMT experiences I will discuss at length in later chapters. One particular facet of cognition assesses the reality bases of the DMT and prophetic states. This is the appraising capacity. We see it at work when someone asks "What is this?" "Where am I?" or "Is this real?"

As with the other categories, the beings also affect cognitive function; for example, they may clarify an otherwise confusing situation. In addition, they possess cognitive attributes: sentience, awareness, and intelligence. In fact, these cognitive attributes are some of the beings' most striking characteristics.

LEVEL OF CONSCIOUSNESS

A common definition for *consciousness* is what we might call "level of awareness" or "alertness." As medical students on the wards, we quickly learned how to determine someone's "level of consciousness" and subsequently communicate that information to our colleagues. The spectrum ranges from coma to hyperalert. Responsiveness to the outside environment is an important factor that contributes to this assessment.

🦎 DMT

Volunteers were generally unaware of what was happening either in the hospital environment or to their own bodies because of the dissociation present at the peak of the DMT effect. They were nearly always "functionally deaf," oblivious to any outside sounds. Neither did they feel the uncomfortably firm grip of the blood pressure recording machine two minutes post-injection. This latter phenomenon was such a routine part of the experience that I didn't write it down during my otherwise assiduous note-taking and therefore don't have excerpts to present.

At the same time, volunteers were quite alert internally to the subjective effects of the drug. William commented on how he maintained mental clarity: *When I'm there, I'm not intoxicated. I'm lucid and sober* (*DMT,* 195).

🦎 PROPHECY

A word that appears in the Hebrew Bible to describe one's level of consciousness in prophecy is *tardeimah.* Its three-letter root *R-D-M* means to be in, or fall into, a deep sleep. A closely related Arabic word means to stop up or close; for example, a door or gap. *Tardeimah,* therefore, conveys the notion of reducing sensitivity to the outside world by stopping up the external senses. The onset of *tardeimah* in prophecy is rapid, and one often feels an accompanying fear or dread. This sudden and emotional onset of dissociating from the outside world is reminiscent of the DMT effect, as is the maintenance of alert awareness of what then takes place in the altered state.

Immediately before God speaks to Abraham: *as the sun was about to set,* tardeimah *fell upon [him], and behold, a great dread* (Gen. 15:12).

A being may effect sleep or stupor, as in Daniel's case: *As [the angel] spoke to me, I fell into a deep sleep with my face earthward* (Dan. 8:18).

With Adam, it's God who stupefies: *And YHVH God cast* tardeimah *upon the man, and he slept* (Gen. 2:21).

On the other hand, an angel may wake one up from sleep. Elijah, fleeing for his life from the king and queen of Israel, whom he has been relentlessly admonishing, lies down to die in the wilderness: *He lay and slept . . . and behold, an angel touching him, and he said to him: "Rise and eat"* (1 Kings 19:5).

CONFUSION OR LOSS OF INSIGHT

While one might maintain mental alertness during either the DMT or prophetic state, confusion may nevertheless figure prominently.

✖ DMT

Ida: *I looked down at my feet and didn't recognize them as my own* (*DMT,* 250).

Carlos: *I didn't know what was going on* (*DMT,* 229).

✖ PROPHECY

In recounting his prophetic dream to Daniel, the king of Babylonia tells him: *My thoughts upon my bed and the visions of my head bewildered me* (Dan. 4:2).

Daniel says about his own prophetic state: *I was bewildered by the vision* (Dan. 8:27).

THE AWARENESS, SENTIENCE, AND INTELLIGENCE OF BEINGS

These features of the beings are quite striking and contribute to much of the perplexity that confronts us when we attempt to understand their nature and function.

🦎 DMT

Dmitri commented on how the beings expected him when he appeared in an alien laboratory: *They had a space ready for me. They weren't as surprised as I was* (*DMT*, 197).

On the other hand, beings may not expect someone to enter into "their" world. Kevin described the female African warrior: *I have surprised her. She takes an aggressive and defensive posture. She says, "YOU DARE COME HERE?!"* (*DMT*, 261).

Chris noted this aspect of the beings' intelligence: *They were recognizing and identifying me* (*DMT*, 191).

William commented on their sapiency: *I felt like an infant. Not a human infant, but an infant relative to the intelligences represented by the Gumby* (*DMT*, 193).

🦎 PROPHECY

We rarely, if ever, read explicit comments about beings' cognitive characteristics in the prophetic state. It's as if the person apprehending the being is thinking, "Of course, the angel or God is sentient, intelligent, and aware; otherwise, how else could this conversation be taking place?"

One of the cognitive qualities of biblical beings is their capacity to interpret the sometimes obscure contents of the prophetic vision. This implies that the being-explicator possesses intelligence greater than that of the questioner. During Zechariah's vision of the golden candelabrum, he asks the accompanying angel: *"What are these, my lord?"* . . . *[He] said to me, "Do you not know what these are?" I said, "No, my lord." He replied and said to me, saying, "This is the word of YHVH"* (Zech. 4:4–6).

ASSESSMENT OF REALITY

A strikingly common finding in my research was that volunteers were convinced that intravenous DMT administration transported them to a world as real as everyday reality, perhaps even "more real."

Several factors play a role in our assessing how real a particular experience feels. *Temporal continuity* is one and consists of sensing that time is passing as it normally does. In a related manner, we also experience cause and effect operating in ways with which we are familiar. Things are how they are now because of how they were before. Additionally, we recognize our "self" as "I" or "me." We feel who we are and identify that self as the one who is observing or participating in the ongoing experience. Physical solidity also contributes to our sense of reality. Finally, we may compare our present state to other, more familiar ones, such as normal consciousness or a dream.

I will present more examples of how real the DMT state seemed than for the prophetic one because, as in the case of the beings' sentience, the issue rarely raises its head in the Hebrew Bible. The men and women we read about in the text simply assume the reality of their experience without questioning or commenting on it. We can infer how real the biblical prophetic state seems by the absence of any mention of its seeming unreality. In the DMT experience, however, the reality sense was something the volunteers and I were certain to discuss because of its surprisingly consistent and convincing quality.

Uncertainty of Reality

James Kugel, a contemporary Hebrew Bible scholar, refers to "the moment of confusion" in prophecy.[1] Similar to the DMT experience, this confusion occurs at the onset of the state. In both, once people get their bearings, much of what takes place consists of relatively normal interactions with the newly visible world.

✍ DMT

Ken recounted, as his horrifying encounter with crocodiles began: *At first I thought I was dreaming, having a nightmare. Then I realized it was really happening* (DMT, 252).

✍ PROPHECY

At the site of the burning bush, his first prophetic experience, Moses wonders if he's "seeing things": *He saw, and behold, the bush was burning in the fire, but the bush was not consumed. Moses said, "Why will the bush not be burned?"* (Exod. 3:2–3).

Similarly, young Samuel wonders if he's "hearing things" or if his teacher, Eli, is calling him: *YHVH called to Samuel, and he said, "Here I am." He ran to Eli and said, "Here I am, for you called me." And he said, "I did not call; go back and lie down"* (1 Sam. 3:4–5).

Familiarity and Recognition

When confronting circumstances that are especially novel, we use our memory to recognize elements in the experience and to compare and contrast them with those from a more familiar state. We might say to ourselves, "Does this feel like I'm dreaming?" "My blurred vision reminds me of taking too much anti-histamine," "Is this like alcohol intoxication?" Sometimes the present state may only allude to another more familiar one rather than obviously resemble it.

✸ DMT

Shanti was thirty-eight years old and the domestic partner of another volunteer, Cal. She was a therapist by trade, and her troubled son occupied much of her time. She described a sense of familiarity with the DMT world: *It's not what it was or was like, but more like what it reminded me of.*

Déjà vu is a French expression meaning "already seen." It refers to a situation feeling familiar even though it's not. In Allan's case, he had never before experienced DMT. When describing his session, he recognized the feeling as déjà vu. He said: *"This is just like the last time," I thought. . . . But this is my first time* (DMT, 223).

✸ PROPHECY

Those experiencing prophecy may remember previous visions or earlier events in the same vision. This seems to assist the prophet to understand what is presently taking place by adding a sense of temporal continuity.

Ezekiel invokes the memory of an earlier vision to identify the beings in his present one: *These were the Chayot that I had seen beneath the God of Israel at the Kevar River. And I knew that they were Cheruvim* (Ezek. 10:20).

Daniel: *I still was speaking in prayer, and the man Gabriel, whom I saw in the beginning vision, approached me* (Dan. 9:21).

Reality vs. the Dream State

DMT volunteers were nearly unanimous in labeling their experiences "not a dream." In the Hebrew Bible the situation is slightly more complex because many prophetic experiences take place in "visions of the night," an expression that means for some, but not all, medieval Jewish commentators a nocturnal dream. If there is a moment of confusion regarding whether the experience is a dream, as in Samuel's case above, it resolves quickly and there is no doubt that the state is prophetic.

🐾 DMT

Sean: *It seemed so natural and complete as it was happening. It wasn't like a dream at all* (*DMT,* 183).

🐾 PROPHECY

Biblical figures sometimes express their realization of the prophetic nature of their dream by using the term *behold.* This word seems to indicate the resolution of the moment of confusion. For example, after God assents to Solomon's request for wisdom, we read: *And Solomon awoke, and behold, a dream* (1 Kings 3:15).

Another king, this time of Egypt, dreams a particularly portentous dream of an upcoming terrible famine: *And Pharaoh awoke, and behold, a dream* (Gen. 41:7).

Death

Despite my warning the DMT volunteers that the rapid dissociation of the mind from the body might feel like death, some were uncertain whether they had died. In prophecy, while the awesomeness of the state may cause one to fear for one's life, we never read about someone thinking he or she died.

🦗 DMT

Rex: *I was certain I was dying* (*DMT,* 206).

Marsha: *I thought I had died and that I might not ever come back* (*DMT,* 163).

As Real as Everyday Reality

There are few if any explicit references in the Hebrew Bible to how real a prophetic encounter seemed. However, this feature was more striking for the DMT volunteers and they were certain to mention it.

🦗 DMT

While this world and the DMT one are quite different, volunteers considered them existentially equivalent. They also noted how the two levels of reality appeared to be operating simultaneously, in parallel with each other. Recognizing that they were inhabiting the DMT world because of an injection of a drug rarely diminished their conviction of its reality. They considered the drug to have *revealed* what they now apprehended rather than having *created* it. It was there all along, simply previously invisible.

Philip addressed the relationship between the two worlds. Before we asked all volunteers to wear black eyeshades, he described the first few minutes of his session: *It was so real I had to open my eyes. When I did the scene was overlaid on top of the room. I closed my eyes, and that removed the interference with what I had been seeing* (*DMT,* 182).

Rex noted the same phenomenon: *It's strange being in this state but feeling your hand on my arm and conversing, while all the alien activity is going on.*

Dmitri alluded to how the DMT world's ordinariness supported its being as real as this one: *It was incredibly un-psychedelic* (*DMT,* 197). He added: *My vision there is the same here as it is there.*

William's extended comments astutely captured another aspect of the DMT world: its convincing sense of being external and free-standing:

This is real. It's totally unexpected, quite constant and objective. One could interpret your looking at my pupils* as being observed, and the tubes in my body† as the tubes I'm seeing. But that is a metaphor, and this is not at all a metaphor. It's an independent, constant reality. . . . This is too proximal. It's not like some kind of drug. It's more like an experience of a new technology than a drug. You can choose to attend to this or not. It will continue to progress without you paying attention. You return not to where you left off, but to where things have gone since you left. It's not a hallucination, but an observation. (DMT, 195)

More Real than Real

No one in the prophetic text uses the expression "more real than real," but several DMT volunteers did.

✍ DMT

Willow: *It was so much more real than life* (DMT, 224).

Allan pointed out how slippery the notion of reality became when two such highly disparate realities appeared to exist side by side: *It's more real than reality. As it gets more familiar, it seems to be more and more alien.*

SUMMARY

In the cognitive sphere, the DMT and prophetic states overlap to a substantial degree. In both we find frightening initial mental confusion as one loses contact with the outside world. However, the confusion usually resolves quickly, and individuals in either state then demonstrate intact cognitive function and a rather striking clear-headedness, lucid-

---

*We checked the size of subjects' pupils by using a reference card held next to their briefly open eyes.

†We inserted an intravenous line into each arm before sessions began, one for administering the drug or placebo and one from which we drew blood samples.

ity, and intact memory. Those in the DMT state more often struggled to determine the reality bases of their experience and consistently concluded that the DMT world felt as least as real as this one. In prophecy, we need to infer the "as real as real" quality because we rarely read anything to the contrary. In both syndromes the beings possess and exercise cognitive functions. They are sentient, intelligent, and aware of those apprehending them.

14 Volition and Will

Volitional effects of the DMT and prophetic states manifest in alterations in the ability to willfully interact with one's own body and mind, as well as with the outside environment. This category is not as clear-cut as the ones we have already covered because direct effects on other functions may indirectly elicit what appear to be explicitly volitional ones. That is, the will to do or think something may exist, but not the ability. In the DMT state, for example, a volunteer may have wished to move, but somatic effects, the immobility that DMT usually caused, precluded doing so. Similarly, the cognitive effect confusion may indirectly impact volition in that one is simply too confused to direct one's will. Nevertheless, I will include examples of these types of indirect volitional effects in this chapter because they appear primarily volitional.*

There are a limited number of volitional effects in the DMT and prophetic states. They concern movement, speaking, and overall self-efficacy. As in the other categories, the beings play a significant role.

---

*These issues may underlie both our findings and those of other research groups that the volitional category of the Hallucinogen Rating Scale is generally less sensitive to various drug effects than are the other categories.

MOVEMENT

Cannot Move

✍ DMT

In her visions, Brenda's "nonphysical" self was unable to move through a distracting curtain of colorful light: *The most intense part of each trip was spent tangled up in these colors* (*DMT,* 214).

Karl commented on how the beings affected him: *One of them made it impossible to move* (*DMT,* 188).

✍ PROPHECY

Ezekiel also cannot pass through a visual obstacle: *a stream I could not cross . . . a stream that could not be crossed* (Ezek. 47:5).

Forced to Move

✍ DMT

I previously noted how Cassandra felt something physically grab her hand and yank her. Here, Robert described a similar sense of a being moving his "self" passively: *This thing sucked me out of my head and I was taken into space, a black sky with a million stars* (*DMT,* 189).

✍ PROPHECY

God moves Moses passively at the beginning of the Mount Sinai revelation: *Moses was drawn to the thick cloud where God was* (Exod. 20:18).

Ezekiel provides a fascinating and baffling observation regarding what appear to be volitional characteristics of the beings. These are effects of the will of one set of beings, the Chayot, on the impulse to move in another set of beings, the Ofanim. Note that the word for *spirit** in these verses may also mean *will* or *disposition.*

Ruach, whose "ch" is pronounced gutturally.

Each in the direction of its face[s]* they would go; toward wherever there was the spirit to go, they went. . . . When the Chayot go, the Ofanim move by their side, and when the Chayot were lifted from upon the earth, the Ofanim were lifted. . . . To wherever there was the spirit to go they would go, to there the spirit would go. The Ofanim were lifted opposite them for the spirit of the Chayot was in the Ofanim. When they moved, they moved, and when they halted, they halted. And when they were lifted from upon the earth, the Ofanim were lifted opposite them, for the spirit of the Chayot was in the Ofanim. (Ezek. 1:12, 19, 20–21)

SPEAKING

Cannot Speak
🦎 DMT

In Ken's vision of the crocodiles, he noted that in addition to their pinning and immobilizing him: *I couldn't speak* (*DMT*, 252).

🦎 PROPHECY

God tells Ezekiel: *I will make your tongue cleave to your palate and you shall become mute* (Ezek. 3:26).

David describes how God indirectly, through emotions, effects a similar outcome: *You grasped my eyes and I was agitated and could not speak* (Ps. 77:5).

Forced to Speak
🦎 DMT

Many volunteers excitedly began to describe their experiences while still under the influence of the drug but after peak effects had resolved. They seemed to feel a pressure to share, as Cleo's enthusiastic inarticulateness demonstrated: *I had the expectation that I would be going "out,"*

---

*The Hebrew word for "face" and "faces" is the same.

but I went in, into every cell in my body. It was amazing. It wasn't just my body . . . themselves . . . themselves . . . it's all connected. Oh, that's what I did. Okay (DMT, 237).

✎ PROPHECY

One theory of how prophecy works is that God simply compels one in a prophetic state to speak by putting words into one's mouth. The person acts as nothing more than a mouthpiece for God. Some of the examples below reinforce that notion by explicitly excluding any contribution from the human speaker.

When God promises to raise prophets among the Hebrews after Moses dies, He says: *I will place My words in his mouth; he shall speak to them everything that I will command him* (Deut. 18:18).

Balaam the gentile prophet is keenly aware of his inability to affect his own utterances: *Am I empowered to say anything? Whatever word God puts into my mouth, that shall I speak* (Num. 22:38).

And Jeremiah describes his inability to resist the pressure to speak: *I labored to contain [God's prophecy] but was unable* (Jer. 20:9).

SENSE OF CONTROL

Volitional effects may extend beyond specific functions such as movement and speech to a more general sense regarding how much one feels in control of oneself as a whole. Feelings of decreased self-control are much more common than those of a heightened sense of control in both the DMT and prophetic experiences.

Decrease of Control
✎ DMT

Sean: *I think I've learned what it's like to die, to be completely helpless in the throes of something* (DMT, 223).

Chris: *I try and program it and I go in with an idea of what to see, but I just can't* (DMT, 191–92).

Several volunteers felt that they had received a mission, something that the experience had imposed on them. Cal reported: *I feel a responsibility, being conscious of what I need to do. I felt the words come to me, "Teach, learn."*

Dmitri: *Somehow we had a mission. . . . Their work definitely had something to do with my presence. Exactly what remains a mystery* (*DMT,* 197).

Occasionally, a volunteer reported feeling that the beings manipulated his or her physical makeup. By doing so, the effect of the DMT encounter would continue to influence the passive volunteer. Rex stated: *The thought came to me with certainty that they were manipulating my DNA, changing its structure* (*DMT,* 206).

William similarly noted: *The machine felt as if it was rewiring me, reprogramming me* (*DMT,* 194).

In addition, recall Ben's experience of the cactus beings inserting a rod under the skin of his forearm, presumably to continue influencing him after his session.

✒ PROPHECY

A common phenomenon in the prophetic state is the sense that God "happens upon" someone and initiates the experience, instead of it occurring as a direct result of one's own efforts.

God tells Moses how to explain the origin of Aaron's and his mission to Pharaoh to release the Hebrews from Egyptian bondage: *YHVH the God of the Hebrews happened upon us* (Exod. 3:18).

Similarly: *God happened upon Balaam* (Num. 23:4).

Jeremiah is resigned to his inability to resist God's commands: *You enticed me, YHVH, and I was enticed; You overcame me and You prevailed* (Jer. 20:7).

God commands Ezekiel: *Do not be rebellious . . . open your mouth and eat that which I give you* (Ezek. 2:8). Ezekiel's response: *So I opened my mouth, and He fed me this scroll* (Ezek. 3:1–2).

God informs Ezekiel of how He also will force upon him a fundamental change in his nature, a sort of rewiring: *I will give you a new heart, and a new spirit I will put into your innards. I will remove the heart of stone from your flesh and give you a heart of flesh* (Ezek. 36:26).

Samuel tells Saul that when the latter encounters the band of prophets: *The spirit of YHVH shall pass over you, and you will prophesy with them and be changed into another man* (1 Sam. 10:6).

Increase or Maintenance of Control

The maintenance of "ordinary" self-control in the face of the overpowering DMT or prophetic experience may be noteworthy in and of itself.

✒ DMT

Cleo commented on her ability to direct her will: *Then the patterns began. I said to myself, "Let me go through you"* (DMT, 237).

Brenda: *A pulsating "entity" appeared in the patterns. . . . It was trying to coax me to go with it. At first I was reluctant* (DMT, 213).

In one of the rare examples of a volunteer feeling a greater sense of control, Sean described: *I felt like something of a god: "Put away that sound! Remove the feeling of needing to pee!"*

Elena's paradoxical comment suggested feeling more in control by having lost control: *I didn't have to wonder what to do next* (DMT, 241).

✒ PROPHECY

Isaiah describes how he maintains his decision-making power during his initial prophetic call: *I heard the voice of my Lord, saying, "Whom shall I send, and who will go for us?" And I said, "Here I am; send me"* (Isa. 6:8).

Zechariah experiences a complex vision of the Temple's High Priest, the Satan, God, and God's angel. At a certain point, Zechariah commands an angel, representing a greater sense of efficacy than normal: *I said, "Let them put a pure turban on his head." And they put a pure turban on his head* (Zech. 3:5).

SUMMARY

While volitional effects occupy a relatively small portion of our comparators, robust and convincing similarities exist between the DMT and prophetic states in this category. These include modifications in the ability to influence movement and speech, as well as more global effects on self-efficacy and self-control.

15 Relatedness

A Unique Prophetic Category

As I have previously emphasized, Buddhist psychology played a signifi-cant role in the DMT study. Not surprisingly it also has influenced my approach to the prophetic state. The Abhidharma, the Buddhist psy-chological canon, helped shape the construction of the new rating scale our team developed for statistical analyses of the DMT effect. In addi-tion, Abhidharma psychological notions have guided my comparison of the DMT and prophetic states. Just as I deconstructed the drug effect into the familiar Buddhist categories of physicality, affect, cognition, perception, and volition, so I have done in the case of the prophetic state in these last several chapters. This method has provided us with a highly effective side-by-side examination of prophecy and the DMT effect.

However, in *DMT: The Spirit Molecule* I devoted substantially more effort to describing the narratives of my research volunteers than I did to analyzing the component parts of their experiences. This is because the narratives captured the fullness of drug sessions to a much greater degree than did lists of heuristically useful but relatively disconnected individual phenomenological elements. By treating the narratives and the phenomenology as mostly distinct from one another, I missed an element that may have bridged the two approaches. This element is what I refer to as a category of "relatedness." In retrospect, my focus on the Buddhist model, especially the expectation that DMT would occasion mystical-unitive enlightenment-like experiences, may have interfered with my seeing that bridge at the time.

In enlightenment, relatedness becomes moot as the subject/object dichotomy drops away. If there is no object and no subject, there is no relationship. However, the DMT volunteers consistently described interacting with the contents of their experiences, especially with the beings, in a thoroughly engaged and reciprocal manner. On the other hand, "a-relational" enlightenment-like states were extraordinarily rare. Sean's account is the only truly typical one:

> *I immediately saw a bright yellow-white light directly in front of me. I chose to open to it. I was consumed by it and became part of it. There were no distinctions—no figures or lines, shadows or outlines. There was no body or anything inside or outside. I was devoid of self, of thought, of time, of space, of a sense of separateness or ego, or of anything but the white light. There are no symbols in my language that can begin to describe that sense of pure being, oneness, and ecstasy. There was a great sense of stillness and ecstasy (DMT, 244).*

While Buddhism does analyze relatedness, it does so in order to do away with it. The Abhidharma describes a twelve-step model called "dependent origination"[1] that is consistent with Buddhism's view that the phenomenal world, both inner and outer, has no inherent reality. This world is conditioned, composite, and ephemeral, and our restless, painful, unenlightened state results from mistaking the unreal for the real. More precisely, it is the result of a flawed *relationship* with the unreal, treating it as if it were real. Dependent origination teaches practitioners to treat all these seemingly real things as objects of meditation, the practice of which leads to a more enlightened consciousness.

Buddhism consequently has developed meditation practices that deconstruct the components of consensus reality. This process results in apprehending reality's essential lack of substantiality and the futility of hoping to derive satisfaction from it. The practitioner "de-realizes" every object with the intended result of distancing "the self" from "it," effectively precluding what we might traditionally consider a "relationship" with anything.

Some of these meditation methods proved helpful in the DMT studies. I might suggest them to volunteers who felt "stuck" in particular aspects of their experience.* The successful application of techniques for redirecting attention from those distracting elements usually led to a more fulfilling session. However, this approach to the DMT experience was remedial and technical rather than directing entry into a unitive-mystical experience. Instead, it helped provide a more highly articulated and deeper relationship with the next level of content, not emptiness, that lay behind the distracting phenomena.

RELATEDNESS, THE DMT EXPERIENCE, AND PROPHECY

As I began studying the Hebrew Bible, I noticed how in a general way the DMT and prophetic states corresponded better than did the DMT and enlightenment experiences. Gradually, the quality of relatedness appeared as one of the bases of that superiority. In the Hebrew Bible, the relationship between one experiencing prophecy and God or His angels is first and foremost. It is the summit of the prophetic state. One does not abandon the relationship or neutralize it. There is never "becoming one with" anything; rather, one "is with" or "in" new relationships. He or she engages in as full a manner as possible with an alternate reality that possesses a higher value than that which he or she normally perceives. Prophecy shares this feature with the DMT state, a feature that suggested to me the new metric of relatedness. In a way, it is a "biblical skandha."

Most of the interactions in the DMT and prophetic states occur with the beings; thus, they figure prominently in this discussion. I already have characterized the beings' properties, such as their color

---

*For example Brenda, *DMT: The Spirit Molecule,* pages 213–14.

or form, sentience, and intelligence. I also have presented examples of their effects on someone perceiving them using the familiar somatic, emotional, and other categories. They may frighten someone (affect) or may carry him or her through space (somatic). Here, I describe more complex interactions.

It may at first glance appear that the previous categories I've used provide a sufficient framework for characterizing all of the subjective features of the DMT and prophetic states, and that a new category is unnecessary. Admittedly, some of the examples in this chapter may fit as well into one or the other of those I've already reviewed. However, I believe that the utility of the notion of relatedness will become clearer as you work your way through this material, because it captures features of the experiences that other categories do not. For example, it helps highlight how communication takes place between a being and someone perceiving it. The notion of relatedness also exerts an organizing effect on seemingly unrelated subjective effects, serving as a kind of metacategory, subsuming other functions under its domain.

PHYSICAL RELATEDNESS

Sometimes the body is the medium of the relationship, rather than words.

DMT

Dmitri noted a "physical" relationship with one of beings: *It was almost a sexual bond, but not sex like intercourse, but a total body communication* (*DMT,* 197).

PROPHECY

Isaiah describes an angel touching his mouth with a glowing coal. This act removes his guilt, perhaps from maligning his fellow Jerusalemites. Physical contact thus effects a moral transformation: *He touched it to my mouth and said, "Behold, this has touched your lips; your iniquity has gone away and your sin shall be atoned for"* (Isa. 6:7).

AFFECTIVE RELATEDNESS

I have previously noted how beings may elicit emotional effects in those apprehending them; for example, fear or reassurance. In addition, emotions may act as the currency of exchange. These interactions were rare in the DMT state and never occurred in the prophetic one.

🦋 DMT

In the beginning of Rex's session, he feared for his life as insectlike beings threatened to overwhelm him: *As I accepted my death and dissolution into God's love, the insectoids began to feed on my heart, devouring the feelings of love and surrender. . . . It was an empathic communication, a telepathic communication (DMT, 206–7).*

NONVERBAL PERCEPTUAL COMMUNICATION

Auditory

While most of what people "hear" in either the DMT or prophetic state is verbal in nature, sometimes a more inchoate sound is the medium of exchange.

🦋 DMT

Rex: *The intense pulsating-buzzing sound and vibration are an attempt by the DMT entities to communicate with me (DMT, 208).*

🦋 PROPHECY

God tells Elijah that He does not communicate through wind, earthquake, or fire, but in: *a still, thin sound* (1 Kings 19:12).

Visual

The following excerpts are examples of a being causing one to see a particular visual phenomenon and thereby communicating certain information.

✍ DMT

Karl described beings standing on the side of a highway: *They held up placards, showing me these incredibly beautiful, complex, swirling geometric scenes in them* (*DMT,* 188).

Sean noted a green female being standing by his side while he watched a city in the distance: *She had her right hand on a dial that seemed to control the panorama we were watching* (*DMT,* 244).

Rex commented that the beings: *were sharing all this with me, letting me see all this* (*DMT,* 208). He also described relatively undifferentiated light as a medium of communication: *There were rays of psychedelic yellow light coming out of the face of the reassuring entity. She was trying to communicate with me* (*DMT,* 209).

Chris reported a type of sign language that three reptilian beings used to direct him toward an information-rich visual display: *They were . . . trying to make me understand, not with words, but with gestures. They wanted me to look into their bodies. I saw inside them and understood reproduction, what it's like before birth, the passage into the body* (*DMT,* 191).

✍ PROPHECY

God instructs Moses in how to build particular Tabernacle utensils: *See and make, according to their form that you are shown on the mountain* (Exod. 25:40).

In his final address to the Hebrews before his death, Moses recounts how God manifested to them at the Sinai revelation: *and on earth It caused you to see Its great fire* (Deut. 4:36).

During one of Zechariah's visions: *YHVH caused me to see four carpenters* (Zech. 2:3).

Jeremiah: *YHVH caused me to see, and behold, two baskets of figs* (Jer. 24:1).

Elisha's attendant cannot see what Elisha does until: *YHVH opened the lad's eyes and he saw, and behold, the mountain was full of fiery horses and chariots* (2 Kings 6:17).

COGNITIVE COMMUNICATION

The aspect of cognition that receives, processes, and transmits concepts is the intellect. It is the arena in which verbal communication takes place. Many elements are operative in verbal communication occurring in the DMT and prophetic states.

Spoken vs. Telepathic

Do those in the prophetic and DMT states apprehend verbal information with the ears or only with their minds? While this issue is rarely explicit in the prophetic literature, it frequently appeared in my conversations with the DMT volunteers.* They (and we) are so accustomed to hearing the spoken voice with the ears that any evidence to the contrary was noteworthy.

✐ DMT

Gabe, a thirty-three-year-old rural family physician, was one of the few volunteers with previous experience using vaporized DMT. He described seeing "spirits of life" during his study session: *They were talking to me but they weren't making a sound (DMT, 190).*

Sean added this detail regarding the green female being: *She turned slightly toward me and asked, "What else would you like?" I answered telepathically, "Well, what else have you got?" (DMT, 244).*

✐ PROPHECY

While I have already referred to this verse in chapter 12, Perception, under the heading "Silence," I wish to present it again here as one of the only instances I could find in which someone experiencing prophecy may be referring to telepathy. Job's friend describes how a being communicates with him: *I heard silence and a voice* (Job 4:16).

---

*As I will discuss later, the predominance of the "spoken voice" in biblical prophetic experience distinguishes it from the DMT state. One solution to this apparent disparity is to consider most, if not all, the verbal exchanges the Hebrew Bible describes as taking place telepathically.

Quality of Communication

In most cases of prophecy, the quality of verbal exchange is relatively clear, typical of a normal conversation. In the DMT state, it was more often difficult for the subject to establish effective communication with the beings. Some volunteers observed that the beings and they did not share a common language. In addition, anxiety may inhibit effective converse in both sets of experiences.

✥ DMT

Brenda: *A male presence tries to communicate with me, but I don't understand. I use my mind to ask, "What?" The reply is garbled (DMT, 212).*

Dmitri: *They were waiting for me to acquaint myself with the environment and movement and language of this space (DMT, 197).*

In Rex's case, the intensity of communication precluded effective exchange: *They were pouring communication into me but it was just so intense. I couldn't bear it (DMT, 209).*

In a reversal of roles, Cleo needed to monitor the strength of her own attempts to communicate: *I had to be careful not to ask it too much or it would wane.*

Roland noted how clear communication could be: *Then a voice came, like the voice of God. . . . It was explaining things, just like a good friend would sit down next to you.*

✥ PROPHECY

Hundreds of examples exist in the Hebrew Bible of "typical" conversations between someone in a prophetic state and God or His angels. However, this is not always the case, and effective communication may require special effort.

God presses Ezekiel to pay better attention to improve his comprehension of His instructions: *Son of man, set your heart, and see with your eyes, and hear with your ears all that I am speaking with you (Ezek. 44:5).*

There are several explicit references in the text to how familiar and clear verbal communication may be when it uses the expression "face to face": *YHVH spoke to Moses face to face, as a man would speak to his fellow* (Exod. 33:11).

Patterns of Communication

Certain patterns emerged when I carefully examined exchanges between beings and those who perceive them. One factor is directionality. Is communication one-way or two-way, or are the parties relatively detached from each other, with the humans receiving information as "bystanders"?

MINIMAL ENGAGEMENT

Research subjects sometimes reported that they or the beings observed, studied, treated, and regarded each other with various levels of involvement.

Simple Witnessing by the Experient

Someone in a DMT or prophetic state may just passively observe the activities of beings. Ezekiel's observation of the "chariot" is a prophetic example.

DMT

Lucas described a similar phenomenon: *They were doing some kind of routine technological work and paid no attention to me* (*DMT,* 189–90).

Disinterested Observation by Beings

DMT

William described the Gumby-like figure watching over him: *It was aware of me, but not particularly concerned. Sort of a detached concern, like a parent would feel looking into a playpen at his one-year-old lying there* (*DMT,* 193).

Robert: *I felt observed by the insect-thing and others like it. Then they lost interest* (*DMT,* 189).

Overhearing

An indirect means of communicating occurs when one overhears a voice speaking about him or her or about something else.

🦎 DMT

William, after finding himself in a high-tech playpen, remarked: *Then I heard two to three male voices talking. I heard one of them say, "He's arrived"* (*DMT,* 193).

🦎 PROPHECY

Isaiah describes overhearing a being-to-being exchange, as angels call to each other in God's presence: *One called to the other and said, "Holy, holy, holy is YHVH of Hosts*; the whole earth is full of Its glory"* (Isa. 6:3).

Zechariah is privy to a conversation between God and the Satan: *YHVH said to the Satan, "YHVH will rebuke you, the Satan"* (Zech. 3:2).

UNIDIRECTIONAL

Sometimes one-way communication takes the form of charging or ordering. This is much rarer in the DMT state than in the prophetic one.

🦎 DMT

Brenda: *They told me to "embrace peace"* (*DMT,* 214).

🦎 PROPHECY

An angel commands Ezekiel after transporting him to the Temple in Jerusalem: *"Son of man, now excavate the wall." And I excavated in the wall. . . . Then he said to me, "Enter and see the evil abominations which they do there"* (Ezek. 8:8–9).

The Ten Commandments are paradigmatic examples of charging, as for example: *Remember the Sabbath day* (Exod. 20:8); *Honor your father and your mother* (Exod. 20:12); and *Do not steal* (Exod. 20:13).

---

*Hosts usually refers to the "heavenly hosts"; that is, the celestial bodies comprising the moon, planets, stars, constellations, and spheres.

Sometimes beings order or charge each other, as Ezekiel describes: *[God] commanded the man clothed in linen, saying: "Take fire from between the Galgal, from between the Cheruvim"* (Ezek. 10:6).

Zechariah overhears two angels speaking about him, and one charges the other: *Behold, the angel who was speaking to me was going forth, and another angel was going forth toward him. He said to him, "Run, speak to that young man over there"* (Zech. 2:7–8).

BIDIRECTIONAL

We find in both the prophetic and DMT states the "question and answer" format. A being asks what someone sees, and then confirms, corrects, or expands upon the answer. This pattern mimics what sometimes occurs in normal discourse when a question functions to initiate a conversation, or to point out the obvious, rather than reflect the questioner's desire to know the ostensible answer. On the other hand, when someone in a DMT or prophetic state asks a question, there is an overwhelming desire to learn the answer. This reflects how the beings usually occupy a higher ranking in the relationship with respect to power, knowledge, and other variables.

DMT

Sean captured the essence of this phenomenon: *I'm asking questions and getting answers (DMT, 243).*

A unique property of the DMT beings' "speech" is its sing-song quality, lilting and repetitive. Leo reported an example: *Welcoming, curious, they almost sang, . . . "Now do you see? Now do you see?" Trilling, sing-song voices (DMT, 344).*

Rex also spoke of this phenomenon, when after telling the insectlike beings that God is love, they replied: *Even here? Even here? (DMT, 206)*

PROPHECY

The Hebrew Bible presents a general description of this type of communication: *Moses would speak and God would answer him in a voice* (Exod. 19:19).

In these examples, a rhetorical question serves to initiate a conversation. An angel appears to Sarah's maidservant, Hagar, in the wilderness: *He said, "Hagar, maidservant of Sarai,* from where have you come and where are you going?" And she said, "I am running away from Sarai, my mistress"* (Gen. 16:7–8).

Elijah arrives at a cave on God's mountain, where He asks: *Why are you here, Elijah?* (1 Kings 19:9).

God repeatedly asks Ezekiel: *Do you see what they do?* (Ezek. 8:6); *Have you seen?* (Ezek. 8:12); *Do you see?* (Ezek. 8:15, 17).

Implying the higher rank of an angel's knowledge than that of a prophet, Zechariah frequently asks an angel to clarify the meaning of his visions, as for example: *"What are these, my lord?" The angel replied and said to me . . .* (Zech. 6:4–5).

Here two beings engage in a question and answer format to help clarify for Daniel when a certain prediction might come to pass: *I heard a holy one speaking. And the holy one said to the anonymous one who was speaking, "Until when, this vision . . . ?" And he said to me, "Until nightfall"* (Dan. 8:13–14).

Contention

A subtype of bidirectional exchange consists of arguing, complaining, testing, and bargaining with a being, attempting to change a course of events leading toward an undesirable outcome. The Hebrew Bible reports many examples of rather edgy exchanges with beings, while this is much less common in the DMT state. Problems with communication may impair the DMT volunteers' ability to engage in this rapid give-and-take manner. However, it also may be that the frequently catastrophic message of the prophetic state and the prophet's attempt to prevent such dire predictions coming to pass makes this type of exchange less relevant to the DMT experience.

---

*Sarah's original name.

✍ DMT

Research subjects described more frequently their *inability* to negotiate or argue with the beings. Kevin, when presented with an opportunity to push back against the frightening African war goddess, quickly retreated: *She says, "YOU DARE TO COME HERE?!" I mentally reply, "I guess so" (DMT,* 261).

Ben remarked on his inability to negotiate with the beings who inserted a probe into his arm: *There were no reassurances with the probe. Simply business (DMT,* 199).

✍ PROPHECY

Moses resists God's charge to lead the Hebrews out of Egyptian bondage despite God's reassurance, guarantee of success, and anger at his refusal. The following distills their exchange, in which Moses begins: *"Who am I that I should go to Pharaoh and that I should take the children of Israel out from Egypt?" And He said, "Because I will be with you."* Moses argues that Israel's elders won't believe it is God who sent him. *Moses said to God, "[When] they say to me, 'What is His name?'—what shall I say to them?" God said, "I shall be as I shall be"* (Exod. 3:11–14). Still not convinced, Moses rejoins: *"But they will not believe me"* (Exod. 4:1). He then offers a more specific excuse: *"Please my Lord, I am not a man of words, not since yesterday nor since the day before yesterday . . . for I am heavy of mouth and heavy of speech."* God's patience begins to wear thin: *YHVH said to him, "Who makes a mouth for man, or who makes one dumb or deaf, or sighted or blind? Is it not I, YHVH? So now, go! I shall be with your mouth and teach you what you will say." [Moses] replied, "Please, my Lord, send through whomever [else] You will send." The wrath of YHVH burned against Moses* (Exod. 4:10–14). Finally, God compromises and assigns Aaron, Moses's older brother, to be his spokesman.

We read eleven verses describing Abraham's challenge to God to be a true judge, attempting to shame the deity in the process, and spare Sodom and Gomorrah despite their overwhelming wickedness:

Abraham approached [God] and said, "Will You also wipe out the righteous along with the wicked? What if there are fifty righteous ones in the midst of the city? Would You still wipe it out rather than spare the place for the sake of the fifty righteous ones in its midst? It would be a sacrilege for You to do such a thing, to kill the righteous with the wicked, so the righteous will be like the wicked.* *It would be sacrilege for You. Shall the judge of the earth not do justice?" YHVH said, "If I find in Sodom fifty righteous ones in the midst of the city, I will spare the entire place on their account."* (Gen. 18:23–26)

Abraham persists and gets God to agree to spare Sodom for the sake of forty-five, forty, thirty, twenty, and finally ten. Unfortunately, even ten do not exist.

Jacob bargains with the angel with whom he just wrestled, and while he is able to extract a blessing from him, he fails to learn the angel's name:

[The angel] said, "Let me go, for the dawn has arisen. [Jacob] said, "I will not let you go unless you bless me." He said to him, "What is your name?" He said, "Jacob." He said, "No longer will it be said that your name is Jacob, but rather 'Israel,'\† for you have striven with God and with man and prevailed." Jacob asked and said, "Tell me now your name." He said, "What is this that you ask my name?" And he blessed him there. (Gen. 32:27–30)

PURPOSE OF THE RELATIONSHIP

Interactions with beings nearly always possess a function. I divide these into three broad types: beneficial, detrimental, and ambiguous.

---

*Suffer the same fate, even though they don't deserve it.

† One possible translation of *Israel* is "he who strives with God."

Beneficial: Guide, Guard, Bless, and Supervise

🦎 DMT

Willow: *The larger beings were there to sustain and support me* (*DMT,* 225).

Blessing may occur in the DMT state. Gabe reported: *It was more as if they were blessing me, the spirits of life were blessing me* (*DMT,* 190).

Roland reported a being guarding him: *Two spiders, white and black, the white was protecting me from the black one, which tried to eat me last time.*

Rex described beings protecting another being; in this case, his beneficent bee-like ally: *I guess the guardians were keeping me from seeing her* (*DMT,* 208).

Dmitri noticed one of the beings supervising the others, implying a hierarchy among them: *There was one main creature, and he seemed to be behind it all, overseeing everything* (*DMT,* 197).

In a role reversal, Brenda helped the beings: *I reached out my hands across the universe and prepared to be a bridge. I let this energy pass through me to them. I said something like, "See, there I did it for you. You have it." They were grateful* (*DMT,* 215).

🦎 PROPHECY

Abraham fears that he has used up all his merit after defeating a much more powerful military opponent. God assures him of his protection: *I am a shield for you; your reward is very great* (Gen. 15:1).

Jeremiah doubts his ability to withstand the people's assaults on him when carrying out his mission. God similarly promises: *I am with you to rescue you* (Jer. 1:8). He then "fortifies" the prophet with a feeling of courage: *I have made you this day as a fortified city, as an iron pillar, and as copper walls against the entire land* (Jer. 1:18).

After awakening Elijah, who had laid down hoping to die, an angel also feeds him:

An angel was touching him and said to him: "Rise, eat." And he gazed, and behold, near his head a coal-baked cake and a flask of water. He ate and drank and went back and lay down. The angel of YHVH returned to him a second time and touched him and said; "Arise, eat, as the journey is too much for you." He arose and ate and drank and went on the strength of that meal.* (1 Kings 19:5–8)

In this example, which I previously noted in chapter 12, Perception, a being is guarding another spiritual object. After expelling Adam and Eve from the Garden of Eden, God: *stationed at the east of the Garden of Eden the Cheruvim and the flame of the turning sword, to guard the way to the Tree of Life* (Gen. 3:24).

Blessing is common in the prophetic experience. We read above how Jacob forces the angel with whom he wrestled to bless him. Here God blesses him: *And God appeared to Jacob again . . . and blessed him* (Gen. 35:9).

In Ezekiel's vision of the Valley of the Bones, he provides the beings with a benefit, as did Brenda, in this case, revivifying them: *I prophesied as I had been commanded, and the spirit entered them and they came to life* (Ezek. 37:10).

Teaching and Instruction
The primary relational role of the beings is to impart information. I will detail that message in chapters 17 and 18, but for now, I wish to simply note this function.

✒ DMT
Chris remarked on the being's educative role: *They were trying to show me as much as possible* (*DMT,* 192).

✒ PROPHECY
Zechariah beholds a complex scene containing horses, a pool, and trees. He asks an angel in the vision: *"What are these, my lord?" The angel who*

---

*Again, hoping to die.

was speaking to me said to me, "I will show you what these are" (Zech. 1:9).

An angel likewise tells Ezekiel: *for in order to show you have you been brought here* (Ezek. 40:4).

Harmful
☚ DMT
Experiences of injury or a threat of harm are rare in the DMT experience. I've described Ken's assault by crocodiles and Kevin's confrontation with the African war goddess. Volunteers did comment on a less explicit but real sense of danger. For example, Gerry, a psychiatric resident in his late twenties, heard a frightening jack-in-the-box-like being say to him: *Now I've got you; there's no place to go.*

☚ PROPHECY
The angel with whom Jacob wrestles: *struck the socket of his hip; so Jacob's hip-socket was dislocated as he wrestled with him* (Gen. 32:26). The next morning: *and [Jacob] was limping on his hip* (Gen. 32:32).

While dire predictions abound in the prophetic literature regarding the Hebrew and other nations, sometimes these are more personal, as with the DMT volunteers. In chapter 11, Emotions, I described how the diviner of Endor allows Saul to behold the dead Samuel's spirit. That spirit informs Saul of his imminent death on the battlefield: *YHVH has turned away from you and has become your adversary. . . . Tomorrow you and your sons will be with me* (1 Sam. 28:16, 19).

The king of Babylonia sees a hand, part of a being, write words on the wall of his palace, and Daniel assumes the role of the interpreting angel: *God has measured your kingship and terminated it; you have been weighed in the scales and found wanting. Your kingdom has been broken up* (Dan. 5:26–28).

Balaam sees a sword-wielding angel on the road only after his female donkey does. The angel then tells him: *Had she not turned away from me, I would now even have killed you* (Num. 22:33).

Ambiguous

🦎 DMT

Cassandra commented on this feature of the beings: *I had a feeling they could turn on me, a little less than completely friendly* (*DMT*, 169).

Ben: *They weren't benevolent but they weren't non-benevolent* (*DMT*, 198–99).

🦎 PROPHECY

Joshua, at the head of the Hebrew forces invading Canaan, encounters a being whose attitude he cannot clearly assess. He asks the angel: *Are you with us or with our enemies?* (Josh. 5:13).

This exchange points to another example of how the Hebrew Bible might inform a psychedelic drug experience. That is, when faced with uncertainty regarding a being's beneficence or malevolence, one solution is to simply ask.

SUMMARY

At face value, this novel category of relatedness appears to serve at least two valuable functions. First, it detects unique elements of subjective experience that the other categories do not. Second, it exerts an organizing influence on different categories that may at first glance appear unrelated. For example, we may understand individual affective and volitional effects as part of a particular relationship rather than, or in addition to, two independent phenomena.

Impressive similarities emerge when using this metric to compare the Hebrew Bible's reports of prophetic experience with those of the DMT volunteers. In both states, the currency of exchange consists of several different modalities: sound, vision, the body, and emotions. In most cases, however, the relationship is verbal and occurs in the cognitive field of the intellect. These verbal exchanges are more or less understandable, display varying levels of reciprocity, and sometimes follow stereotypical patterns such as "question and answer" and the "rhetorical question." The effects of these various interactions extend into a number of domains: blessing, overseeing, healing, guarding, guiding, and informing. In addition, harm may accrue to someone as a result of their interaction with a being.

Differences exist between the two states. Emotional communication occurs in the DMT state but not the prophetic one, verbal "sparring" with beings occurs in prophecy but not in the DMT state, and only DMT volunteers felt the beings regarding them in a detached, impersonal manner. While this latter finding may reflect the clinical setting in which drug sessions occurred, I also am aware of similar reports from those who use DMT in more social and shamanic non-research settings.

The most salient difference between the two experiences, however, is simply that the interactions are much more complex in the prophetic than in the DMT state. One gets the impression that these types of exchanges are part and parcel of what one might expect to encounter in the world of our biblical figures. In contrast, the existence of and interactions with the beings frequently nonplussed research subjects, and this impeded effective communication. Perhaps with greater regularity of contact and longer exposure, we might begin to see the level of relatedness in the drug state approximate that of the prophetic one. In addition, learning more about the beings through study of the prophetic text, in which interaction and relatedness play a critical role, may provide useful information regarding the beings' nature, function, and methods of interacting with them more effectively.

16 Kavod

God's Glory

The term *kavod* frequently appears in the Hebrew Bible. The most common translation is "glory"—in particular, God's glory. When I first came across *kavod,* I treated it as I did many of the other new and confusing terms that my investigation of prophecy was revealing. I noted it and put it "on the back burner," knowing I would return to it when larger and more pressing matters had become clearer. Once I began reexamining the concept, kavod appeared quite puzzling.

The notion of kavod challenges a neat association between the DMT and prophetic states. As the preceding chapters have demonstrated, an impressive correspondence exists between these two syndromes when we look at their phenomenology. And while upcoming chapters will show that the information content of each differs substantially in quantity and sophistication, there is a general thematic comportment between the two. However, kavod possesses several features that are less "typical" of prophecy itself and also are more difficult to locate within the DMT experience.

In the Hebrew Bible, it is uncertain whether kavod is an angel, God, both, or something else. This option of "something else" is certainly viable because unlike other features of prophecy, kavod is visible and audible to the masses. In addition, interactions with kavod are substantially more rudimentary and less verbal than prophetic interactions in general. These two features suggest that kavod is an object somehow straddling the worlds of spirit and matter.

Kavod's properties are relevant to the psychedelic drug state because understanding them may shed additional light on how the Hebrew Bible may inform and guide one's sessions with these substances. In a drug session, are we seeing God, an angel, or God's glory? What are the differences among them? Do they matter? Can we relate to kavod in the same manner as we relate to the beings, God, or angels, or does kavod's atypical nature require that we approach it differently?

BIBLICAL AMBIGUITY

The three-letter root of kavod is *K-V-D,* which signifies "to be heavy, weighty, honored." It also can mean "grievous, stubborn, burdensome." We see already how even its basic definition is highly pliant. Thus, context determines the exact definition of words containing this root. For example, the Hebrew word for *liver,* the body's "heaviest" visceral organ, is *kaved* (Exod. 29:13). The text also uses the word *kaved* to describe Pharaoh's heart when he repeatedly refuses to grant freedom to Egypt's Hebrew slave population despite the devastation that God's ten plagues are inflicting upon his country (Exod. 8:28).

Kavod is more abstract than the Hebrew Bible's anthropomorphic representations of God possessing hands or a mouth, but more concrete than the medieval Jewish philosophers' notion of an incorporeal being without any conceivable or perceptible attributes. Kavod shares certain qualities with God. It possesses power, appears fiery, and interacts with those who perceive it; for example, it may benefit or harm. Unlike God, however, the text never states that kavod feels or expresses human emotions such as anger or love. While one may apprehend God's kavod visually, the text also tells us that what we see may not exactly be kavod. Instead it is "the appearance of the glory" (Exod. 24:17) or even "the appearance of the semblance of the glory" (Ezek. 1:28). This adds another layer of ambiguity to any discussion of the term.

These shifting and transitional properties of kavod within the matrix of the prophetic literature have led translators to attempt to bring some order to the concept. In particular, "presence"—*Shechinta* in Aramaic,* rendered *Shechina* in Hebrew—is how most contemporary English versions of the Hebrew Bible[1] translate *kavod* (e.g., Exod. 40:34). However, "the Shechina" has taken on a life of its own, variously appearing as God's wisdom, word, or logos[†]; the feeling of God's presence; God's care and love for His creation; providence in general; or even an autonomous anthropomorphic object of veneration in later Kabbalah.[2]

This transmogrification of *kavod* has caused many to overlook the original Hebrew Bible word and, as a result, to overlook its dynamic and liminal nature, a nature that simultaneously straddles several different realms. Consistent with my approach throughout this book, I am limiting myself to the Hebrew Bible when characterizing *kavod* as well, and we never find the noun *Shechina* as a synonym for it there. Avoiding later, nonbiblical interpretations of *kavod* leads to a more unruly approach to the concept, but is intellectually more honest and provides a more spacious approach to its various meanings.

APPEARANCE AND IDENTITY: CLOUD AND FIRE, ANGEL AND GOD

Kavod may reside in a particular object, be that object itself, or lack association with any object. The relationship among kavod, God, and an angel is similarly fluid. We gain some insight into kavod's shifting identity when the Hebrew Bible describes its visual properties in the same or adjacent verses in which appear God or His angels (or both). Those visual properties resemble fire, a cloud, smoke, a smoky cloud, or a fiery cloud rather than the more highly articulated forms we are now familiar with.

The cloud-kavod relationship: *When Aaron spoke to the entire assembly of the Children of Israel, they turned to the wilderness, and behold, the glory of YHVH appeared in the cloud* (Exod. 16:10).

---

*The language of the first translation of the Hebrew Bible that the rabbis endorsed, appearing in the first or second century CE.
[†]The rational principle developing and governing the universe.

The relationship between God and the cloud, the cloud ostensibly representing kavod: *YHVH went before them by day in a pillar of cloud* (Exod. 13:21).

And that between God's angel and the cloud: *The angel of God who had been going in front of the camp of Israel moved and went behind them, and the pillar of cloud journeyed from in front of them and went behind them* (Exod. 14:19).

A unique visual characteristic of the kavod cloud is its density, as when God tells Moses: *Behold, I come to you in the thickness of the cloud* (Exod. 19:9).

Kavod often appears as fire: *The appearance of the glory of YHVH was like a consuming fire on the mountaintop before the eyes of the Children of Israel* (Exod. 24:17).

Similarly, after King Solomon inaugurates the Temple in Jerusalem, the entire populace witnesses kavod: *All the Israelites were watching when the fire and the glory of YHVH descended upon the Temple* (2 Chron. 7:3).

God Itself may be in the fire: *YHVH went before them . . . by night in a pillar of fire to give [the Israelites] light* (Exod. 13:21). Or God may be in the fire and cloud: *YHVH gazed out . . . in the pillar of fire and cloud* (Exod. 14:24). Fire and cloud may encompass God: *Cloud and thick darkness surround It. . . . Fire goes before It* (Ps. 97:2–3).

Here, God, kavod, and the fire all interweave with each other: *The glory of YHVH appeared to the entire people. A fire went forth from before YHVH* (Lev. 9:23–24).

Sometimes God *is* God's glory, not simply residing in it, in its cloud, or in its fire: *The glory of YHVH appeared. . . . YHVH said to Moses . . .* (Num. 14:10–11).

KAVOD OCCUPIES SPACE

Ezekiel explicitly refers to the "place" of God's glory: *Blessed is the glory of YHVH from its place* (Ezek. 3:12). That place is located above the beings: *The Cheruvim lifted their wings and rose up from the land . . .*

and the Ofanim were opposite them. . . . And the glory of the God of Israel was upon them from above (Ezek. 10:19).

It fills volume: *The cloud covered the Tent of Meeting, and the glory of YHVH filled the Tabernacle* (Exod. 40:34).

It comes: *Behold, the glory of the God of Israel came by way of the east. . . . The glory of YHVH entered the [Temple] by way of the gate which opened by way of the east* (Ezek. 43:2, 4).

It ascends: *Then the glory of the God of Israel rose up from atop the cheruv on which it had been to the threshold of the [Temple]* (Ezek. 9:3).

Kavod descends and also stands: *YHVH descended in the cloud and it stood with [Moses] there* (Exod. 34:5).

Kavod possesses sides. When Moses requests seeing God's glory, He replies: *You will see My back, but My face may not be seen* (Exod. 33:23).

SOMATIC EFFECTS

When witnessing God's smoke and fire, presumably Its glory, atop Mount Sinai as the revelation begins: *the entire people that were in the camp shuddered* (Exod. 19:16).

Kavod similarly physically overwhelms Ezekiel: *Behold, there the glory of YHVH was standing, like the glory that I saw by the River Kevar, and I fell upon my face* (Ezek. 3:23).

AFFECT

Job describes the emotional quality of kavod during his theophany: *On God there is an awesome glory* (Job 37:22).

At the Mount Sinai revelation the members of the Hebrew camp: *were afraid of the fire* (Deut. 5:5).

VOLITION

A property of kavod that appears throughout the Hebrew Bible is its preventing entry into the space it occupies. After dedicating the Tabernacle:

Moses was not able to come to the Tent of Meeting, for the cloud rested upon it, and the glory of YHVH filled the Tabernacle (Exod. 40:35).

Similarly, subsequent to King Solomon dedicating the First Temple: *The priests were not able to stand to minister because of the cloud, for the glory of YHVH filled the House of YHVH* (1 Kings 8:11).

PERCEPTION

Vision

I have already discussed the fiery, smoky, and cloudy visual properties of kavod. Additionally, kavod may possess a bright or shining quality: *Like the appearance of the bow that would be in the cloud on a rainy day, so was the appearance of the brilliance all around. That was the appearance of the semblance of the glory of YHVH* (Ezek. 1:28).

Sound

While the visual aspects of kavod predominate, there also are auditory ones. The sound may be nonverbal: *The glory of the God of Israel came by way of the east, and its sound like the sound of great waters* (Ezek. 43:2).

One may hear God's spoken voice emanate from the kavod cloud: *YHVH descended in a pillar of cloud ... and He called, "Aaron and Miriam"* (Num. 12:5).

Or God's voice emerges simply from kavod itself without any associated visual image: *The glory of YHVH appeared to [Moses and Aaron], and YHVH spoke to Moses* (Num. 20:6–7).

The masses also hear God speak from the kavod fire. In this case, as with the visual aspects, the auditory effects are not especially well articulated, being in the manner of a "voice" and not "words": *Behold, YHVH our God has shown us His Glory and His greatness, and we have heard His voice from the midst of the fire* (Deut. 5:21).

This excerpt is unusual and hints at synesthesia. God informs Moses that It appears visually as a kavod cloud so as to be audible to the masses: *Behold! I come to you in the thickness of the cloud, in order that the people will hear as I speak with you* (Exod. 19:9).

RELATEDNESS

Interactions between kavod and the people who perceive it are generally less complex than what we have read about with respect to interactions with more typical beings or God.

Kavod may be dangerous. For example, after Moses asks God to reveal to him His glory, God replies: *You will not be able to see My face, for no man can see Me and live* (Exod. 33:20).

It portends danger. Immediately before the earth opens its mouth to swallow a group rebelling against Moses: *the glory of YHVH appeared to the entire assembly. YHVH spoke to Moses and Aaron saying, "Separate yourselves from amidst this assembly, and I shall destroy them in an instant"* (Num. 16:19–21).

On the other hand, kavod may shield an individual from God's own destructive power. The Hebrew nation declares how perceiving God through kavod has spared them from death: *Behold, YHVH our God has shown us His glory and His greatness, and we have heard His voice from the midst of the fire. This day we saw that YHVH will speak to a man and he can live* (Deut. 5:21).

Kavod feeds. When the Israelites complain of hunger in the wilderness, Moses and Aaron reassure them: *In the morning you will see the glory of YHVH, that He has heard your complaints . . . when, in the evening, YHVH gives you meat to eat and bread to satiety in the morning* (Exod. 16:7–8).

Kavod may appear in response to prayer: *Moses and Aaron came to the Tent of Meeting, and they went out and they blessed the people,* and the glory of YHVH appeared to the entire people* (Lev. 9:23).

Falling upon one's face seems to indicate prayer, and as such elicits kavod: *Moses and Aaron went . . . and fell on their faces. The glory of YHVH appeared to them* (Num. 20:6).

Kavod instructs. In this example, we get a sense of the profundity of what a high-ranking prophet may learn from directly experiencing

---

*Prayed for their welfare.

kavod. After Moses asks to see God's glory, He prepares Moses for what His glory is like: *I shall make all My goodness pass before you, and I shall call out with the name YHVH before you; I shall show favor when I choose to show favor, and I shall show mercy when I choose to show mercy* (Exod. 33:19).

In the Messianic Era, kavod will gather in all the exiled Israelites to their homeland, as Isaiah foretells: *The glory of YHVH shall gather you in* (Isa. 58:8).

In this intriguing passage, we wonder if the psalmist is suggesting that after death, God's glory will accompany him: *In Your counsel guide me, and afterwards, glory, You shall take me* (Ps. 73:24).

This example may be the only one in which someone in a prophetic state "becomes one with," "enters into," or "merges with" God or Its glory. Before receiving the Ten Commandments on Mount Sinai: *Moses came into the midst of the cloud* (Exod. 24:18).

DMT

Here I note examples from the DMT reports of descriptions that share features with kavod.

Cloud

In chapter 12, Perception, I presented two excerpts describing clouds. Sean's description was simply of clouds, while Philip mentioned colored clouds and a humanoid face emerging from them. In neither case did the cloud possess any of the other properties of kavod.

Fire

There are many instances of fire-like phenomena in the DMT state, and I provided examples in chapter 12. Only rarely do these amorphous, fiery visions partake of kavod's additional characteristics, such as volitional effects, as when Brenda feels "tangled up" and unable to move through the curtain of colors.

Relatedness

The only instance in the DMT study of a volunteer "entering into" an amorphous bright light, akin to Moses entering the cloud on Mount Sinai, is Sean's case, in which he merged with the bright, yellow-white light: *I chose to open to it. I was consumed by it and became part of it* (*DMT,* 244).

SUMMARY

The Hebrew Bible's descriptions of kavod indicate that it occupies a transitional position between a formless God and an apprehensible being. It morphs along a rather fluid continuum: being God or an angel, the physical location of God or an angel, or a proxy for God or an angel. Kavod possesses phenomenological characteristics with a lower level of articulation or complexity than what we find in other aspects of the prophetic state. Visually it is fiery, smoky, or cloudy (or a combination of those) and never takes a recognizable form, such as animal or human. At the same time, it occupies space and moves through it. Kavod is powerful, eliciting falling upon one's face as well as precluding movement into the space it occupies. It may benefit or harm, feed or protect. Kavod also is unique in that it is visible and audible to the masses. In addition, the cloud of kavod is the only manifestation of God that one may "enter into," similar to the mystical-unitive types of experiences more common in Buddhist enlightenment.

Kavod is unusual within the spectrum of the prophetic state, and we also don't encounter many kavod-like effects in the DMT experience. Its atypical features offer mechanistic challenges, both biological and metaphysical. Perhaps endogenous psychedelics other than DMT play a role in how it manifests. In addition, different metaphysical mechanisms may mediate the apprehension of kavod than those mediating more typical prophetic experiences. I return to these issues when discussing the metaphysics of prophecy and of DMT as well as areas of future research.

17 Message and Meaning I

Belief and Behavior

The previous chapters comparing the Hebrew biblical prophetic and the experimental DMT states provide powerful evidence in support of my contention that they share phenomenological similarities. Compelling correspondences were found in all mental categories we investigated: bodily sensations, emotions, perception, thought processes, volition, and relatedness. As always, however, we must continue asking ourselves, "If so, so what?" Why does it matter that the prophetic and DMT experiences share these features? How is the world a better place knowing that such similarities exist?

We may look for answers to these questions by examining the impact of the two sets of experiences. If the psychedelic state has exerted an influence on our civilization comparable to that of the prophetic one, then these resemblances are more than skin deep. In other words, the psychedelic state would be not simply a facsimile of prophecy, but truly accesses its same moral and ethical universes. This would indicate that we may experience prophecy through the psychedelic experience. However, I believe the evidence does not support this conclusion.

In the case of the psychedelic drug experience, its aesthetics—visual, emotional, and auditory—have had a much greater impact on our culture than has its message. We see this in the presence and popularity of psychedelic art, music, and other media. However, as yet there is no cogent psychedelic philosophy, law, theology, economics, or religion. These latter fields depend to a much greater extent on cognitive information than aesthetics.

When psychedelic drugs have demonstrated a non-aesthetic impact on our culture, it has been primarily in the area of "therapy." We consider them to exert effects akin to psychiatric medication, and they can be used as tools to enhance various forms of psychological treatment. If spiritual issues do arise within a non-aesthetic context, such as occasioning spiritual states, we usually consider them to provide primarily psychological benefit. We see this in the field of "transpersonal psychology," which developed in response to the infusion of psychedelic and Eastern religious sensibilities into mainstream psychology in the 1960s.[1]

In contrast, the Hebrew Bible has set the course for many if not all the bastions of Western civilization for thousands of years. Its message endures and influences to a much greater extent than do its aesthetics, even though its aesthetics are at least as impressive as those of the DMT experience. For example, the Ten Commandments are widely known, but it's unlikely we could describe the visual, emotional, and auditory components accompanying their revelation at Mount Sinai despite the experience itself being thoroughly mind-boggling.

I found this aesthetics-rich and message-poor dichotomy to exist in my DMT data as well. Volunteers' experiences did contain information, both personal and spiritual. However, they wrestled mightily with how to articulate what they had learned, how to integrate it into their personal and social lives, and by what means to communicate it. Dmitri alluded to this in chapter 14, "Volition and Will," when he sensed that the beings and he had a mission, but he didn't know what it was.

Jay, a student in his early twenties, even more cogently captured this conundrum when after his first high-dose DMT session he remarked: *I was trying to capture the meaning, the knowledge, not knowing what to do; to put it in some kind of context, some kind of anchoring. How do you manifest it? Where's the blueprint, the longevity? I don't want it to just steal away.*

The most striking insight that the DMT subjects attained through their sessions was that there existed a level of reality parallel to and interacting with this one just a few heartbeats away. They noted its solidity and temporal continuity, and catalogued its contents. When they received a message during their sessions, it usually contributed significantly less to their experiences' overall impact than did their descriptions of the DMT state itself. And when the message was prominent, it nearly always involved personal psychological issues, rather than ones of a larger social or spiritual nature, such as we soon will read about in the prophetic literature.

THE CANONICAL VS. NONCANONICAL MESSAGE

We must not prematurely conclude that prophecy inherently possesses a richer message than the DMT state. It is important to note that much of the prophetic message that has come down to us resides in the books of the canonical prophets like Isaiah, Jeremiah, Ezekiel, and the twelve minor prophets, and does not come from those who ostensibly lack a prophetic mission. Nevertheless, those latter individuals may have attained the highest possible levels of prophecy.

For example, Hagar, Sarah's Egyptian maidservant, sees and speaks with angels, who accurately predict the future to her. The content of that prophetic state she experienced, that her son Ishmael would become the patriarch of a powerful and numerous people (Gen. 16:10; 21:18), is relatively brief and has little relevance to ethical, legal, or theological matters compared to the communications of the canonical prophets. However, the brevity and personal nature of a prophetic message does not detract from its truth value. In Hagar's case, the prediction turns out to be true—her son indeed becomes the progenitor of the numerous and powerful Arab people.

PREPARING FOR WHAT FOLLOWS

This and the next chapter contain an enormous amount of information, and I feel some conflict between my desire to paint as full a picture as possible of the prophetic message and my concern for losing the reader's interest. In this spirit, I often simply will refer to scriptural verses rather than quote them in full.

For those already familiar with the prophetic message, I beg these readers' forbearance regarding this chapter's length, especially if the message of the DMT state lacks enough sophistication to keep their interest. This especially may occur if one is seeking the same degree of correspondence between the two states as the preceding chapters have demonstrated in the phenomenological realms. Nevertheless, the information content of the DMT and prophetic states do share significant correspondences, albeit not to the same extent that exist in the phenomenological arena. In addition, my method of categorizing elements of the prophetic message may appeal to this group of readers.

The detail these chapters contain also may serve those interested in prophecy who do not possess much knowledge of the Hebrew Bible. Explicating the prophetic message to the extent that I do will demonstrate how much fuller is the informational content of biblical prophecy than simply predicting or foretelling. And for those who are reading this material through the lens of their interest in the psychedelic drug state, it may provide the intellectual and ethical "context, anchoring, and meaning" that Jay was seeking in his attempt to answer "If so, so what?"

Most important, however, is that the thorough explication of the prophetic message compared to the DMT one continues our examination of how the two syndromes do and do not resemble each other. As these next two chapters will demonstrate, the message of the prophetic state significantly differs from that of the DMT experience in its possessing greater depth, breadth, complexity, and profundity. When they do share features, we can hypothesize shared mechanisms. And when they do not, we need to search for how those mechanisms differ. It is only through rigorous hypothesis building that we can work toward modifying those mechanisms in order to bring the two states into closer alignment. The ultimate aims of this juxtaposition are to make the psychedelic experience more prophetic in its message and impact, and to make the prophetic experience more accessible to students of the Hebrew Bible.

As I discussed in the chapter introducing the comparison between the DMT and prophetic states, the organization of the following two message chapters differs from the phenomenology ones. It quickly became apparent that the informational content of the prophetic state is substantially greater and more sophisticated than that of the DMT experience. Therefore, instead of binning biblical excerpts into my pre-existing phenomenological categories—perception, emotion, and so on—I developed ad hoc message categories using the Hebrew Bible as my frame of reference. I then binned DMT excerpts into them. For example, one such biblical category might pertain to God being merciful. If a DMT report contained a reference to God's mercy, I would place that excerpt into that biblical grouping. In addition, because much of the prophetic message does not have a counterpart in the DMT volunteers' reports, there are many categories that contain only biblical references and no DMT ones.

ELEMENTS OF THE
PROPHETIC MESSAGE

The message of the Hebrew Bible covers a vast scope, and its seeming inconsistencies tax our capacities. It tells us that humans are created in God's image, but accepts the institution of slavery. It teaches us not to murder and that one day humanity will disarm and live in universal peace, but also permits the taking of life in certain circumstances such as capital punishment and war. The text teaches kindness to and empathy with animals while prescribing all manner of animal sacrifice. The message of the Hebrew Bible is as challenging as it is all-encompassing.

Belief and Behavior
We may divide the information one obtains in any spiritual experience into two related categories: those pertaining to belief and those pertaining to behavior. Beliefs concern the nature of the physical and spiritual worlds. In the Hebrew Bible, information regarding God's attributes

and actions are essential to any such set of beliefs. Behavior involves how we relate to our bodies and minds as well as to the outside world—natural, social, and spiritual. The Hebrew Bible conjoins these two categories of belief and behavior by teaching that accurate beliefs about God lead to specific ethical behavior based thereon.

Foretelling, Including the "World to Come"

Prediction figures prominently in the Hebrew Bible, as it explicates God's involvement in history. Foretelling also occurs, though rarely, in the DMT state. The time span of prediction in both sets of experiences may be uncertain. Of great interest are descriptions, relatively common in prophecy and occurring occasionally in the DMT experience, of the "world to come." When describing this "world to come," we begin to encounter allusions in the Hebrew Bible to certain DMT-like elements characterizing this qualitatively different level of future existence.

False Prophets and False Prophecy

Accuracy of prediction is important in differentiating "true" from "false" prophecy, a topic of great concern to the Hebrew Bible and the medieval Jewish philosophers. However, several other factors play at least as important a role in recognizing the false prophet and false prophecy, including the nature of the message and the character of its bearer. False prophecy is relevant to the psychedelic state because we must exercise great care in deciding whether the information we obtain during a drug experience is accurate, true, and beneficial rather than simply another way in which we delude ourselves and others.

Wisdom and Poetry

The Hebrew Bible contains a wisdom literature: Job, Proverbs, and Ecclesiastes being representative of the genre. Here we explicitly learn about proper attitudes and behavior by which to live one's life. In addition, the 150 poetic prayers of Psalms and the tale of love that the Song of Songs recounts have provided inspiration and solace to hundreds of generations throughout the world.

WHAT GOD IS

The prophetic articulation of God's nature and actions constitutes a significant portion of the Hebrew Bible. When information about God appears in the DMT reports, it generally comports with the prophetic text. In addition, there are regular examples in my DMT notes of volunteers describing "something" that for all intents and purposes could have been "God" if that something manifested within the prophetic context. Therefore, I include these examples, too, as concerning God.

Knowledge of God includes seeing His role in our personal lives, in nature, and on the stage of world history. That knowledge dovetails with guidelines for the conduct of individual and public life, the complex scaffolding of laws in the Hebrew Bible. Such laws oversee every aspect of our existence: commerce and exchange, diet, agriculture, medicine, war, family life, rites and rituals, and so on. Our degree of compliance with these guidelines determines the operation of God's "justice." This term represents overlaying cause and effect with an anthropomorphic cognitive filter that assumes a certain value system. Generally speaking, compliance with God's precepts leads to the "rewards" of happiness, health, peace, and similar boons, and noncompliance leads to the "punishments" of war, illness, natural disasters, and similar banes. We also learn that it is possible to petition God by various means to temper with mercy His strict application of justice.

While reviewing this material, remember that God's attributes are, strictly speaking, inconceivable. References to them partake of homonymy, as I discussed in chapter 7, God. They are the "next best thing" to an accurate description. By saying, for example, that God is "eternal," this simply means that It is not limited by time, because It "existed" before existence and will continue to "exist" after existence. These are notions that we cannot possibly comprehend. However, "eternal" as an approximate description is better than a wrong one, such as "temporary," or positing that God does not exist at all.

God Exists

The most essential attribute of God is that It exists, or more precisely, doesn't not exist. We usually find the name YHVH in this context. Moses sings a song to the Hebrew nation just before his death, in which he speaks for YHVH: *For I, I am It* (Deut. 32:39).

God Lives

God lives, or rather, is not dead. In the context of God "taking an oath" to fulfill His word, He expressly states: *as I live* (Num. 14:28).

God Is One

The expression "one" may mean several things: qualitatively unique among its kind, indivisible, or the only one of its species. In this verse, which makes up part of the Shema, the most well-known Jewish prayer, "one" may refer to all three of these definitions. *Hear, Israel: YHVH is our God, YHVH is one* (Deut. 6:4).

God Is Eternal

As the rabbinical adage has it, "Time exists within God, but God does not exist in time." God tells Isaiah: *Even before there was a day I am It* (Isa. 43:13), whereas the psalmist compares the temporal nature of heaven and earth with God's eternality: *They will perish, but You will endure* (Ps. 102:27).

God Possesses Will and Unlimited Power, Knowledge, and Presence

These different attributes are difficult to isolate in a pure and distinct manner. For example, there exists an ineluctable relationship between God's omnipresence and omniscience; in other words, because God is everywhere, It is aware of everything. And God's omnipresence and omniscience make possible the execution of His will through His omnipotence.

God's answer to Moses's question regarding His name reflects the simple possession of will: *I shall be what I shall be* (Exod. 3:14).

God's power is limitless: *When I do, who can reverse it?* (Isa. 43:13).

Will and power combine in the act of creation: *God said, "Let there be light," and there was light* (Gen. 1:3).

God's omniscience extends to the inanimate world: *There is no rock that I do not know* (Isa. 44:8); to the entire universe: *He reveals the deep and the mysterious, knows what is in the dark* (Dan. 2:22); to our own hearts and actions: *For YHVH is a God of thoughts, and to Him are deeds counted* (1 Sam. 2:3); no matter where we are: *If I ascend to heaven You are there; if I make my bed in the lowest depths, behold, You are there* (Ps. 139:8).

✍ DMT

Elena witnessed the universe's creation as an act of cosmic will: *Then the words "just because it is possible" emerged out of nothingness* (*DMT*, 240). She also referred to God's power: *It was all-powerful, all-immense; it was Yahweh.*

Cleo referred to God's omnipresence: *I was looking for God outside. [The beings] said, "God is in every cell of your body"* (*DMT*, 238).

Incorporeal and Corporeal Descriptions of God

God's omnipresence seems incompatible with Its possessing a body or occupying space. We read accounts of both God's corporeality, such as the occasion when the prophet sees God "standing on a wall" (Amos 7:7), and incorporeality, as when Moses reminds the Hebrews that they "saw no form" at the Mount Sinai revelation (Deut. 4:15). King Solomon captures this conundrum when he rues that while the "heavens cannot contain" God, how is it possible for It to dwell in the Jerusalem Temple (1 Kings 8:27)? While kavod, a "limited version" of God, may answer this question, anything to do with the notion of God's glory sooner or later stumbles over its paradoxical nature. To wit, Isaiah overhears angels declaring that "God's glory fills the entire world" (Isa. 6:3).

Enigmatically, when God creates humans, He says: *Let us make man in our image, after our likeness* (Gen. 1:26). To forestall an anthropomorphic interpretation of this phrase, the medieval Jewish philosophers suggest that this refers to a real, although not physical, resemblance. For example, man shares God's creativity, free will, and rationality.

God Is Holy

While the notion of holiness is enormously complex, the Hebrew word for it, *kadosh,* provides some insight into how the Hebrew Bible understands it. The three-letter root *K-D-Sh* implies such ideas as separation from the profane, mundane, and everyday. It is sacred, hallowed, and sanctified.

Isaiah hears the angels in his vision say: *Holy, holy, holy is YHVH of Hosts* (Isa. 6:3). And God's name itself is holy (Ps. 33:21).

✍ DMT

Siggie, in his early thirties and one of several Jewish volunteers, worked in a residential school for disturbed children. He described his overall impression of his DMT session: *There's a certain holiness to it.*

Direct Perception of God Is Incompatible with Life

One possible and extreme conclusion regarding the fundamental dichotomy between holiness and the ordinary is that direct contact with God is incompatible with life. We previously read that direct perception of God's glory may kill (Exod. 33:20). Despite this, we never find that someone viewing God or an angel actually dies. Rather, there is surprise at still being alive, as Jacob noted after wrestling all night with an angel (Gen. 32:31).

✍ DMT

Gerald may have been referring to this threat: *It seemed potentially dangerous to venture into it unless you were versed in how to handle it.*

God Is Zealous

An attribute of God we read about in the Hebrew Bible is "jealous" or "zealous."* Both terms refer to an intense commitment to a particular

---

*The Hebrew root is *K-N-A,* and the exact definition of specific *K-N-A*–related words depends upon context.

thing: a person, nation, belief, or practice. When something sunders or threatens to sunder that relationship, adverse consequences result. The term usually appears in connection with God's "feelings" about idolatry in its various forms (Exod. 20:5).

WHAT GOD DOES

Providence is the term we use to express the relationship between God and the phenomenal world. God created and sustains the world by means of providence, including its moral and natural laws. The notion of homonymy also is critical in this discussion. Recall, for instance, the biblical concept of God rewarding and punishing that I discussed in chapter 7, God. The expression "God rewards" represents one way to label the end result of the operation of cause and effect that regulates existence. "God rewards" is shorthand terminology that militates against wrongheaded propositions such as "God is unaware of what we do," "God has no power in this world," or "God possesses no moral compass." This is where the anthropomorphic notion of God's providence proves useful. That is, if we received benefits (or suffering) for our actions from a person, we would interpret them as reward (or punishment). While this "reward" or "punishment" simply reflects the operation of cause and effect, that cause and effect is set up in such a manner as to encourage certain beliefs and behaviors and to discourage others.

God Created and Sustains the Natural and Moral Worlds
The first words of the Hebrew Bible describe how God imposed the order of natural law upon preexisting chaos: *In the beginning of God's forming* the heavens and the earth . . . (Gen. 1:1).

With respect to both the natural and moral worlds, God: *forms light and creates darkness, makes peace and creates evil* (Isa. 45:7). God enlivens (Ps. 36:10) and kills (Deut. 32:39), created consciousness (Ps. 139:13) and the soul (Isa. 57:16), and placed these into His creations

---

*Usually "creating," but "forming" lends more accuracy to the act.

on earth (Isa. 42:5). God created the means of communicating, such as eyes, ears, and the mouth (Exod. 4:11).

✣ DMT

DMT volunteers also noted the process of creation. Roland spoke "for" God in this excerpt: *The first thing I created was chaos, the mother and father of all things. It gives birth to the patterns and everything else.*

Volunteers described "slowing down" as a necessary stage in creation. Carlos experienced himself as "the Creator" and then: *watched the universe's creation down from fundamental mental energy to a vibratory rate to material things* (*DMT,* 230–31).

God Exercises Justice and Righteousness

God is the ultimate judge because He is omniscient and has the power to judge: *I YHVH search the heart, test the will in order to give to each person according to his ways, the fruit of his deeds* (Jer. 17:10).

The rewards for living in accordance with God's guidelines are manifold: spiritual benefits such as achieving closeness to God (Amos 5:14), attaining His love (Gen. 18:19), realizing the knowledge (Jer. 22:16) and awe (Deut. 6:2) of God, and acquiring prophecy (Ps. 17:15). The rewards also include a long life (Prov. 3:2), many descendants (Gen. 26:4), good health (Exod. 15:26), favorable weather (Deut. 11:14), and being a blessing to the world (Gen. 22:18).

✣ DMT

Elena's experience countered the suggestion that God "searches" or "judges": *It doesn't seek or impose.*

Ken alluded to the relationship between suffering and being punished in his horrifying encounter with the reptilian beings: *It was as if I were being punished* (*DMT,* 252).

God Loves, Comforts, and Heals

While we never read in the Hebrew Bible that God *is* love, the text notes that God *does* love: *for YHVH is good, for His loving-kindness is forever* (Jer. 33:11). God: *loves the stranger to give him bread and garment* (Deut. 10:18), and provides comfort to the distraught (Isa. 57:15) and healing to the ill (Deut. 32:39). His mercy extends to animals, as manifest in their having enough to eat (Ps. 147:9).

✒ DMT

When Rex's panic-stricken entry into the DMT state tested his faith, he came to the realization that: *all is God, and that God was love* (*DMT,* 206).

God Teaches and Instills Wisdom

While the highly abstract God of the medieval Jewish philosophers seems rather removed from the mundane human sphere, we encounter the opposite notion in the Hebrew Bible itself. For example: *I am YHVH your God, who teaches you for your benefit* (Isa. 48:17). In particular, He teaches those most capable of learning (Dan. 2:21).

✒ DMT

In the prophetic milieu, Heather might have been referring to God: *Maybe it was trying to teach me something* (*DMT,* 179).

God Tests

God sets challenges before humanity, especially regarding one's faith in It. Abraham passes such a test by simply agreeing to sacrifice Isaac, his son, after God requests that he do so. The willingness is sufficient (Gen. 22:16–17), and Isaac lives through the ordeal. Similarly, God feeds the Hebrews manna for forty years in the wilderness to teach them that It, and only It, provides sustenance (Deut. 8:3).

God Responds to Entreaties

God's power and will allow Him to "relent" in a "merciful" manner. These expressions refer to how He may, as the creator and sustainer of the laws of cause and effect, modify their strict application in cases in which "punishment" would normally occur. A more modern "scientific" iteration of God's relenting relates to a certain degree of "uncertainty" regarding the operation of cause and effect.[2] That is, one need not evoke a non-natural explanation for the uncertainty that attaches to particular outcomes devolving from particular antecedents. This "scientific" explanation, however, simply explains *how* God may bend the rules of cause and effect, not *why* the possibility of such bending exists in the first place.

The text expresses the notion that repentance—admitting to a wrong, promising not to repeat it, making restitution when possible—may effect God's relenting: *Return to Me, and I will return to you, says YHVH* (Mal. 3:7). In a related manner, God may relent in response to people changing their behavior by becoming more merciful and just (Jer. 7:5–7), through confession (Isa. 57:16), and suffering exile (Lev. 26:34).

GUIDELINES FOR LIVING: PROPER RELATIONSHIPS

This material begins introducing us to the practical applications of the knowledge one obtains in the prophetic state. To the extent that the prophetic and DMT states resemble each other, the guidelines that the Hebrew Bible lays down may have relevance to the drug experience. That is, they may provide valuable direction in developing a Western model for a way of life that resonates more closely with one's psychedelic sensibilities.

In the introduction to this chapter, I present the idea that knowledge of God leads to particular ethical behavior based on that knowledge. For example, if God loves the stranger or hates idolatry, then by loving the stranger or hating idolatry, we are emulating God. Emulating God is one way to establish a closer relationship with It. By following certain guidelines we partake in God's holiness: *You are to sanctify yourselves* and you shall become holy, for I am holy* (Lev. 11:44).

The basis of a Godly life is knowing the difference between right and wrong, or in biblical terms, between good and evil, that which ulti-

---

*By following God's guidelines.

mately avails and that which ultimately does not. Sometimes we can make that determination using common sense or rational deliberation. At other times the Hebrew Bible suggests we need revealed guidance. Isaiah chastises those who make up their morality as it suits them, equating this behavior with a denial of reality: *Woe to those who speak of evil as good and of good as evil, who make darkness as light and light as darkness, who make bitter as sweet and sweet as bitter* (Isa. 5:20).

The revelation at Mount Sinai is replete with somatic, emotional, perceptual, and other properties of the prophetic state. More important, there the Hebrew nation learned certain things about God's nature, how to optimize their relationship with It, and how to optimize their relationships with their inner and outer worlds. The climax of the revelation is Moses receiving the Ten Commandments, what we might consider a distillation of the entire prophetic message. They first appear in chapter 20 of Exodus, and they appear again in chapter 5 of Deuteronomy with minor variations. The first subset of the Ten Commandments contains guidelines for relating to God. The second subset concerns social relations. I will begin with the former.

Relating to God

1. *I am YHVH your God [Elohim]* (Exod. 20:2). YHVH exists, and is Elohim, the creator of heaven and earth. This fixes in the mind a belief, not a specific behavior.
2. *You shall have no other gods before Me* (Exod. 20:3). There is only one God.
   2a. *You shall not make yourself a carved image nor any likeness of that which is in the heavens above or on the earth below or in the water beneath the earth* (Exod. 20:4). Don't make idols.
   2b. *You shall not prostrate yourself to them nor worship them* (Exod. 20:5). Don't bow before idols or the spiritual forces they represent or contain.
3. *You shall not take the name of YHVH your God in vain* (Exod. 20:7). Contemptuously and falsely swearing by God diminishes Its stature on earth.

4. *Remember the Sabbath day to sanctify it* (Exod. 20:8). This is a
    reminder that God created the heavens and the earth and then
    ceased from creation, and that God took the Hebrews out of Egypt.
    God also enjoins us, our workers, and our beasts of burden to rest
    on the Sabbath.

In One's Attitude

The primary feelings toward God that the Hebrew Bible attempts
to inculcate are love (Deut. 6:5), knowledge (Exod. 6:7), closeness
(Deut. 13:5), and awe (Deut. 10:12). Awe of God is one way to attain
knowledge of It (Prov. 2:5). In addition, awe and love conduce to obedience. For example, Abraham obeys God's command to uproot himself from his family at the age of seventy-five and travel to a destination
that God will reveal to him only after he has arrived (Gen. 12:1).

✤ DMT

Similarly, Cal received a call to journey. Note how in this excerpt a relational issue occurs regarding the quality of communication between the
being and Cal: *There was some guy there speaking in English so I could
understand it. He said, "Go to Chaco Canyon."* He repeated it and told
me to repeat it three or four times to make sure that I remembered it.*

Ritual and Prayer

The Hebrew Bible recommends certain practices, rites, and rituals
that increase closeness to God. Some are effective when priests in their
official capacity perform them on behalf of the community, and others
require individual performance. Offerings are one example, and these
include sacrifices, donations, and loans—of animals, agricultural products, valued possessions, money, or land.

The crucial variable affecting the efficacy of any ritual is sincerity,
which the text defines as following God's guidance in other areas of one's

---

*Ancient Native American ruins in New Mexico that possess spiritual significance for
many contemporary spiritual seekers.

life. In fact, the Hebrew Bible equates oppressing the disadvantaged with idol worship (Jer. 7:6). That is, worshipping God in one's prayers while not being charitable is as if one were actually worshipping the idols of wealth and possessions and not the charitable and loving God. Rather, God desires: *loving-kindness and not sacrifices, and knowledge of God more than burnt offerings* (Hosea 6:6). Insincerity negates the efficacy of prayer (Isa. 29:13), as does acute alcohol intoxication (Lev. 10:9). Rituals one directs at any entity other than God also are ineffective (Isa. 44:9).

Prayer is another form of ritual, in which one may petition for things, such as healing or salvation (Jer. 17:14), or express praise and thanksgiving (1 Chron. 16:8–10). Prayer may effectively substitute for ritual sacrifice (Ps. 141:2).

✒ DMT
Research subjects rarely explicitly prayed. Heather addressed a God-like presence in her vision: *Show me, oh powerful one.*

STUDYING NATURE
One may know God, and thus approach Him, by studying His works. Job advises: *Ask the beasts and they will instruct you, the birds of the sky and they will tell you. Or, speak with the earth and it will teach you, the fish of the sea will tell you* (Job 12:7–8).

Relating to the World: The Golden Rule
A proper relationship with the world is tantamount to knowledge of God, as we learn from the prophet who bemoans the absence of both among the people and their rulers: *There is neither truth nor loving-kindness nor knowledge of God in the land* (Hosea 4:1).

The second subset of the Ten Commandments thus concerns our relationships with everything "other than" God: ourselves, other people, and the natural world.

5. *Honor your father and your mother* (Exod. 20:12). Your parents are partners with God in your creation.

6. *You shall not murder* (Exod. 20:13). Wanton murder is prohibited.
7. *You shall not commit adultery* (Exod. 20:13). People shouldn't be unfaithful to each other.
8. *You shall not steal* (Exod. 20:13). Stealing deprives others of what is rightfully theirs and often leads to swearing falsely.
9. *You shall not bear false witness against your fellow* (Exod. 20:13). This is a prohibition against lying, as well as gossip.
10. *You shall not covet your fellow's house. You shall not covet your fellow's wife, nor his manservant, nor his maidservant, nor his ox, nor his donkey, nor anything that belongs to your fellow* (Exod. 20:14). This is the only prohibition against a feeling and not an overt behavior.

This set of statements finds its distillation in the "Golden Rule," which in turn derives from love. Love is the antidote to hatred, the emotion with which the introduction to the seminal verse opens: *You shall not hate your brother in your heart. . . . You shall not take revenge and you shall not bear a grudge against the members of your people; you shall love your fellow as yourself—I am YHVH* (Lev. 19:17–18).

Several medieval Jewish commentators note that the wording of the Golden Rule points to its revealed nature. While it may be possible to rationally deduce much of the prophetic message, when the text adds the words "I am YHVH" to the end of a precept, it appears to be emphasizing that rational thought alone could not lead to it.*

One may derive many corollaries from the Golden Rule: "Don't do to your fellow what you don't want done to you," "Don't do to yourself

---

*The French exegete Rashi proclaims in his comments to these verses that the Golden Rule is "the Torah's great principle." The Spaniard Nachmanides says in his commentary to the Golden Rule: "This is an expression by way of an overstatement, for a human heart is not able to accept a command to love one's neighbor as oneself." His solution follows ibn Ezra's exegesis: that the rule means to love your fellow's well-being as much as you love your own well-being. Buber suggests that the Golden Rule tells us to act "as if" we love our fellow, which then may lead to actually establishing a more loving relationship with that person.[3]

what you wouldn't want your fellow to do to you," "Love yourself as you wish your fellow to love you," "Treat your fellow as you would like him or her to treat you," and others.

Empathy plays an enormously important role in understanding and applying the Golden Rule, as we read when God states: *Do not oppress a stranger. You know the feelings of a stranger, for you were strangers in the land of Egypt* (Exod. 23:9).

✒ DMT

Allan referred to the Golden Rule and its basis in empathy when he saw angry Hispanic young men in his vision and told them: *If you hate me, you hate yourself. . . . Their culture, our culture, they were co-real, existing simultaneously* (*DMT,* 180).

APPLICATIONS OF THE GOLDEN RULE

General Applications

The Hebrew Bible establishes general categories of proper behavior: practicing righteousness, charity, and love, and shunning unrighteousness and hatred. God tells Isaiah: *Cease to do evil, learn to do good, aid the wronged, uphold the rights of the orphan, take up the grievance of the widow* (Isa. 1:16–17). Seeking peace is an especially high priority, as when the psalmist preaches to "seek peace and pursue it" (Ps. 34:15).

✒ DMT

I previously noted how the beings charged Brenda with "embracing peace" (*DMT,* 214).

Specific Applications

The Hebrew Bible contains a vast number—Maimonides lists 613— of specific laws that address the multitudinous exigencies of daily life using its particular moral compass.[4] In the pursuit of peace, it condemns gossip and slander (Ps. 34:14). In honoring our creator, it eschews self-mutilation (Lev. 19:28) and maladaptive intoxication (Isa. 5:11). The text spells out specific health-related regulations, including dietary ones

(Lev. 11), that are conducive to having the closest possible relationship with God. These latter precepts include, among others, avoiding the consumption of blood, which the Hebrew Bible identifies with an animal's soul or life (Lev. 17:14).

✖ DMT

Gerald received a specific pointer regarding his health: *There was a verbal message that I got, directing me to work with my nasal congestion.*

✖ PROPHECY

The text teaches compassion to animals; for example, mandating that we chase away the mother bird before collecting her eggs for food (Deut. 22:6–7) and that we not cook a kid in its mother's milk (Exod. 34:26).

Several laws expand on the general prohibition against stealing: respecting property boundary lines (Deut. 19:14) and maintaining honest weights in the marketplace (Deut. 25:15). In fact, dishonest weights are "an abomination to God" (Deut. 25:16), the same expression the text uses to describe idol worship and its practices, up to and including child sacrifice (Deut. 12:31). Lending serves as a corrective against greed (Deut. 15:7–8). While the Hebrew Bible condones slavery, it sets time limits to enslavement: *He shall work for six years and in the seventh he shall go free* (Exod. 21:2).

With respect to the administration of a nation, we learn that a prophet should anoint the king (1 Kings 19:15), and the latter should not enrich himself through his office (Deut. 17:16). When waging war, the military must accept the peaceful surrender of its foes (Deut. 20:10–11). God tells the Hebrews to appoint "judges and officers" throughout the land (Deut. 16:18) to ensure the greatest possible degree of righteousness and justice.

SUMMARY

This first chapter comparing the information content of the prophetic and DMT states demonstrates how much more complex, sophisticated, and voluminous is the prophetic message relative to the DMT one. When the two sets of data do address the same or similar issues, volunteers' statements generally resemble those in the Hebrew Bible. For example, both point to similar qualities of God, or a God-like presence, such as Its power, creativity, and holiness. Volunteers also alluded, albeit rather indistinctly, to a Godly force's involvement with the world, including such notions as loving, punishing, charging, and instructing. However, they spoke relatively little about moral principles, ethical teachings, or practical guidelines for living, such as the Hebrew Bible's benchmark Golden Rule and the numerous precepts that devolve from it.

18 Message and Meaning II

History, the World to Come, the Messiah,

Resurrection, False Prophecy, Wisdom, and Poetry

The Hebrew Bible teaches that God guides human affairs across the entire spectrum of history, on a scale that ranges from the individual to the global and even cosmic. Thus, the past is the fulfillment of God's will. This is the source of the paradoxical notion of history as fulfilled prophecy; or to state it more precisely, that history reflects accurate prophetic foretelling. The past as well as the future reveal God's "hand" in history: *The Lord YHVH-God will not do anything unless He has revealed His secret to His servants the prophets* (Amos 3:7).

The accuracy of prophetic foretelling, however, is not as cut and dry as it may seem, as many biblical predictions clearly have never taken place.[1] As a result, there are many theories regarding the arena in which prophetic predictions reside, if that arena is not actual history *qua* history. Perhaps predictions are simply metaphors and teach theology; for example, that God is eternal and rewards and punishes according to one's deeds. Or predictions that haven't yet materialized may do so in the relatively distant future. Or the fulfillment of certain foretellings is happening now or will in the extremely near future.[2]

Taking into account this caveat regarding the ambiguity of prophetic predictions, I have adopted a particular approach to categorizing them. The primary criterion is how far in the future they apply.

"Almost-immediate" predictions deal with hours to days, as when God tells Samuel to expect Saul the next day (1 Sam. 9:16), or as in Joseph's accurate dream interpretation regarding the fate of his two fellow prisoners in an Egyptian jail (Gen. 41:13). An example of an almost-immediate prediction in a DMT volunteer occurred with Brenda: *It (he) is trying to tell me I will see something. But what? I try to ask, "Will I know it when I see it?" The presence tells me I will see something* (DMT, 212). This example also illustrates how impaired communication interferes with the apprehension of the information that the DMT state contains.

"Near-term" predictions fall within months to years, as when Joseph interprets Pharaoh's dreams as indicating years of plenty and years of famine (Gen. 41:25–31). "Long-term" predictions occupy a time span of decades to generations, in which case we begin losing specificity and sensitivity. An example is Moses's prediction of the Israelites' exile from their land (Deut. 28:64). While this event occurred several hundred years after the conquest of Canaan, Moses's prediction lacked any temporal precision. "Very long-term" predictions are the most confusing regarding when they will occur, among whom, and where.

The World to Come

The notion of very long-term predictions, what the text often refers to as "at that time," leads us into *eschatology,* which my dictionary defines as: "The branch of theology that treats of death, resurrection, immortality, the end of the world, final judgment, and the future state."[3] The vagueness of statements regarding when this end will occur provides the basis for the belief that that time may be in the remote future or may occur at any moment. The paradox of the inconceivably remote future being a heartbeat away is part and parcel of the confusion and hope that such a concept elicits. The Hebrew Bible conveys a sense of the enormity of this radical shift of circumstances, as for example when Daniel's angel calls it "the end" (Dan. 8:17) and Jacob on his deathbed refers to "the end of days" (Gen. 49:1).

As my study of the Hebrew Bible progressed, the nature of this future world increasingly drew my attention. This is because of how similar many of its properties appear to those of the DMT state. I began to consider how endogenous DMT may play a role in this phenomenon, and it is for that reason I describe the "future world" in as much detail as I do below.

TRANSITION PHASE

Between this world and the next, a momentous and unpleasant transition is often predicted, which then evolves into a beatific state: *For that day is great, with none like it, and it is a time of distress for Jacob, through which he shall be saved* (Jer. 30:7). Its onset may be sudden (Mal. 3:1), and a loud noise may accompany it: *I will whistle to them and gather them* (Zech. 10:8). These characteristics are comparable to what we have already encountered in the movement between the normal waking state and either the DMT or prophetic one.

OVERWHELMING SENSE OF REALITY

God tells Isaiah how our current reality will pale in comparison to the new one, so much so that the old will fade from memory: *For behold, I am creating new heavens and a new earth, and the first ones shall not be remembered, neither shall they come into mind* (Isa. 65:17). The psalmist predicts that the past will seem like a dream (Ps. 126:1).

DIFFERENT LAWS OF NATURE

Some descriptions of the new reality focus on changes in the natural world: *The heavens shall vanish like smoke, and the earth shall rot away like a garment* (Isa. 51:6). The light of this new world is preternaturally intense: *The light of the moon will be like the light of the sun, and the light of the sun will be seven times as strong—like the light of seven days* (Isa. 30:26).

The human body becomes more highly perfected. All physical ailments and disabilities cease (Isa. 35:5–6) and childbirth becomes painless (Isa. 66:7). Human nature becomes more sublime: war ceases (Hosea 2:20) and "sorrow and sighing flee" (Isa. 51:11). God will change human nature in order to increase our love of and closeness to Him:

YHVH your God will remove the barrier of your heart* and the heart of your offspring, to love YHVH your God with all your heart and with all your soul (Deut. 30:6). It is a time of boundless joy: *The righteous will be glad, exult before God, and rejoice with gladness* (Ps. 68:4). Most striking, everyone from the highest to the least will prophesy. Joel, a Second Temple–era prophet, predicts: *Your sons and daughters shall prophesy, your elders shall dream dreams, your young men shall see visions. Even also upon the slaves and the maidservants in those days I shall pour out My spirit* (Joel 3:1–2).

✍ DMT

The notion of a future world also appeared in some of the DMT volunteers' reports. William described learning of a better "world to come": *I felt evolution occurring. These intelligences are looking over us. There is hope beyond the mess we are making for ourselves* (*DMT*, 193).

Rex saw a new type of "loving and sensual" hive-like human dwelling: *[The being] said to me that this is where your future lay* (*DMT*, 210).

Roland referred to a world in which conversing with God will be the norm: *There's a barrier between us and the divine; we made it; it's not real; if it weren't there God could talk to us like we talk to each other.*

Willow intimated that such a rarified state must be incorporeal: *There is no limit to love except the body.* She also referred to its utterly sublime nature: *If we all knew what was waiting for us, we'd all kill ourselves* (*DMT*, 225).

Resurrection and Eternal Life

The Hebrew Bible offers inconsistent hints regarding its views on eternal life, resurrection, the soul's survival after death, and rebirth. Daniel's angel tells him: *Many of those who sleep in the dust of the earth will awaken* (Dan. 12:2). This notion of resurrection provides the medieval Jewish philosophers with a solution to theodicy—seemingly unjustifiable suffering or success—as the second half of this verse in

---

*Literally, "circumcise your heart."

Daniel indicates what will occur after resurrection: *some to eternal life; others to reproaches, to everlasting abhorrence* (Dan. 12:2). However, the author of Ecclesiastes remarks about the dead: *nor will they ever again have a share in whatever is done under the sun** (Eccles. 9:6).

The medieval Jewish philosophers offer a compromise position by suggesting that death is permanent in this world of normal, natural law. However, when the new world comes into being with different laws of nature, death is more malleable. Job captures the essence of this solution: *A man lies down and does not rise. They do not awaken until the heavens are no more; only then, aroused from their sleep* (Job 14:12).

✵ DMT

Willow referred to the seeming deathlessness of her disembodied existence: *Eternity is an attribute of that place. It would have to be* (*DMT*, 226).

Elena remarked on her own rebirth: *I have practiced dying and returning* (*DMT*, 222).

Brenda saw how rebirth might occur: *The essence of who I am was alone in the void, back in the staging area for life where souls wait to incarnate* (*DMT*, 212).

The Messiah

The prophetic message contains references to a herald, most likely human, of the transition from this world to the next. That person also may be that world's sovereign. Specifics vary among the medieval Jewish philosophers regarding the nature of this "messiah." The word itself derives from a three-letter Hebrew root, *M-Sh-Ch,* that means "to anoint" or "smear with oil." Prophets anoint and thus sanctify their successors, as well as kings, priests, and the structures and implements of the sacrificial service. It is of note that while DMT volunteers described certain qualities of the "future world," none referred to the notion of a messianic figure.

---

*That is, in the world of the living.

The Hebrew Bible predicts that the messiah will be a prophet (Isa. 11:2); wise, heroic, mighty, understanding, and reverent (Isa. 11:2–3); and a universal leader (Isa. 49:6). His success is certain, as God tells the prophet: *Behold, My servant will succeed* (Isa. 52:13). Maimonides suggests that the messiah will appear around the time of the resurrection and will oversee an era of great peace, the ingathering of all Jews to Israel, universal worship of YHVH, and extraordinary longevity. He also posits that the era of the messiah will be a prelude to the soul's eternal life in a discarnate state.[4]

FALSE PROPHETS AND FALSE PROPHECY

The legitimacy of prophets and their messages is an issue that troubled people of biblical times, and has continued as a concern to the religious for millennia, and is also relevant to the contemporary psychedelic drug experience. That is, how do we determine the truth value of our own or someone else's spiritual encounter?

The Hebrew Bible clearly states that there are true and false prophets; for example, when God compares the true prophet to "wheat" and the false prophet to "chaff" (Jer. 23:28). While it may be clear to God, Moses recognizes our own struggle to make such a distinction when he predicts that prophets will arise after he dies, and the people will ask: *How can we know the word that YHVH has not spoken?* (Deut. 18:21).

Contributing to this ambiguity, we find that when the Hebrew Bible discusses "false" prophets, it nearly always employs the word "prophet" without qualification. There are times, however, when it does specify false prophets as "prophets of the lie" (Jer. 23:26). The Greek translation of the Hebrew Bible, the Septuagint, uses the word *pseudoprophetes* in several places, thus providing us with some additional guidelines in specific contexts.[5]

The Hebrew Bible proposes several criteria for differentiating true prophecy from false. These include (1) the presence or absence of confirmatory "signs," such as miracles or the accuracy of a prediction; (2) the character of the prophet; (3) the source of the message; and (4) the message itself. However, as I will demonstrate, for every example of a criterion's utility, we find other examples that militate against it.

Signs

Failure to bring about a promised sign may indicate a false prophet: *If the prophet will speak in the name of YHVH, and that thing will not occur and not come about, that is the word that YHVH has not spoken* (Deut. 18:22). However, the text also points out that even if the prediction comes true, the content of the message—for example, encouraging people to serve idols—indicates that the prophet is false (Deut. 13:2–6).

Character

Conviction may vouch for a prophet's authenticity. The true prophet Michaiah announces: *As YHVH lives, that which YHVH will say to me, that will I speak* (1 Kings 22:14). Hananiah the false prophet also believes he speaks in the name of "YHVH of Hosts, the God of Israel" (Jer. 28:2), but his predictions do not materialize, and his advice is faulty.

False prophets are greedy (Mic. 3:5), whereas true prophets refuse payment (2 Kings 5:16). Nevertheless, Solomon, who experiences prophecy, amasses unimaginable wealth and burdens his country with staggering taxes and forced labor to construct both the Temple and his private palace (1 Kings 5:6, 27–30).

False prophets are adulterers (Jer. 29:23). However, David commits adultery with the wife of a man whom he then sends to the front lines to ensure his death (2 Sam. 11). False prophets are alcohol abusers (Isa. 28:7), but we read in Genesis how Noah the prophet drank himself into an indecent stupor (Gen. 9:21).

False prophets lie, as in the case of a particular false prophet who entices a true one (1 Kings 13:18), which results in the latter's death. However, true prophets also lie, as when Isaac tells his neighbors that his wife is only his sister (Gen. 26:7). In a related vein, a true prophet's advice may not be prophetic. Nathan, David's court prophet, tells him that God is "with him" in his desire to build a Temple. Later that night, in a true prophetic dream, God informs Nathan otherwise (2 Sam. 7:3, 13).

True prophets are humble. The text describes Moses as the "humblest man in the world" (Num. 12:3). However, he regularly berates the Hebrew nation in anger (Num. 20:10), and his impetuousness precludes his entering Canaan with them (Num. 20:12), even after forty years of faithful stewardship in the wilderness.

✍ DMT

With respect to the personal characteristic of humility, Brenda noted: *I guess I don't feel comfortable in my role as an earthly spiritual emissary* (*DMT*, 215).

Message

A "false" message bespeaks the falsity of the prophet who delivers it, while the falsity of the message is proportionate to how much it deviates from the Hebrew Bible's guidelines. For example, false prophets encourage drunkenness (Mic. 2:11) and promise salvation to the unrepentant (Jer. 23:14). However, while the true prophet's message is often disturbing (Jer. 1:10), he or she may also preach unconditional salvation and consolation (Isa. 60:1), just as do false prophets.

Varieties of False Prophecy

One species of false prophet speaks for idols, what the text refers to as "the gods of others," rather than for God (Deut. 18:20). Another relies on divination or magical practices rather than inspiration, as in the case of the king of Babylonia who: *shot arrows, inquired of the teraphim,** *and looked into the liver*† (Ezek. 21:26). However, divination may be accurate, as Jacob's avaricious father-in-law Laban tells him: *I have learned by divination that YHVH has blessed me on account of you* (Gen. 30:27). Astrology is another form of divination that the Hebrew Bible

---

*Most likely small clay idols.

† Of a ritually slaughtered animal, in search of anatomic patterns indicating the proper course of action.

considers false: *the stargazers who foretell by new moons about what will happen to you* (Isa. 47:13).

The Hebrew Bible suggests that one can recognize false prophecy when it is plagiary, the product of: *those who steal My words from one another* (Jer. 23:30). However, true prophets may plagiarize. Compare Isaiah's description of the person and reign of the messiah with Micah's:

> *He shall judge between the nations and reprove many peoples. They shall beat their swords into plowshares and their spears into pruning hooks; nation will not lift sword against nation, and they will no longer study warfare.* (Isa. 2:4)

> *He will judge between many peoples and will reprove mighty nations far away. They shall beat their swords into plowshares and their spears into pruning hooks; nation will not lift the sword against nation, and they will no longer study warfare.* (Mic. 4:3)

Societal Response

Many of the missionary prophets, those whose prophetic experience compels them to preach, neither pursue nor relish their role because of the reactions to their message in their target audiences. True prophecy often causes nearly pathognomonic* responses in those who receive it. This is due to the message's admonishing and chastising content as well as its dire predictions. The text refers to prophecy as a "weight" or "burden" (Zech. 9:1; Mal. 1:1). The emotional, interpersonal, and physical strains are crushing, and many called to a prophetic mission attempt to avoid it.[6] The true prophet may receive physical abuse (Isa. 50:6) or death threats (Jer. 11:21), or people may simply shun and ignore the prophet (Jer. 25:3). In fact, people usually prefer false prophecy, as Isaiah laments their request: *Speak to us with smooth talk* (Isa. 30:10).

---

*A medical term referring to a sign or symptom uniquely characterizing a particular disease or condition.

WISDOM

The books that make up the Hebrew Bible's formal wisdom literature are Proverbs, Job, and Ecclesiastes, although wisdom courses through the entire text. These books contain very little, if any, legal, historical, or narrative content. Instead, they emphasize theological and ethical issues, and lead to a clearer knowledge of God as well as help us attain well-being, dignity, and decency in this life. There are no visions in Proverbs and Ecclesiastes, only succinct observations and advice, and the Book of Job is nearly entirely a dialogue about theodicy. The wisdom books of the Hebrew Bible possess a degree of sophistication that matches anything one might encounter in the Eastern wisdom traditions; for example, Proverbs lists eleven types of wisdom or wise individual and six types of folly or foolish person.[7]

In the spirit of a wisdom text, the Hebrew Bible opens by directly addressing whether creation is good or bad. This heads off any potential sense of disheartenment, nihilism, or weariness regarding this world. *And God saw all that He had made, and behold, it was very good* (Gen. 1:31).

✿ DMT

Gabe confirmed this positive viewpoint: *[The beings] were saying that life was good* (*DMT,* 190).

We Determine the Quality of Our Lives

The Hebrew Bible establishes early on its teaching about self-determination when describing the delicate balance between doing good and doing evil, a decision over which we generally exert free will. Cain is angry that God accepted his brother Abel's sacrifice and not his own. In response, God tells Cain: *Surely if you improve yourself, you will be forgiven. But if you do not improve yourself, sin rests at the door. Its desire is toward you, yet you can conquer it* (Gen. 4:7).

🪰 DMT

Andrea encapsulated the results of not "improving oneself": *Humans and I are just plodding along, not going anywhere.*

Wisdom's Nature and Value

Wisdom predates creation. It says of itself: *I was created when there were yet no deeps* (Prov. 8:24). Wisdom is theocentric: *Let not the wise man glorify himself with his wisdom. . . . For only with this may one glorify himself: contemplating and knowing Me* (Jer. 9:22–23); ethical: *Behold, the awe of my Lord is wisdom, refraining from evil is understanding* (Job 28:28); and consists in knowing the value of seeking it: *The beginning of wisdom [is to] acquire wisdom, and with all your possessions acquire understanding* (Prov. 4:7).

🪰 DMT

Using the Greek term for the intelligent order that regulates existence, Allan reported perceiving: *the Logos, . . . the core of meaning and semantics* (*DMT,* 179).

Limits to Human Knowledge

The Hebrew Bible's position is that our ability to understand God's wisdom is not sufficient for the task. Solomon suggests that our very nature precludes attaining ultimate knowledge: *[God] has also put an enigma into their minds so that man cannot comprehend God's work that He did from beginning to end* (Eccles. 3:11). God tells Isaiah that our use of the term "wisdom" is only homonymous in relation to His: *For as the heavens are higher than the earth, so are My ways higher than your ways and My thoughts [higher] than your thoughts* (Isa. 55:9). In addition, our inability to fathom God's wisdom is at the root of the problem of theodicy, as we read in the concluding chapters of the book of Job.

🪰 DMT

Elena commented on the limited ability of her conceptual knowledge to grasp the essence of existence: *There was no benevolent god, only this primordial power. All of my ideas and beliefs seemed absurdly ridiculous* (*DMT,* 240).

POETRY

We usually equate the Book of Psalms and the Song of Songs with biblical poetry. However, several other songs appear in the Hebrew Bible. They all provide a lyrical mode of prayer—petitioning, praising, giving thanks, or expressing love. Psalm 23 probably is the most popular:

> *YHVH is my shepherd, I shall not lack. In lush meadows He lays me down, beside tranquil waters He leads me. He restores my soul. He leads me on paths of righteousness for His name's sake. Though I walk in the valley overshadowed by death, I fear no evil, for You are with me. Your rod and Your staff, they comfort me. You prepare a table before me in view of my tormentors. You anointed my head with oil, my cup overflows.*

COMPARING MESSAGES OF THE HEBREW BIBLE AND BUDDHISM

Traditional Buddhism teaches that there is no God external to us, one with whom our self attains a deeper and more highly developed relationship in the spiritual state. Instead, one reaches the goal of enlightenment by deconstructing that self and thereby experiencing absolute identification with an imageless, formless, and concept-free state of "emptiness." The emptiness of enlightenment lacks any attributes, teaches no precepts, and possesses no personality, expectations, nor feelings.

Ethical–moral precepts do play a role in Buddhist practice, but they result from, rather than make up the essence of, the spiritual experience. In my Zen community, the three basic precepts were: (1) cease from evil, (2) do only good, and (3) do good for others. While these comport with the prophetic message, they represent an enlightened response to reality rather than constitute the message of enlightenment itself, because enlightenment by definition contains no message.

Buddhist ethics developed after the core enlightenment experience of the Buddha. He returned, as it were, with certain knowledge; for example, that there is no abiding self in the mind-body complex, that everyday existence is impermanent and therefore an improper relationship with it begets suffering. Therefore, deconstructing our relationship with the phenomenal world leads to inner peace. Buddhist interactive-relational guidelines, such as acting charitably, are secondary, not intrinsic, to a higher-order a-relational mystical-unitive experience.

In prophecy, there exists the maintenance and even intensification of one's self in a highly dynamic and interactive relationship with a speaking, feeling, acting, and teaching God. Through prophecy, God communicates specific guidelines for beliefs and behavior that are consistent with the natural and moral laws He created and sustains. The prophetic experience is full of intelligible information, not devoid of it. The message, not its absence, is the soul of prophecy—its essential feature.

SUMMARY

This chapter has compared the informational content of the prophetic and DMT states with respect to God's role in history, as well as the world to come, the messiah, resurrection, false prophecy, poetry, and wisdom. As in the previous chapter, the degree of overlap is not especially impressive. Prediction, especially near- to long-term, is virtually absent in the DMT experience compared with the prophetic one. And while eschatological elements appear in both states, those of prophecy are much more highly articulated. However, it is of great interest that biblical descriptions of the world to come share phenomenological properties with the DMT state. These common characteristics have led me to consider the role of endogenous DMT in the "eschaton," and I will discuss this issue in chapter 20, The Metaphysics of DMT.

I have addressed at some length the notion of false prophecy. I believe it is necessary to keep this phenomenon in mind if and when we use the information and ideas in this book to attempt a renaissance of contemporary prophetic experience. We must approach any such effort with utmost care, within both the religious and the psychiatric/psychedelic communities, to minimize false prophecy's potential for adding more, rather than less, confusion and misunderstanding to our world.

While the DMT experience and prophecy appear to open the door to a very similar phenomenological universe—sights, sounds, feelings, and so on—it is less clear whether they open the door to the same theological and moral ones. In prophecy, especially that type we associate with the canonical prophets, there is information that consists of beautiful language, ideas, and guidelines for living that have shaped Western civilization for thousands of years. While the information contained in moments of inspiration and insight in the drug state usually are consistent with those of prophecy, the message of the DMT experience does not begin to approach the prophetic one's breadth, depth, complexity, and profundity. And even in the case of non-canonical prophets, the truth value and relevance of the message they receive is far greater than that which the DMT volunteers return with.

At the same time, it may be that we are only now beginning to see a greater influence of the psychedelic "message" in the non-aesthetic worlds. In chapter 17, I referred to the development of transpersonal psychology as an intellectual response to the influx of psychedelic and Eastern religious sensibilities into Western culture in the 1960s. More recently, there is evidence for a similar effect on the disciplines of modern physics[8] and personal computing.[9] I remain uncertain, however, whether such developments are truly non-aesthetic. More precisely, do these developments provide us with greater ethical and moral values or superior wisdom? Do they truly represent the workings of a higher order or are they simply hypertrophied manifestations of the ordinary?

How might we understand the discrepancy between the degree of resemblance between the two states' phenomenology and their information content? One possible solution to this problem is that the DMT volunteers did indeed enter into the same theological and moral worlds as do the prophets, but simply lacked the relevant concepts and vocabulary to recognize, understand, and communicate the information they contain. The alternative explanation is that the two states only superficially resemble each. One is true prophecy and the other is false or, more accurately, a simulacrum or facsimile.

This is a critical issue. If it simply is a matter of education and training, it is theoretically possible to make the prophetic experience more likely in those who seek it using psychedelic drugs. However, if the two sets of experiences differ fundamentally, then no amount of training or education will lead to the contemporary psychedelic drug state developing into true prophecy. These issues lead us to the investigation of the mechanisms underlying the prophetic and DMT experiences, the topic that now follows. Can we, by understanding those mechanisms, affect them in such a manner as to occasion true prophecy in our time?

PART IV

Mechanisms:
Spiritual and Material

19 The Metaphysics of Prophecy

I have established in the preceding chapters that the prophetic and DMT experiences share many phenomenological features. And while the informational contents—the messages—that the two states present are relatively comparable with respect to their broadest outlines, the prophetic state's is much greater in breadth, depth, profundity, and impact. The two syndromes' phenomenological resemblances suggest shared underlying mechanisms. The discrepancies in message content point toward significant differences in how the two states develop. Understanding these processes, how they do and don't resemble each other, will help us build more sophisticated models for understanding prophecy and the DMT experiences. These new models then may lead to intriguing practical applications, such as attempting to experimentally elicit prophecy.

In the next two chapters, I will engage in a dialectic between two perspectives in order to explicate the mechanisms underlying the prophetic and DMT states. One is a spiritual-metaphysical model that takes prophecy as its reference point, and the other is a scientific-material model that takes DMT as its reference point. In this chapter, I will treat spiritual mechanisms, the metaphysics of prophecy, especially as the medieval Jewish philosophers have written about them. In the next chapter, I will attempt to integrate what we know about the DMT effect into these metaphysical theories.

The medieval Jewish philosophers' system of metaphysics constitutes a sophisticated internally consistent model for understanding spiritual experience. I also have found it extraordinarily useful for understanding the DMT effect. As this project has progressed and I learned more about the metaphysical processes operating in prophecy, I began to see how I had been limiting my idea of "similar underlying processes" in the two states to only biological ones. It appeared that similar metaphysical processes also were at work. To the extent that the two sets of experiences overlap, they may share a common metaphysics as well as a common biology.

The metaphysical processes take place at levels that presently are objectively invisible but whose effects are subjectively evident. The biological processes are objectively observable but not subjectively evident. In other words, we directly apprehend thoughts, feelings, sights, sounds, and other phenomena in our minds, but we do not apprehend the alterations in serotonin receptor function, for example, that underlie them. In contrast, we can objectively measure effects on serotonin but not objectively measure our subjective experience. An "explanatory gap" exists between biological processes and inner experience. The medieval Jewish philosophers' metaphysics provides a potential bridge spanning that gap.

The hallmark of this book's theoneurological model is its placing spiritual mechanisms on at least equal footing in discussing mechanisms for how these states come about. Theoneurology proposes that God communicates with humans prophetically using the brain as the physical agent of communication. It is a top-down model, rather than a bottom-up neurotheological one.

In neurotheology the brain "gives the impression" of communicating with God. In theoneurology, the brain allows that process to take place through a process that metaphysical theories help model. A theoneurological perspective provides a useful counterpoint to contemporary neurotheological models in its reversing the direction of causality. By utilizing metaphysics, it attempts to integrate a sophisticated religious worldview into a rigorously scientific one.

RELEVANCE TO
THE SCIENCE OF SPIRITUALITY

Contemporary research into spiritual experiences generally conflates all such experiences with the mystical-unitive type, resulting in its having become the "gold standard" for this research. A recent academic article[1] listed contemporary research criteria for a "spiritual experience": unity, a noetic quality,* and sacredness; a positive mood; the transcendence of time or space (or both); and ineffability.† However, by now it should be apparent that these criteria fail to capture many of the salient properties of the highest form of Hebrew biblical spirituality, prophecy, or of the DMT effect. In these interactive-relational syndromes we find the maintenance, if not enhancement, of one's sense of self, a self that interacts fulsomely with the highly articulated contents of the altered state. One enters into another world, rather than merging with pure experience, or even God Itself, and that other world is replete with processes and contents that occupy time and space. Finally, prophecy is rarely ecstatic and nearly always highly verbal.

By restricting the definition of spiritual experience to the unitive-mystical type, we do two disservices to our investigation of the prophetic state and, by extension, to our investigation of the DMT one. First, by ranking the unitive-mystical syndrome higher than the interactive-relational experience, researchers are automatically ranking lower the benchmark spiritual experience of the Hebrew Bible, the spiritual text that serves as a scriptural foundation for half of the world population's religious traditions. If current research considered the two sets of experiences as equal, albeit qualitatively different, examining these differences would lead to a broader theoretical,

---

*Resulting in new insights or a deep intellectual realization.
†Denoting the inadequacy of words to characterize the state.

biological, and practical understanding of spirituality in its various forms. It also would provide a more equitable theoretical foundation for using DMT, which elicits an interactive-relational experience, to conduct serious inquiries into spiritual experience. Because DMT effects are interactive-relational, one may argue that its effects are somehow "inferior" to those resulting from administration of compounds that more reliably occasion a unitive-mystical one.[2]

Second, and in a consciously or unconsciously related manner, relegating to lower status the interactive-relational prophetic and DMT states allows researchers to dispense with the "embarrassing stigma"[3] of both, stigmata one can avoid when dealing solely with the nonverbal and content-free unitive-mystical state. In prophecy, these embarrassing stigmata are the beings and the prophetic message. The message contains ethical and moral values, and is transmitted by a God external to us. This God possesses specific attributes, holds expectations for our beliefs and behavior, and metes out reward and punishment according to our adherence to certain guidelines. In the DMT state, the embarrassing stigma is the presence of the beings, who seem to serve certain functions. It is much easier to sidestep both of these "problems" by focusing on the mystical-unitive experience, which is absent such controversial content.

MEDIEVAL METAPHYSICS: A BRIEF REVIEW

In general, the Hebrew Bible does not present a metaphysical model of prophecy. Instead, the text simply records that God or His angels appear to one or more humans and say and do various things. The development of a systematic metaphysics of prophecy awaited the medieval Jewish philosophers. Most of these writers agree on a general framework for how prophecy works.[4]

There are three pillars of prophecy: its source, its recipient, and the process of communication. I have already discussed the source of prophecy, God, in some detail in chapter 7, from an abstract perspective, and in chapters 17 and 18, Message and Meaning I and II, I presented textual examples of those abstract notions. In chapter 8, Prophet and Prophecy, I summarized characteristics of those who experience the prophetic state, as well as methods, training, and other factors that may conduce to its occurrence. The process of interaction between God and one experiencing prophecy I reviewed in chapter 15, Relatedness.

However, for the discussion that follows, I'd like to briefly review and synthesize the information the preceding chapters contained under the umbrella of the medieval Jewish philosophers' metaphysics, the system of spiritual objects and processes that fill their intellectual and theological worlds. By so doing, we'll be better prepared to approach their theories explaining the occurrence of prophecy and prophecy-like phenomena.

For those medieval Jewish philosophers who believe that an incorporeal God does not interact directly with a corporeal world, "intermediaries" fill that role. The Hebrew Bible refers to this notion when it states that God: *makes the winds* * *His messengers, the flaming fire His ministers* (Ps. 104:4). Others believe that God does directly interact with the phenomenal world. In either case, all the medieval Jewish philosophers posit an overflow, emanation, or efflux† of divine influence from God or His intermediaries‡ onto the natural world, including that of humans.

The subjective experience of divine influence occurs in the mind, in particular through the operation of two mental faculties: the "rational" and the "imaginative." The *imaginative faculty*§ is not what we usually consider the "imagination," that which "makes things up," but rather it is the mental mechanism responsible for mediating perceptions, emotions, and somatic experiences. In more modern terms, we might call it the circuitry of the mind-brain complex mediating those functions. It also reproduces sensory experience using images of perceptions and

---

*Alternatively, "His spirits."

†These terms are interchangeable.

‡The Active Intellect is the earth's most proximate intermediary and thus exerts the most direct influence upon it.

§I use *imaginative faculty* and *imagination* interchangeably.

sensations whose immediate causes no longer exist; that is, the imaginative faculty possesses memory. Finally, the imagination combines these images in novel ways; for example, we might have seen a horse and a human in the real world, and then we imagine a centaur.

The medieval Jewish philosophers consider the imaginative faculty more physical or corporeal than the rational one because it deals with body-based data: perceptions, emotions, and the like. Therefore, the imagination, dependent as it is on the body, is something whose degree of development, what the medieval Jewish philosophers call its "degree of perfection," is more fixed at birth and is relatively less modifiable by education or training.

The *rational faculty** cognizes. It performs intellectual functions, logically processing formless ideas. It assesses truth and makes rational decisions. Because the rational faculty deals with less "solid" or corporeal objects, the philosophers consider it the higher ranking of the two, as it more closely resembles God in this aspect of incorporeality. The rational faculty also can recall concepts and combine them in novel ways. The rational faculty is more amenable to training and education than is the imagination. Through education, one's intellect may be potential and then become actual.

METAPHYSICAL EXPLANATIONS OF PROPHECY

All the medieval Jewish philosophers except Saadiah believe that the prophetic experience exists in the subjective realm. Only Saadiah teaches that prophecy results from God forming a "created sound" or "created light" that one perceives while awake, with the external senses in the objective world. He equates the "created light" with kavod, which in his model comprises every element of what one apprehends in prophecy. Saadiah's theory takes us into the realm of the "miraculous" appearance of physical objects, a notion that leads us away from the approach I have been taking throughout this book. Rather, I have been focusing on

---

*I use the terms *rational faculty, intellect,* and *intellectual faculty* interchangeably.

characterizing and developing models of prophecy as a subjective experience. In this, I follow all the other medieval authors.

My taking the default position that prophecy is a subjective experience also is consistent with how I previously addressed the beings when I wrote *DMT: The Spirit Molecule*. There I proposed a spectrum of "contact" experiences, with one pole consisting of consciousness-to-consciousness interactions and the other pole consisting of body-to-body interactions. Because no beings materialized in our research room and no volunteers demonstrated physical signs, such as implants or burns, I chose to build my model on the consciousness-to-consciousness platform. Saadiah's model of the objective reality of the prophetic experience is more in line with the body-to-body perspective, which I chose to de-emphasize.

All our writers except Saadiah teach that what one sees, hears, and feels in the prophetic state, its phenomenological content, consists of what one's imaginative capacities allow. Angels, beings, and other forms, while they exist in the perceiver's mind, are not their "real" form. What we see are "insensible" processes, forces, and objects existing in previously invisible realms. The imagination's raw materials garb or enclothe the previously invisible things to make them apprehensible.

Maimonides' theory is that divine influence emanates on the two faculties consistent with their degree of perfection or development. Those with a highly developed rational, but not imaginative, faculty become wise, as in the case of philosophers or scientists.* When the imagination is more perfect than the intellect, one may become a statesman, lawgiver, or diviner. Only when both faculties are equally and highly developed is one capable of attaining prophecy. Gradations occur in prophetic rank due to gradations in development of those faculties.[5]

All that being said, the presence or absence of prophecy ultimately depends on God's willing that the person experience it. In this context,

---

*This is most likely how he would have conceptualized the state of Zen enlightenment, when the field of the imagination becomes empty through the practice of meditation and the rational faculty alone is operative at a high level.

our authors teach that possessing imaginative and rational perfection makes one "qualified" for prophecy but does not ensure it. Nevertheless, the more qualified one is, the more likely it is that God will choose that person.

When divine influence affects someone with highly and equally developed rational and imaginative faculties, the stimulated rational faculty, the higher of the two, overflows "downward" onto the imaginative. This allows the imagination to make "sensible" the "insensible" or formless contents of the rational faculty. The intellect then interprets and communicates the contents of the imagination that the imagination generates in response to this overflow of originally insensible information. Differences in the imaginative faculty, which is corporeal and thus varies across individual bodies, explain why prophetic visions vary whereas their messages do not.

The prophet receives an abstract notion that can't be conveyed in concrete terms, and therefore he or she uses the imagination to present the message in a pictorial or metaphorical form. Because the visions and voices of the prophetic state belong to the imagination, prophets treat them allegorically, at least when the subject is a theological or metaphysical truth. The message is divine, but one cannot apprehend nor transmit it without the seen images and heard words filling the imagination. Due to the allegorical nature of much of prophecy, communicating it may be as difficult as, or even more difficult than, attaining it, as the majority of Daniel's and Zechariah's visions attest. Nevertheless, the highly developed imagination of a prophet produces parables conveying important information of their own, what Maimonides, quoting Proverbs 25:1, refers to as "silver settings" for "golden apples."[6]

Using this model, one may suggest that Isaiah's vision in chapter 6 of his book and Ezekiel's vision in chapter 1 of his both had the same "vision" of the chariot. However, Isaiah's superior intellect allowed him to communicate its meaning better than did Ezekiel. In the case of Moses, the Hebrew Bible's outstanding prophet, his perfected intellect and imagination allowed him the most unimpeded prophetic experience: nearly entirely verbal information that he readily communicated to his audience.

THE PROPHETIC MESSAGE

The medieval Jewish philosophers laud biblical prophecy and its message; that is, all but Spinoza, who had his reasons not to.* They believe that the prophetic message emanates from God or His intermediaries and therefore possesses ultimate truth value. Prophecy provides unique insights and teachings about moral, theological, and natural law because its divine source possesses all of this knowledge. The information one attains in the prophetic state is either inaccessible through the rational methods of philosophy or science, or if it were, would require more time, aptitude, and training to acquire than most of us possess. This latter point is one made especially forcefully by Saadiah.

In addition, the prophetic message presents itself in a form that the masses are capable of accepting, if not thoroughly understanding. For example, the notion of an "angry" God, while not strictly true, because God does not have feelings, teaches obedience to laws with a divine origin that promote individual and social welfare.

The Location of the Prophetic Message
Does divine overflow contain the information one apprehends in prophecy? Or does it instead simply illuminate our own latent knowledge? The medieval Jewish philosophers discuss this issue, and while the nuances they raise are subtle, it is worth considering the general question. This is because we need to consider how message-poor the DMT experience is relative to that of prophecy. If one of the outcomes of this book is the development of projects attempting to elicit prophecy

---

*Spinoza's goal in writing his *Tractatus Theologico-Politicus*,[7] in which he lays out his theories of prophecy, was to wrest from the clerics of his day the authority to legislate and police proper thought, speech, and behavior. Spinoza realized that clerical power, both that of the Church and that which he believed Maimonides' writings implied, relied on the assumed divine nature of prophetic scripture. By belittling the vast majority of biblical prophecy and placing what he did find meritorious in it, such as the Golden Rule, outside of philosophic and scientific discourse, Spinoza sought to undermine abusive clerical power that relied on prophetically inspired scripture as its justification.

or prophecy-like states by means of judiciously using psychedelic drugs, there needs to be some way to increase the informational content of the drug state. Therefore, understanding how the medieval Jewish philosophers conceive of the location, nature, and accessibility of the prophetic message is relevant for our purposes.

Some of our medieval authors suggest that there is no information as such in divine efflux; rather, it simply strengthens one's faculties in order to access information that the mind already possesses in some form or another. This is a model positing the "embedded" nature of the prophetic message. Others propose that divine overflow strengthens one's faculties in order to apprehend the message that the emanation contains; that is, emanation both contains information and enables us to comprehend it. While the particulars may differ, the consistent theme is that something—divine emanation—from outside the individual affects him or her, resulting in attainment of the prophetic message.

Canonical vs. Non-canonical Prophetic Figures

Here I would like to clarify an issue that I referred to previously. This concerns the distinction between canonical prophets, such as Moses, Isaiah, and Jeremiah, and non-canonical ones. The criterion for this distinction is not necessarily the level of prophetic attainment. Both types communicate with angels or God (or both), and the message is true and highly relevant. These non-canonical figures such as Abraham, Jacob, Samson's mother, and many others attain high prophetic stature but do not leave a book or teachings behind. If we are to assume that both types attain prophecy by means of identical metaphysical mechanisms, divine emanation overflowing onto equally highly developed rational and imaginative faculties, we must look elsewhere for the source of this difference. Several solutions are possible.

The social and political circumstances of the canonical prophets differ from those of many of the non-canonical figures. The canonical prophets preached during a highly tumultuous historical era, to an often corrupt and recalcitrant monarchy, through two catastrophic exiles. The absence of such situations facing the non-canonical prophets may account for the lack of canonical figures, except for Moses, during pre-monarchical times. Regarding Moses, his circumstances were even more extraordinary, in that he acted as midwife for the birth of the Hebrew nation, and was responsible for transmitting its new laws, rituals, and other requirements.

Another place to search for an explanation of the difference between canonical and non-canonical prophecy is in the information content of the experience itself. If divine efflux contains information, then the information that God or His intermediaries is communicating is more complex in the case of the canonical prophet. On the other hand, if the divine overflow illuminates something that the prophet's mind already somehow possesses, then the difference lies in the prophet's personality, eloquence, morality, sense of social obligation, and so on.

The cases of Elijah and Elisha are illustrative in this context. Both attained to the highest rungs of prophetic experience but did not leave behind teachings, despite living during the tumultuous monarchical era. This suggests that the informational content of the experience itself differed in their cases rather than personal or sociocultural factors playing the determinative role.

HOW ONE BECOMES A PROPHET

The medieval Jewish philosophers debate whether prophecy is a "mission" or a "perfection." The prophecy-as-a-perfection viewpoint posits that one trains for prophecy and then attains it. This requires possessing optimal physical capacities from birth, especially the brain—where the medieval Jewish philosophers believe the imagination resides—and undergoing suitable education and training of the rational faculty. Some commentators add the variables of love, virtue, piety, and courage. When one has met these conditions, she or he attains prophecy.

The notion of prophecy-as-a-mission proposes that God chooses someone for prophecy simply because of necessity. The time and place require God's communication with an individual or group. As a concession to the medieval authors who consider prophecy a perfection, proponents of the "mission" viewpoint add that God perfects the intellect and imagination of such people to suit the requirements of the moment.

This issue has significant implications with respect to whether prophecy today remains within our reach. If prophecy is a perfection, then we may strive for it, and some of us may attain it. There have been, and will continue to be, athletic, artistic, scientific, and political geniuses whose constitutions and training have allowed them to attain such heights. However, if prophecy is strictly a mission, in the sense that God chooses whom He will regardless of one's qualifications, there is little we can do to experience it.

In support of the view that prophecy is a mission, we read about a nameless foreign foot soldier telling his friend one morning about a prophetic dream that accurately predicts a Hebrew military victory (Judg. 7:13–14). Amos explicitly proclaims his lack of qualifications and the missionary nature of his career: *I am neither a prophet nor the son of a prophet, but a cattle herder and an examiner of sycamores. YHVH took me from behind the flock, and YHVH said to me, "Go prophesy to my people Israel"* (Amos 7:14–15).

Most medieval authors take a compromise position and suggest that God chooses for His mission someone who is qualified. Jeremiah's call to prophecy exemplifies the interplay of mission and perfection. God tells him: *Before I formed you in the womb, I knew you, and before you left the womb, I sanctified you. I established you as a prophet unto the nations* (Jer. 1:5). This suggests that Jeremiah's biological constitution at birth, the bases for his imaginative faculty, qualified him for his mission.

Jeremiah's reply supports the idea that a suitable constitution alone is necessary but not sufficient, for he lacks intellectual maturity: *Alas my Lord YHVH, see, I do not know how to speak, for I am just a youth* (Jer. 1:6). God responds by strengthening his intellectual and verbal capacities, which were previously lacking, and thus Jeremiah becomes qualified: *YHVH stretched out His hand and touched my mouth, and YHVH said to me, "Behold, I have placed My words in your mouth"* (Jer. 1:9). God then tests Jeremiah's ability to interpret the visions He causes him to see, and confirms Jeremiah's new status (Jer. 1:11–14).

Objections to Prophecy as a Perfection

Maimonides' view of prophecy as a perfection, that God is more likely to choose a perfected individual, is not especially defensible. Those who attain a superior level of prophecy may actually lack a very well developed rational faculty. For example, Adam and Eve, who are privy to an easy conversational relationship with God, thought that they could hide from Him in the Garden of Eden and thus avoid the consequences of eating the proscribed fruit (Gen. 3:8). In other words, they lacked the basic knowledge of God's omnipresence, something the medieval Jewish philosophers believe one may attain through rational deduction. And Abraham's arguing with God to save Sodom and Gomorrah, if there existed ten righteous men within the two cities (Gen. 18:23–33), suggests that he did not possess knowledge of God's omniscience, also attainable through the application of a highly developed intellect.

Spinoza refers to these and other examples in contending that what passes for prophecy in the Hebrew Bible are the utterances of individuals whose vivid imaginations are more active than their intellects. Consistent with his attempt to debunk the authority of biblical prophecy—or more precisely, the revealed nature of the Hebrew Bible— he offers his low opinion of the imagination relative to the intellect in its ability to obtain truth.

Spinoza points to how the imagination is more active when people are asleep, ill, dying, afraid, or otherwise reduced in their rational faculties. Opposing Maimonides, he opines that the intellect and imagination function in opposition to, rather than in synergy with, each other. One waxes only when the other wanes. And because the intellect can't control the imagination, the imagination usually is wrong. At the same time, Spinoza believes that the Hebrew prophets were genuinely devout and moral. The combination of these two factors, a powerful imagination and virtue, led to teachings that are morally useful, but have nothing to do with either natural or theological truths.

Several medieval Jewish philosophers suggest that a high degree of moral development is also necessary for attaining prophecy. Living a pious life helps prevent indulging in beliefs or behavior detrimental to perfecting one's intellect and for maintaining one's physical health that is necessary for optimal imaginative function. However, Balaam the Canaanite prophet, despite his requesting and receiving regular congress with God seemingly as easily as Moses, hires himself out to a local king to curse the camp of God's chosen people on its way to Canaan (Num. 22:2–24:25). And Moses's volatile temper results in his smashing the original pair of God-inscribed tablets containing the Ten Commandments (Exod. 32:19). His impetuousness also precludes his entering into Canaan, as I mentioned in the previous chapter.

How then to determine whether prophecy is a mission or perfection? The stance I am most comfortable taking in this debate is as follows: First, Hebrew biblical prophecy exists as the text explicates it. It is communication with God or His intermediaries. This, of course, is the basis for the theoneurological model I am proposing. Second, we cannot really know why God chooses whom He does. Thus, a reasonable approach is that prophecy is *both* a perfection and a mission. Being qualified makes it more likely that one will receive prophecy, if God decides to bestow it.

FORETELLING

The medieval Jewish philosophers note that prediction may occur through non-prophetic as well as prophetic means. In the case of a "self-fulfilling" prophecy, the prediction influences the future. Or there may exist only a coincidental relationship between the event and its foretelling. Sometimes a highly developed imagination operating in the absence of a commensurately powerful intellect combines past events in a novel manner, resulting in an accurate prediction. Finally, successful prediction may result from deductive reasoning by an expert; for example, a meteorologist predicts the weather more accurately than not.

When the medieval Jewish philosophers do invoke metaphysical mechanisms for predicting, they draw upon their understanding of God's omniscience and will. Within God, or the Active Intellect, exists the knowledge of all possible outcomes.* As one who is capable of deciphering divine efflux, the prophet captures one particular set of outcomes resulting from the present set of circumstances that God may will into actuality.

KAVOD

Kavod's nature is liminal and highly dynamic. It possesses attributes and actions somewhere between, or as a hybrid of, God and Its intermediaries. Kavod's elusive, and allusive, properties contribute to the variety of explanations that the medieval Jewish philosophers have developed regarding how it operates.

One of the properties of kavod upon which turn mechanistic hypotheses is its apprehensibility by the masses. It is difficult to explain how all of the Hebrew camp qualified for prophecy, constitutionally or by training. However, Saadiah's explanation of prophetic phenomenology responds to this qualm: kavod is a light or sound that God creates for a special purpose. It is an external object that the physical senses perceive. In a related fashion, the luminous visual properties of kavod prompted Judah Halevi to speculate that it somehow combines material *and* spiritual properties. He proposes that it is a very subtle physical, visual aura surrounding a spiritual entity, or that it is a physical reflection of divine light, like the light of dusk from the sun. His definition equivocates regarding whether one must be a prophet to perceive it.

If we assume, however, that prophecy is solely a subjective experience, we need to fall back upon the notion of prophecy as a mission. God temporarily perfected the masses' rational and intellectual faculties for a specific purpose. Kavod's ill-defined visual and auditory properties point to a lower-level, stopgap quality consistent with this expedient granting of prophecy to essentially unqualified individuals. Evidence in support of this latter notion is that when kavod does manifest its "voice" to people, those who hear formed words (such as Moses and

---

*In this model, God "knowing" the future doesn't necessarily affect it.

Aaron) rather than unformed sounds (as do the masses) have already attained to prophetic stature.

FALSE PROPHECY

The Hebrew Bible provides several self-evident processes by which false prophecy may occur, such as plagiary and deliberate fabrication. However, the medieval Jewish philosophers suggest other mechanisms by which false prophecy may operate; for instance, cases in which the false prophet is sincere and the determination of the falsity of the message is more difficult.

The metaphysical mechanism common to our authors' explanations of false prophecy is that false prophets do experience visions, but the visions are not the result of divine influence. Rather, they occur in the setting of an overactive imagination absent of a highly developed intellect.* Jeremiah captures this notion when, speaking for God, he says: *The prophet with a dream tells a dream, but the one with My word speaks My word of truth* (Jer. 23:28).

The other mechanism the Hebrew Bible, but not necessarily the medieval Jewish philosophers, posits for how false prophecy works is that God Himself delivers to the false prophet a deliberately spurious message. I raise this issue only reluctantly, because it leads into a very murky theological quagmire. The classic example of this phenomenon is when God wishes King Ahab to die in a war because of his many sins. A "lying spirit" volunteers to deceive the king's court prophets. Their *true* prophetic reception of a *false* prediction of victory encourages the king to enter the battle. Another true prophet, who has no court affiliation, that the king summons to validate the court prophets' advice, notes: *YHVH has put a spirit of falsehood in the mouths of all these prophets of yours, for YHVH has decreed evil upon you* (1 Kings 22:23). This is another example of how subtle and complex is the notion of false prophecy.

---

*Ironically, this definition is consistent with what Spinoza believes is the mechanism for nearly all of Hebrew biblical prophecy. Thus, his definition of a biblical prophet might be Maimonides' definition of a false prophet with virtue.

20 The Metaphysics of DMT

A Theoneurological Model of Prophecy

In *DMT: The Spirit Molecule,* I hypothesized that DMT elicits its effects by chemically modifying the receiving characteristics of the mind-brain complex. After receiving an injection of DMT, one's mind becomes capable of apprehending previously invisible things. These things may be solely the product of the mind-brain complex, or they may be external to us, existing in parallel levels of reality. In my search for where those additional layers of reality might reside, I first turned to the notions of dark matter and parallel universes, where modern physics is directing its attention in its search for invisible worlds. Contemporary researchers posit the existence of dark matter, for example, to explain how much of the universe's mass appears to be "missing" relative to the gravitational forces that are necessary for it to maintain its visible form. In this manner, physics is continuing in the tradition of medieval metaphysics, attempting to explicate mysterious, observable phenomena by invoking invisible theoretical processes and objects.

In the previous chapter, I outlined how the medieval Jewish philosophers similarly developed metaphysical hypotheses for prophecy, an observable phenomenon of great interest to them but for which no objective mechanisms were forthcoming. In this chapter, I will use their theories to build a metaphysical model for the DMT experience, another matter of great interest for which we have only a limited understanding regarding how it works. I believe I am justified in this attempt because the similarities between the prophetic and DMT states suggest common metaphysical mechanisms underlying them. Once we appreciate how their shared metaphysical and biological processes may occasion their shared phenomenology, we may then consider how their differences, especially regarding their informational content, reflect different metaphysical processes.

As I did in *DMT: The Spirit Molecule,* I will build hypotheses using general notions rather than review particular biomedical research findings. I will not focus extensively on specific psychopharmacologic data regarding DMT, the biological concomitants of spiritual experience, nor the neuroscience of the imagination and intellect. Instead, due to the extremely preliminary nature of this project, I wish to work with as much conceptual freedom as possible in order to begin bridging the psychedelic drug state and prophetic experience using medieval metaphysics. My aim in this exercise is to broadly introduce a top-down theoneurological model for spiritual experience that provides a counterpoint to the contemporary bottom-up neurotheological paradigm. A theoneurological model uses the vocabulary, concepts, and processes of metaphysics and theology while taking into account the presence and properties of endogenous mind-altering compounds such as DMT.

One immediate effect of this new model is that it provides a novel religious answer to the "If so, so what?" conundrum that the biological spirituality research field confronts. A less cryptic version of Dr. Freedman's question is, "Why did nature configure the brain to provide these types of experiences?" Neurotheology provides answers within a biomedical model: Religious experience is good for your health, good for society, and good for the species. Theoneurology provides answers within a religious context: God created and sustains our biological mind-body complex to provide a means of communicating with Him. By communicating with God and following His guidelines, we draw nearer to Him and thus fulfill His wish for closeness with us. The theoneurological model complements the neurotheological one by providing a higher level of abstraction. It places the origin, message, and purpose of the state external to the individual and species while basing itself on a religiously oriented and theocentric worldview.

DMT AND THE PROPHETIC STATE

Now that I have demonstrated convincing evidence regarding similarities between the phenomenology of the prophetic and DMT experiences—their perceptual, emotional, somatic, and other properties—it is possible to state clearly what this suggests at the biological level. The similar subjective effects of biblical prophecy and the DMT experience suggest similar brain activity in both syndromes.

This comparable biology may reflect the presence and activity of elevated brain levels of DMT. On the other hand, elevated brain levels of DMT may not be the most immediate proximate cause. That is, DMT administration in the volunteers may elicit a "downstream" biological effect, say "process X," that is ultimately responsible for the subjective experiences they described. Those downstream effects may take place in prophetic figures as a result of a proximate cause other than endogenous DMT; in other words, something other than DMT may initiate "process X" in prophetic states. Nevertheless, for the purposes of this discussion, it is much easier to focus on DMT because its effects in the research subjects and descriptions of biblical prophecy are so similar. Our working hypothesis is that elevated endogenous DMT may mediate the features of the prophetic experience that it shares with the experimental DMT effect.

IMAGINATION AND INTELLECT, PHENOMENOLOGY AND MESSAGE

The similarities between the prophetic and DMT states are less compelling when we examine their respective messages, especially those of the canonical prophets. Using the medieval Jewish philosophers' system of metaphysics, these findings suggest that DMT administration stimulates or strengthens the imaginative faculty, the locus of the phenomenological contents of both sets of experiences. However, DMT appears to exert little effect on the rational faculty, where the information content manifests. Let's look more closely at the implications of such a hypothesis.

The metaphysical model posits that in prophecy, God's or Its intermediaries' influence emanates onto equally highly developed rational and imaginative faculties. Either this influence first affects the intellect and then the imagination in a qualified individual, or it first emanates directly onto the imaginative faculty. In either case, the intellect extracts comprehensible and communicable information from the contents of the imagination. The critical elements here are that in prophecy (1) the source of this activation is external to the individual and is divine and (2) both faculties are similarly and highly developed.

If endogenous DMT were involved in the workings of the imaginative faculty in prophecy, it is in the service of transmitting God's influence to the experient. The divine overflow bestows perceptible form to fundamentally imperceptible information by using the imagination to generate more or less recognizable objects that are intended to convey that information. Then the intellect more or less accurately interprets and communicates the message that the imaginative contents represent.

After administering DMT in a research setting, the same putative elevation of brain levels of the compound may exist as in the prophetic state. However, in this case, DMT is stimulating the imagination "from below," as it were, not "from above." In addition, it is not affecting the rational faculty in any significant manner. The relative paucity of the DMT state's message may then reflect a difference in what catalyzes elevated brain DMT levels. Divine efflux stimulates the imagination—perhaps through DMT—as well as the intellect, whereas DMT only activates the imagination.

If divine efflux contains information, rather than only illuminating what the mind already possesses in some form or another, this would be another reason why the DMT state's message is so sparse. The substance itself does not contain information; rather, the contents of the imagination that DMT generates reflect intrinsic personal and not extrinsic Godly influences.

Let's now look at the idea that stimulating the imagination by drug administration "from below" is functionally analogous to what may occur in true prophecy. There are many examples in the Hebrew Bible of certain circumstances leading to the prophetic state, which I discussed in chapter 8, Prophet and Prophecy. They include fasting, prayer, delicious food, loneliness, despair, music, proximity to death, sexual abstinence, certain body postures, meditation, and particular geographic locations. These all affect the body, which the medieval Jewish philosophers teach is the basis of the imaginative faculty. Thus, these exigencies may make prophecy more likely by temporarily enhancing the imagination's activity. They also may lead to increasing endogenous levels of DMT through enhanced stress-related synthesis.* The quality of the resultant prophetic state, now manifest because of the DMT-mediated enhanced imagination (in a true prophet), would then depend on the corresponding ability of the rational faculty to extract information from the imaginative contents.

Here I wish to reiterate the notion of being "qualified" to receive divine efflux. God chooses whom He will to experience prophecy. At the same time, it is more likely that God will choose someone who is qualified, the most basic requirements being highly developed rational and imaginative faculties. Endogenous or exogenous DMT may temporarily elevate the function of the imagination and thus make one more qualified in that regard. However, it would have no effect on increasing the intellectual faculty's state of readiness. And it does not automatically ensure Godly efflux.

---

*I discuss possible catalysts for raising endogenous DMT in *DMT: The Spirit Molecule,* especially pages 70–77. However, no data yet exist to confirm or refute the hypothesis that endogenous DMT levels rise in these contexts.

THE EMBEDDED NATURE OF THE
PHENOMENOLOGY AND OF THE MESSAGE

One "neurotheological" way to conceptualize the process I have been outlining is that prophecy and the DMT states represent the stimulation of a reflex that resides in the mind-brain complex. In other words, both phenomenological syndromes are embedded within us, waiting for the appropriate catalyst: DMT injection or hypothetical self-induced stimulation from below, or externally induced stimulation by divine efflux from above. At the same time, we must recognize how interdependent is the relationship between the information the experience contains and the phenomenological contents of the experience. These contents convey the message.

This led me to wonder if the prophetic message also is embedded in the brain, waiting for its appropriate trigger. This notion is consistent with the teaching of those medieval Jewish philosophers who believe that Godly emanation does not contain information but simply sheds light on what the mind already contains. In prophecy, the prophetic state is the trigger for attaining to the prophetic message. Why shouldn't the DMT state, to the extent that it shares biological features with prophecy, similarly occasion apprehension of the prophetic message?

After some consideration of this idea, I again found the answer in the notion that prophecy affects both faculties, whereas DMT affects only the imaginative one. Activation of the imaginative faculty alone, either from above or from below, doesn't strengthen one's ability to understand or communicate the contents of that faculty, regardless of the source of its stimulation.

THE TRUTH OF THE MESSAGE

Recall that DMT volunteers' insights sometimes were consistent with those of the prophetic message. If DMT works primarily on the imaginative faculty, minimally affecting the rational one, how might this occur? We can approach this problem by pointing to the idea that the rational faculty works with the contents of the imagination regardless of their origin. The intellect asks, "What do these contents mean?" and operates on them according to its abilities. The truthfulness of the message the intellect extracts from the imagination's contents, strictly speaking, is not dependent on their source. This is analogous to how a non-prophet may arrive at the same truths as a prophet, although by non-prophetic means; for example, through deduction or intuition.

There is a danger, however, in equating the message one receives in a non-prophetic state of heightened imagination with true prophecy and thus claiming spiritual authority. This is false prophecy inasmuch as the person claims prophetic inspiration but is arriving at his or her conclusions non-prophetically. Endogenous or exogenous DMT may contribute to the imaginations' heightened function, but the information does not derive from a divine source.

In cases of divine efflux solely affecting the imaginative but not the rational faculty, the contents of the imagination reflect true things because their source is divine. However, if the intellect is poorly developed, it may misinterpret what it apprehends in the imagination. This misinterpretation of true images also may qualify as false prophecy. If one recognizes the phenomenon for what it is, however, benefits may still accrue, as Maimonides points out in the case of statesmen or diviners. But it is not prophecy.

THE URIM AND THUMMIM

In chapter 8, Prophet and Prophecy, I described how the Urim and Thummim rested in a compartment behind the Hebrew High Priest's breastplate. The breastplate contained twelve stones of different colors, each of which sat in a metal setting and each of which represented one of the twelve Hebrew tribes, whose names a craftsman had engraved on the stone. The High Priest in an inspired or prophetic state would inquire of the Urim and Thummim, and they provided an answer. These questions were usually simple, in which a "yes" or "no" response, or the selection of a particular Hebrew tribe for a specific task, sufficed.

The etymological relationship between *urim* and *light** suggested to some medieval Jewish philosophers that the breastplate stones lit up in specific patterns that represented the answer to the question. Might it have been the case that in a prophecy-like state resulting from mildly elevated levels of endogenous DMT, modified visual function made the stones seem to "glow"? And if the prophecy-like state truly represented Godly efflux, the rational faculty of the priest would provide the correct interpretation of the glowing stones' pattern.

THE WORLD TO COME

The concept of a "new world" following the "end of days" or other similar transitions has been and continues to be the subject of tremendous speculation and hope. The medieval Jewish philosophers have written extensively on the topic, perhaps in part because the Hebrew Bible's references are vague or contradictory.

Maimonides, for example, differentiates between a messianic era and a world to come.[1] In the former, all the laws of nature exist exactly as they do now. The only difference is that all Jews live in Israel and are free to study and practice their laws without other nations' enmity. He adds that during the messianic era, bodily resurrection takes place.† After resurrection, lifespans are extremely long, similar to those we encounter in the early generations of humanity that Genesis describes, in the range of one thousand years. The messianic era exists in this world as the first stage of a more ideal life after the material world. This more ideal life Maimonides calls the "world to come," an incorporeal state in which disembodied souls exist eternally after the body's death.

When descriptions in the Hebrew Bible refer to fundamental changes in nature, in particular non-corporeal forms and other

---

*The Hebrew word for light is *ohr,* whose three-letter root is the basis for the word *urim,* one translation of which might be "lights" or "things that light up."
†While resurrection's origin is supernatural—outside the realm of scientific scrutiny—the actual processes by which resurrection manifests within the natural world may be as amenable to explication as any other observable phenomenon.

psychedelic-like characteristics, I would like to propose a role for endogenous psychedelics. This should not come as an entirely surprising suggestion because I have already demonstrated how the world to come resembles in some ways the DMT experience.

I began considering a role for endogenous DMT in the world to come after the discovery of the DMT-synthesizing gene in humans and other mammals. This gene is responsible for the enzyme that attaches two methyl groups onto tryptamine, thus forming di-methyl-tryptamine, or DMT. We are only beginning to understand the regulation of this gene, what turns it on and off. Researchers have inserted the human version of this gene into a virus, and when that virus infects mammalian cells in a test tube, those cells produce DMT.[2]

Consider the following scenario: At the onset of the world to come, there is the sudden and profound burst of activity of the DMT-synthesizing gene in all organisms that contain it.* This is the tumultuous transition to the world to come, which then opens up before all of us. The stimulus for such an activation of the gene, of course, remains even more speculative than the activation itself. However, we may consider some possibilities.

External forces such as magnetic field shifts, massive gamma ray bursts, and other large-scale geo-celestial perturbations may act as the trigger for the widespread activation of the DMT-synthesizing gene. Alternatively, the workings of an internal genetic clock might provide the stimulus. This latter mechanism would preclude one's being able to shield oneself, so to speak, against this transitional event, whose universal nature is one of its defining characteristics.

Remember that these are mechanistic speculations regarding the nature of and transition into the world to come. They do not address the ultimate cause of its existence nor of the transition into it. As with prophecy in general, God is that ultimate cause.

It is of interest to consider how the imaginative faculty contributes

---

*Maimonides does not believe animals have a share in the world to come.[3] However, the ubiquity of DMT in the animal kingdom points to the opposite notion.

to this scenario. Because the imagination is a corporeal function, there may be no images or feelings associated with "life without a body." All the sights, sounds, and emotions we have learned to associate with the transition to physical death—the near-death experience—may occur at the transition point, but after physical death and the removal of any corporeality from the equation, we have no idea what is in store.[4]

PROPHECY, DMT, AND THE BEINGS

The beings may be viewed in several ways. They may be thoroughly objective things, or they may be sensible representations of either subjective or objective forces or processes.

As subjective things, the beings might represent our own psychology, in which case their nature would be like that of a dream's contents. At the most superficial level, they may represent residual feelings or thoughts that linger, barely consciously, in the backs of our minds. At a deeper level, they may be symbolic renditions of more significant emotional dynamics that had been previously completely unconscious. For example, a healing being may represent a health-care provider for whom we have strong feelings that we cannot express in everyday life. These psychological notions draw on the implicit assumption of the term *psychedelic* defined as "mind-manifesting." Our apprehension of the beings reflects the workings of our minds.

As objective things, we might understand the beings as residing in alternative levels of reality such as dark matter or parallel universes. Modified consciousness resulting from elevated brain levels of DMT, endogenous in prophecy or exogenous in my research subjects, allows someone to peer directly into those realms and thus view their inhabitants. One approach to assess the objective nature of the beings we perceive in the DMT and prophetic states would be to develop instruments that allow us to capture images of what exists in dark matter or parallel universes. By comparing these images to descriptions of the prophetic and DMT states, we would be able to determine how closely they resemble each other. If they do, we could more confidently posit an "external" location of the phenomena.

Finally, the beings may be sensible representations of essentially insensible processes or forces. For example, the beings appear to consist of light. However, this may not be their true nature but only the visible manifestation of a particular process, akin to how a flame visibly expresses the operation of combustion or light represents our perception of electromagnetic radiation. Our perceptual apparatus, as it were, can see only what it is capable of seeing.

Now, I'd like to expand the field of the term *psychedelic* to include how our minds apprehend forces that are externally, not internally, existent. I believe doing so allows us to interpret the beings as representing previously invisible external objects or forces. However, rather than suggesting that the mind generates those images, this notion proposes that the mind affects how we perceive external objects or forces, how they manifest in our minds.

We apprehend the beings in a more or less clear manner depending on the degree of overlay from our own psychology, constitution, training, and education. If we possess highly developed rational and imaginative faculties, we apprehend in as unadulterated a manner as possible those external things. The less well-developed these faculties, the more we muddy our observations of those external things with our own internal workings, our wishes, hopes, conflicts, ignorance, and so on. That muddying results in our subjective experience being more of a mirror and less of a window.

What are the external forces that the beings may represent? They may include healing and illness, strength and weakness, love and hate, evil and good, wisdom and folly. Using the medieval Jewish philosophers' metaphysics, these are what one might consider God's intermediaries, the vehicles through which Godly efflux works providentially. For example, the angel Raphael may represent healing forces, and Gabriel the force of strength. These world-affecting forces manifest in apprehensible visual, somatic, and other modalities using the repertoire our minds possess.

This model of the beings adds an additional level of sophistication to our discussion of their objective, externally existent nature. That is, they may not be "inhabitants" of other levels of reality, but rather omnipresent forces that exist outside of ourselves that we observe by means of our subjective consciousness. If this is the case, then our "invisible worlds camera," rather than capturing images of localized objects, may capture images of more pervasive forces exerting local effects.

On the other hand, our hypothetical instruments might be unable to capture any images of these external forces or objects—discrete, localized, or local representations of omnipresent forces—because perceiving them requires an interaction between them and our minds. In the case of a local manifestation of omnipresent forces, we might say that lifeless machines cannot apprehend divine efflux; it is simply too subtle to be objectively recorded.

DMT, CONSCIOUSNESS, AND THE NATURE OF REALITY

The more we learn about DMT's role in consciousness, the instrument by whose agency we perceive and think, the more blurred such distinctions between inner and outer become. In chapter 3, I referred to studies demonstrating active transport of DMT across the blood-brain barrier. This suggests that DMT may be necessary for normal brain function. And normal brain function means normal consciousness. In other words, the brain appears to require an endogenous psychedelic substance to maintain normal consciousness.

Recent studies are homing in on additional roles for endogenous DMT in mediating our experience of the world. Experiments in primates have demonstrated that the gene that makes the DMT-synthesizing enzyme is highly active in the retina, and levels of the enzyme itself are correspondingly high in this visual organ.[5] This suggests that our visual perception of the world also may be under the influence of an endogenous psychedelic substance. It should be evident by now that research examining the relationship between endogenous DMT and altered and normal consciousness is a matter of utmost importance to the fields of neuroscience, consciousness, epistemology, philosophy, and spirituality.

While these possible roles for DMT in mediating our worlds of vision and consciousness complicate any definitive answers regarding the "reality" of the beings, this uncertainly has little effect on how they impact one in the prophetic and DMT states. For those who engage with them, they exert tremendous effects, as real, profound, and meaningful as anything we may ever encounter in our lives. We see and hear them, and they see and hear us. In the case of the Hebrew Bible, the messages that the beings related have resonated for millennia and underlie half of the world population's religious beliefs and practices, leaving their indelible imprint on nearly every Western social, scientific, political, and artistic institution.

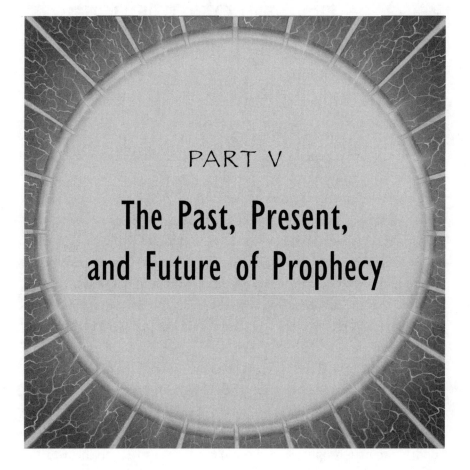

PART V

The Past, Present, and Future of Prophecy

21 The End of Prophecy

We now are in a position to take a long view of prophecy. I have discussed how my psychedelic drug research with DMT led me to the Hebrew Bible's notion of this paradigmatic Western spiritual experience, reviewed salient features of the Hebrew Bible's structure and contents relevant to prophecy, and characterized prophecy's features and compared them side by side with those of the DMT effect. This comparison demonstrated that the two states display striking perceptual, emotional, cognitive, and other phenomenological similarities. It also revealed that the prophetic message, especially in the case of the canonical prophets, is much more abundant, sophisticated, and highly articulated than that of the DMT experience. While the messages of the non-canonical prophetic figures are quantitatively more modest than those of the canonical prophets, they nevertheless contain more truth value and impact than the information acquired by the DMT subjects.

I have reviewed the medieval Jewish philosophers' metaphysical models for how prophecy works and attempted to relate them to the DMT state. Joining the two seemingly disparate phenomena of prophecy and the DMT experience using the bridge of medieval Jewish metaphysics has been one of the primary goals of my theoneurology model. The essential feature of this model is that it proposes that God communicates with humans through the agency of the mind-brain complex. DMT may be a critical component in this exchange.

Now that we have learned what prophecy is and how it may come about, what do the Hebrew Bible and the Jewish tradition say about its presence in our times? As usual, we find opposing views. One opinion is that prophecy has simply continued in much the same form as it did during the biblical era. Moses predicts: *A prophet from your midst, from your brethren, like me, shall YHVH, your God, establish for you—to him shall you listen* (Deut. 18:15).

On the other hand, prophecy may "end." This end may occur in one of two ways. The more sanguine alternative is that in the distant future everyone will prophesy. Thus, prophecy as a unique phenomenon, different from normal consciousness, will cease to exist. This is one of the features of the "next world" that I previously discussed. As God tells the prophet: *My spirit which is upon you and My words that I have placed in your mouth will not be withdrawn from your mouth, nor from the mouth of your offspring, nor from the mouth of your offspring's offspring . . . from now until forever* (Isa. 59:21).

The other "end" of prophecy is a true cessation. No one receives and communicates God's message anymore. The psalmist states: *Our signs we have not seen, there is no longer a prophet, and none among us knows how long* (Ps. 74:9). Similarly, Ezekiel foretells: *They shall seek vision from a prophet, but teaching shall be lost from the priest, and counsel from the elders* (Ezek. 7:26).

One qualifier of this rabbinic proposition modifies the end of prophecy by limiting it to a particular type. The Second Temple prophets refer to the "earlier prophets" as distinct from themselves. Zechariah states: *They did not hearken to the teachings and the words that YHVH of Hosts had sent through His spirit by the earlier prophets* (Zech. 7:12). However, all the canonical prophets speak in God's name and teach essentially the same message. While the form of the message varies across time, place, and personalities, this is the case throughout the entire biblical record. Perhaps these later prophets are alluding to the end of a specific type of a general phenomenon; for example, preaching to Israel's kings.

However, rabbinic authorities who inherited the mantle of Jewish leadership around the beginning of the common era were more consistent in pronouncing prophecy's actual end. They taught that this happened during the early Second Temple period, in the fifth century BCE. The earliest stratum of rabbinic teachings exists in the Talmud, so let's look at a few representative Talmudic statements that make this assertion. Because traditional Judaism is essentially rabbinic, and rabbinic Judaism is essentially Talmudic, we will see how the rabbis laid the groundwork for the two-thousand-year-old Jewish tradition that prophecy has disappeared.

The Talmud states that after the destruction of the First Temple, "only children and fools prophesy" (Bava batra 12b), and "the wise are superior to the prophets" (Bava batra 12a). The Second Temple lacked, among other things, "the spirit of prophecy" and the Urim and Thummim prophetic tools (Yoma 21b). Legal acumen now trumped prophecy; for example, determining correct property boundaries without reference to previous rabbinic rulings is "nothing but prophecy" (Bava batra 12a). And in the spirit of historic revisionism, the Talmud interprets certain biblical references to prophets as "really" referring to legal scholars (Shabbat 119b).

How could prophecy have ended? Did it cease to exist because of some biological change in humans? Or were there perturbations in the theological-metaphysical realms? Did the authorities simply legislate away prophecy? Or did it never end?

METAPHYSICS AND THEOLOGY

An End to Prophecy

The medieval Jewish philosophers propose several reasons why prophecy ended, none of which stand up to biblical scrutiny. For example, Judah Halevi, who wrote when no significant Jewish population inhabited Israel, believes that prophecy can exist only in Israel because its geology and geography possess unique metaphysical properties. Without Jews living in Israel, prophecy could not occur, but once they return in the future, prophecy will also. However, the Hebrew Bible refutes Halevi's assertion that prophecy can take place only in Israel. Ezekiel and Daniel prophesied in Babylonia and Jonah did so in Assyria.

Maimonides posits that prophecy requires an optimal constitution and training, and God's will. He suggests that prophecy ended because of the sorrow of the exile, with depression making prophecy less likely because of its negative effects on the imagination. The Hebrew Bible contradicts this assertion: Jeremiah prophesied for decades in a state of near-continuous despondency. Thus, one needs to discard both these explanations—the presence of despondency and residing outside of Israel—for why prophecy "ended."

As a way out of these and other contradictions, the medieval Jewish philosophers offer a solution to the problem of prophecy's end, if indeed there was one, by placing much greater emphasis on God as the ultimate arbiter of the phenomenon. This is a difficult solution for the Aristotelian Maimonides, who while wearing his scientist-philosopher's hat, notes that God does not stint, saying, "God will never withhold from any creature that which it deserves,"[1] and "The laws of nature demand that everyone should be a prophet" when the proper conditions are met.[2] At the same time, as a Jewish rabbi and community leader, Maimonides cannot go against centuries of rabbinic tradition regarding the end of prophecy. Thus, he proposes that the absence of prophecy in his day is supernatural; one cannot explain it scientifically. It is a miracle: the "miracle of withholding." Despite the laws of nature, one can be qualified and yet not attain prophecy if God so decides.

Spinoza and the End of Prophecy

Spinoza's analysis of prophecy turns on his defining it as any apprehension of the truth through the intellect. Therefore, anyone who attains a truthful certainty about anything experiences a measure of prophecy. Because, according to Spinoza, the Hebrew prophets were wrong about so many natural and theological laws, he writes that they possessed a lower degree of prophecy than many of us. Thus, we can't really say that Spinoza confirmed or denied that prophecy ended because of his unique definition. Prophecy as he defines it has always existed. However, prophecy as those who believe in the literal truth of the Hebrew Bible define it, never existed, at least *qua* prophecy.

Nevertheless, Spinoza did effectuate an end to prophecy in a very real sense. He struck a mortal blow against it as a legitimate area of rational investigation.[3] Because biblical prophecy isn't really "prophetic," scientific inquiry into its nature is akin to studying a mirage. In the case of a mirage, we can study heat, radiation, light, and even people's sense that they are perceiving water, but there is no water. Similarly, for Spinoza, there is no prophecy in the Hebrew Bible. It is also a phantom. The study of "real" prophecy as he defines it is epistemology, the science of how we know things. And if the Hebrew Bible contains any miraculous revelation, such as the Golden Rule, its miraculous nature precludes its being an object of rational analysis. For Spinoza, how revelation works is fundamentally unknowable.

Spinoza's treatment of biblical prophecy resulted in the Hebrew Bible becoming a book like any other book. We may understand it within its historical context as a text solely human in origin and not as a product of revelation. One gains insights into psychology, archaeology, literature, and so on by studying the text, but it is not a record of real prophecy, just as a mirage is not the perception of real water.

Spinoza also drove a stake into the heart of any attempt to reconcile science with prophetic experience. Because the Hebrew Bible contains little if anything prophetic, the text instead became poetic, social, political, anthropological, and psychopathological. No longer was it respectable to consider prophecy—as had the medievalists before him—as a system of intellects, agents, spheres, God, and human mental faculties. Studying prophecy's shadows and reflections replaced inquiry into its essence.

Metaphysical approaches to the text gave way to modern bible studies, secular Western philosophy, and ultimately psychology. Psychiatry is still working within this paradigm. We see this in Freud's writings about religion being a pathological product of unconscious mental processes,[4] as well as in the more recent phenomenon of neurotheology. In this contemporary, if more benign, iteration of Freud's reductionism, neurotheology teaches that religious experience similarly "serves a function," but now it has become an adaptive brain state rather than a way to sublimate unconscious incestuous and murderous impulses. Spiritual experience enhances our physiological, emotional, and social lives. It is good for us, rather than being how God communicates with us in order to draw us nearer to Him. Those interested in studying prophecy from the top down now were seen as reactionaries, saddled by irrational tradition, faith, or even obscurantism. They were not welcome at the table of high-level scientific or philosophic debate. Any attempt to bring a theocentric metaphysics of prophecy back within the purview of contemporary philosophic and scientific discourse had become pseudoscience.

BIOLOGY

Julian Jaynes in his book on the "bicameral mind" suggests how the experience of hearing a spoken voice arose and fell in the course of human evolution.[5] For millennia, those existing in small tribal groups perceived an "outside" voice advising, admonishing, and otherwise guiding individuals who faced various decision points. The spoken voice served as the prototype of self-consciousness and introspection. Jaynes theorizes that this voice was the subjective experience of communication between the brain's right and left cerebral hemispheres.

He proposes that several thousand years ago, certain geo-cultural forces exerted selective pressure on the brain in such a manner as to gradually eliminate this phenomenon. The combined effects of volcanism-induced mass migrations and the establishment of large city-states influenced the evolution of brain structures mediating this exchange between its two hemispheres. A new "unified" consciousness emerged that was more adaptable to the increasingly complex physical and social environments. Jaynes considers the prophets as the last exemplars of "bicamerality," a trait that finally died out with them and whose remnants we observe in those experiencing hallucinatory psychoses. He presents literary and archaeological evidence supporting his views, but the physical anthropological data, evidence of structural brain changes in physical remains of ancient humans, are lacking.

My own contribution to possible biological bases of the "end" of prophecy invokes endogenous psychedelics. If these compounds mediate elements of the prophetic state, decreased activity of this system would result in the disappearance of those experiences. This diminished activity might relate to the synthesis or breakdown of, sensitivity to, or relative proportions of different psychoactive molecules. However, as in Jaynes's case, I know of no data either supporting or refuting this hypothesis.

HISTORY AND POLITICS

The most cogent arguments I have found for the rabbinic declaration that prophecy ended are political ones.[6] That is, it didn't end, but it was expedient to say that it had. Prophecy "ended" because the authorities told us so, and we believed them.

Various explanations exist for the rabbis' pronouncing the death of prophecy. A likely reason pertains to the birth and early growth of Christianity, which temporally and geographically coincides with their edict. The earliest Christians, many of whom were Jews, attempted to convert other Jews to this new religion by claiming that Jesus was a Jewish prophet, if not the promised messiah. By retrospectively proclaiming that prophecy had ended several centuries before Jesus, the rabbis implied that he possessed no prophetic stature.

We can see how the rabbis' response to Christianity affected their attitude toward prophecy when examining their postbiblical writings. There are six times the number of references to the canonical prophetic books in the New Testament compared with the contemporaneous rabbinic Mishnah.*[7] Both of these works were competing for legitimacy among the same groups, and the quantity of Christian references to prophecy indicates how important it was in supporting Christian contentions of the messianic status of Jesus. To counter these claims on the part of Christianity, the rabbis responded by extirpating prophecy from

---

*The earliest part of the Talmud.

their competing version of normative Judaism. The rabbis delegitimized contemporary prophecy and prophetic authority in an attempt to delegitimize Christianity's authority.

Prophecy rails against the corruption of those in power. Perhaps the rabbis wanted prophecy to end in order to maintain the precarious safety of the Jews living within Roman-occupied Judea. They marginalized anyone who claimed prophetic rank as the basis for criticizing the occupying government. This function overlapped with that of refuting anyone's claim to being the messiah, one of whose roles is to redeem the Jewish people from subjugation by other nations. The rabbis had exercised this function throughout the years of the Roman occupation beginning in the first century BCE, not only during the early years of Christianity. If the Jewish religious establishment labeled as imposters those whom the masses considered messianic prophets, the authorities might be more tolerant of eccentrics making overblown claims than they would be of revolutionaries. In fact, the rabbis could claim a greater love for their co-religionists than that of the prophets or so-called messiahs, for the latter two sets of individuals consistently questioned whether the Jews deserved to survive because of their continual transgressions against God's word.

In a related manner, the rabbis may have taught that prophecy ended because it had never been effective and the people no longer needed it. The prophets had not prevented the Jews' exiles to Babylonia and Assyria centuries before, and their continued destabilizing presence would only lead to their destruction again, this time by the Romans. In addition, the kings of the independent nations of Israel and Judea had disappeared. Therefore, the most important and influential audience to whom the prophets preached no longer existed. The prophets' time had passed.

The rabbis also used the canonization of scripture to promulgate the notion that prophecy was no more. By closing off the Hebrew Bible, a prophetic text, to any additional books, they implied that no contemporary individual's utterances qualified as prophetic and therefore worthy of inclusion in the canon. Canonization also suggested that people no longer needed prophecy to know God's word because of its ready availability in an authorized text. If the "new Israel," the nascent Christian religion, could not tack on their "prophetic" narratives to a sealed canon, they had no claim to prophetic authority, at least not within the Jewish stream.

DID PROPHECY REALLY END?

Contrary to their general declaration, the early rabbis conceded that prophecy continued in their time. They referred to people in Israel who are "if not prophets, then the sons of prophets" (Pesachim 66b). If one awakens from a dream and a verse of scripture "falls into one's mouth," this is a "small prophecy" (Berachot 55b). Some sages sought answers in dreams or nighttime visions to questions they could not solve in normal waking consciousness, and considered these answers prophetic (Bava metzia 107b). Rabbinic lore is replete with references to the *bat kol,* the "daughter" or "echo" of a "voice." This auditory phenomenon transmits God's word to its recipients, usually one or several rabbis involved in solving a moral, exegetical, or legal dilemma (Yoma 9b). Halevi, among the medieval Jewish philosophers, states that the Talmudic sages composed "with God's help."[8]

All of these examples lead to the conclusion that the "end of prophecy" points to the end of a particular type that belonged to a group of prophets whose ranks included Isaiah, Jeremiah, and Ezekiel. The rabbis seem to have legislated the end of canonical prophecy, but they tacitly accepted the continuing existence of the non-canonical type among their ranks.

PROPHECY AFTER THE PROPHETS

During the late Second Temple period and afterward, those outside the institution of the rabbinate continued to claim prophetic stature, and the Jewish population of Judea regarded them in that light. As Rebecca Gray, author of *Prophetic Figures in the Late Second Temple Jewish Palestine,* notes: "People said and did in Josephus'* time very much the same sort of things classical prophets said and did."[9] In addition, "prophetic" books continued to appear; in particular, the Apocrypha and Pseudepigrapha. Both are collections of works by Jews and early non-Jewish Christians, who for the sake of authoritativeness, attributed them to ancient biblical personalities, such as Moses and the twelve sons of Jacob.[10] Some of these works found their way into the New Testament, but the redactors of the Hebrew Bible did not include them. The content and style of the Apocrypha and Pseudepigrapha are similar, and are replete with typical prophetic features, describing an "almost psychedelic world."[11]

Certain rabbis who lived after the Talmudic and Second Temple eras also attained a prophetic reputation.[12] Even our medieval Jewish philosophers admitted to their own prophetic or prophecy-like experiences. In his commentary to the verse, Rashi tells us how he arrived at his interpretation of Exodus 28:4: "I don't know but my heart tells me." And Maimonides notes how he attained to a certain insight: "These ideas presented themselves like a prophetic revelation."[13] We most often associate post-Maimonidean spiritual practices and states with the thirteenth-century Spanish kabbalist Abraham Abulafia.[14] Soon thereafter, the highly visionary kabbalistic school of Isaac Luria rose up in Ottoman Palestine in the sixteenth century.[15] The eighteenth century founder of the Hassidic movement, the Baal Shem Tov, recounted numerous prophetic experiences quite similar to those we find in the Hebrew Bible.[16]

SUMMARY

From a naturalistic point of view, concluding that prophecy ended—or survives only as an impulse for good, beauty, or knowledge[17]—is not tenable. I see no reason to assert that the biological and metaphysical mechanisms we've discussed, excluding the miraculous withholding of

---

*A Jewish military leader and historian who wrote during the early first century CE. The occupying Romans destroyed the Second Temple in 70 CE.

prophecy, no longer operate much as they always have. Perhaps, then, it is more accurate to frame the discussion by saying that while canonical prophecy ended millennia ago, non-canonical prophecy has continued, albeit standing much more at the periphery of normative Judaism than it did in the distant past.

If, on the other hand, one wishes to believe that no manner of prophecy exists any longer because God has decided to withhold it, there is nothing preventing us from doing everything possible to bring about its renewal. On the contrary, we read repeatedly in the Hebrew Bible that following God's guidelines will result in humanity's redemption, one of whose features is widespread prophecy. By thoroughly understanding prophecy's nature and mechanisms, we may use that knowledge to make ourselves more qualified for prophecy if and when the time comes that God chooses to grant it again.

22 The Once and Future Prophet

An early subtitle for this book contained the word *birthright,* as in prophecy being our birthright. I composed this subtitle with the notion in mind that prophecy is a type of spiritual experience to which we all have access, despite normative Judaism claiming it disappeared thousands of years ago. I later decided to remove the word from the book's subtitle because prophecy and how it works are much more complex than I first envisioned. I now see certain elements of prophecy as a birthright but not the experience itself. By removing the word from this book's subtitle, I wished to forestall any simplistic interpretation of the term to suggest that we somehow "deserve" prophecy.

THE IDEA OF A BIRTHRIGHT

A birthright is a right, privilege, or possession one receives by virtue of birth or at the time of birth. It may be extrinsic to a person, such as wealth, or be intrinsic, such as race. The word also relates to an inheritance. One may assume a birthright at the moment of birth, after attaining a certain readiness or maturity, or after crossing a threshold. That threshold may require effort on our part to cross; for example, succeeding in an academic or spiritual course of study. Or it may come to us simply by attaining a particular biological state, such as sexual maturity or a specific age. Reaching the appropriate milestone indicates a greater likelihood of receiving, understanding, or utilizing one's birthright.

We may be unaware of our birthright, passively allowing it to exert its influence, both positive and negative, on us. Others learn about and take advantage of its various elements in order to excel in ways otherwise impossible. We might reject our birthright or exchange it for another.

One element of prophecy that I believe is our birthright is its form: its visions, voices, emotions, and other phenomenological elements. The brain-mind complex that nearly all of us possess at birth appears to contain these forms in a latent and easily and reliably accessible manner, as the DMT research convincingly demonstrated. We can stimulate the imaginative faculty pharmacologically in order to occasion prophetic phenomenology. The phenomenology is the body of prophecy, so to speak, its outward appearance. However, the soul of prophecy, its essential feature, is the prophetic message and is not so easily accessible. According to the medieval Jewish philosophers, other factors are at work: the operation of the rational faculty and God's will.

Another element of prophecy that is the birthright of those born into Abrahamitic religions or cultures is the Hebrew Bible. This is the paradigmatic prophetic text of all major Western religions, one that permeates Western civilization at a nearly cellular level. Those born and raised within cultures so infused by the Hebrew Bible may not like this fact, or may even be unconscious of it. Despite one's ignorance of or resistance to the Hebrew's Bible's influence, the prophetic model of spirituality is much more a birthright to such an individual than Asian religious models or Latin American shamanic ones. Adopting these foreign systems is instead an estrangement from thousands of years of collective memory.

The possibility of our becoming qualified for prophecy constitutes another aspect of a birthright. We have determined that the prophetic state requires highly developed rational and imaginative faculties. One's state of readiness to receive overflow from God or His intermediaries is based on the condition of these faculties. While the final decision to bestow prophecy lies with God, we have within our means the ability to enhance the quality of our minds' function, which in turn makes prophecy more likely.

What then are the implications of the Hebrew Bible's model of prophecy for contemporary spiritual seekers? In particular, how might the theoneurological model, which evolved from my study of the endogenous psychedelic substance DMT and medieval Jewish metaphysics, influence the renaissance of a contemporary stream of prophetic experience? In the material that follows, I suggest that in our effort to become qualified for prophecy, we consider the judicious use of psychedelic agents such as DMT to enhance the imagination. And in order to develop our rational faculty, we study, learn, and practice the prophetic teachings that the Hebrew Bible contains.

THE IMAGINATION

According to the medieval Jewish philosophers, the imaginative faculty is the more physical, or corporeal, of the two relevant mental functions. Therefore, in addition to an optimal genetic endowment, other factors such as good health, diet, and avoidance of toxins will optimize its operation. Toxins include physical substances as well as negative emotions and actions, such as hatred, envy, theft, lying, and exposing ourselves to violent and otherwise degrading entertainment.

In addition to maintaining the health of the imaginative faculty, we also may work toward enhancing its function. A more highly developed imagination will contain more cogent or intelligible raw materials with which to manifest Godly emanation. Such an enhanced imagination also may provide a more suitable matrix, and thereby increase one's readiness, to receive that emanation in the first place. Therefore, the Hebrew Bible provides guidelines for maximizing physical and social health through the diet as well as cultivating piety and virtuous emotions and actions such as love, modesty, charity, and empathy. It also encourages exposing our external senses to beautiful and uplifting input.

As the imagination is the more physical mental function, it is logical to intervene in its operation using physical substances such as DMT and other psychedelics. The overwhelming similarities between the imaginative components of the prophetic and DMT states bespeak the rational basis of such a suggestion.

DMT's effects on the imagination, while profound, do not account for the entire spectrum of the imaginative characteristics of prophecy; i.e., its phenomenology. Let's look at two examples of this lack of fit.

The Spoken Word

Most of us assume that when a biblical figure experiences prophecy, he or she hears a spoken voice originating outside the head. If this were the case, it would differ from the DMT experience, in which the verbal exchange usually but not always occurred telepathically, mind to mind and not mouth to ear. Among the medievalists, only Saadiah proposes that God creates a sound in the objective world that one hears with the external ears. All the other authors understand the prophetic experience as subjective, something that the mind's eye sees and the mind's ear hears. However, if the Hebrew Bible is referring to words that someone hears outside the head, are there endogenous compounds that reliably induce this experience?

One such family of pharmacological agents is the *anticholinergic* compounds. These substances block the effects of the ubiquitous neurotransmitter acetylcholine and include atropine, scopolamine, and belladonna. At high doses, such agents produce auditory hallucinations, including that of the spoken voice. Anticholinergic compounds occur in many plants and make up part of the contemporary pharmacopeia for the treatment of medical conditions such as urinary bladder problems and movement disorders like Parkinson's disease. Endogenous anticholinergic substances occur in mammals, including humans.[1]

However, these voices occasioned by anticholinergic substances occur in the context of a delirium, a state of profound confusion and fluctuating levels of consciousness. Maintenance of mental clarity is the rule in prophecy, and this militates against a role for similar endogenous substances in prophetic experience. However, there are several subtypes of the central nervous system receptor that anticholinergic drugs influence, and it may be that some mediate confusion and others affect audition. Future research will help shed light on this subject.

Kavod

While descriptions of the visual properties of kavod—God's glory—and those of the typical DMT experience do overlap, those of kavod do not possess a comparable degree of complexity. In addition, kavod's "cloud-like" nature with which one may merge or "become one with" also alludes to its uniqueness. These properties suggest that another DMT-like compound may contribute to kavod's phenomenology. A strong candidate is 5-methoxy-DMT (5-MeO-DMT), an endogenous mammalian and plant psychedelic substance with profound subjective effects.

While no rigorous scientific data exist, anecdotal reports indicate that 5-MeO-DMT administration elicits a rapidly developing, intense, physically immobilizing, and dissociative state much like that resulting from DMT. In addition, 5-MeO-DMT appears to elicit several kavod-like experiences more often than DMT, such as the visual apprehension of a formless white light, loss of the sense of self, and a highly unitary state of absorption.[2]

It is of great interest to compare the phenomenology of the DMT and 5-MeO-DMT experiences in the same people, as well as comparing descriptions of the latter compound with those of kavod. It also may prove valuable to compare 5-MeO-DMT's effects to descriptions of other religious traditions' mystical-unitive experiences, Western and Eastern. If research demonstrates significant areas of overlap, we may propose a role for this endogenous compound in those states as well.

Kavod is the only prophetic phenomenon that appears to the masses. While we know that stress raises levels of DMT and 5-MeO-DMT in rodents,[3] it may be that less stress is necessary to stimulate production of the latter compound than the former. If this were so, 5-MeO-DMT-mediated experiences in the masses would be more likely than those that DMT mediates.

THE RATIONAL FACULTY

The theoneurological model proposes that DMT primarily affects the imaginative faculty, and this is most likely why it elicits an experience with relatively higher aesthetic than informational content. How might we enhance the capacities of the rational faculty to maximize our attaining to the prophetic message? Here is where the role of education, study, and training come to the fore. Indeed, Maimonides believes that the greatest boon of the peaceful reign of the messiah is that it will allow us to engage in these activities undisturbed in order to perfect our rational faculties and thus qualify for prophecy.[4]

The medieval Jewish philosophers believe that the rational faculty is more amenable to education and training than the imaginative. Study strengthens and develops the intellect through a process of transforming potential knowledge into actual knowledge. Education is part of a positive feedback mechanism. It increases the function of the intellect, which then in turn is more capable of attaining to additional knowledge. Such training helps us recognize, understand, and communicate prophecy's content more effectively.

Studying the Hebrew Bible occupies the highest rank in the hierarchy of intellectual pursuits, but our medieval authors additionally advise mastery of grammar and philology, mathematics, philosophy, astronomy and astrology, and other areas of natural science. Expertise in these fields helps us comprehend the scope of God's creation. As a result, we draw closer to Him—that is, approach prophecy—through love for and awe of His creating and sustaining this unfathomably complex universe.

Biological options also exist and deserve future research; for example, identifying and utilizing compounds that stimulate the rational faculty. Such substances may increase one's readiness to receive genuine divine overflow and increase the intellect's ability to interpret and communicate the contents of the imagination resulting from that efflux. Molecules affecting dopamine neurotransmission are likely candidates, and dopamine-related exogenous and endogenous stimulants impact some of the previously discussed cognitive characteristics of prophecy.[5]

Interestingly, early clinical research combined stimulants with psyche-delics to enhance, prolong, and augment the latter's effects, particularly in psychotherapy.[6] This points to the potential value of modifying imaginative and rational faculties in tandem when using biological means to draw down Godly influence.

Enhancing the rational faculty pharmacologically, however, raises the question of the source of the prophetic message, an issue that I previously discussed. If Godly efflux simply shines a light on information that the mind already somehow possesses, then such biological interventions may potentially elicit true prophecy by similarly accessing embedded information. However, if the message resides in the emanation itself, whatever information someone receives while in this enhanced state would not be prophetic, even if it were true.

HASTENING THE END

Psychological, spiritual, and especially biological attempts to attain prophecy by our own devices raise the notion of "hastening the end"; that is, precipitating the salvific end of days that I have referred to throughout this book. Widespread prophecy is one of the hallmarks of this future world. Thus, accelerating the end means accelerating the establishment of widespread prophetic experience. Since it appears that the world to come also shares features with a non-corporeal DMT-like state, hastening this transition has even greater implications. That is, rather than simply catalyzing widespread prophecy, we may also find ourselves attempting to accelerate a mass entrance into a nonphysical plane.

The Hebrew Bible's attitude toward hastening the end is highly ambivalent. It consistently encourages us to act and believe in accordance with God's guidelines, as this will speed the onset of salvation. At the same time, it inculcates patience: *Let not the believer expect it soon* (Isa. 28:16), and points out the merit of patience: *[Why] . . . disturb the love while it still gratifies?* (Song of Songs 8:4). The text also suggests a mixture of patience and urgency, as God tells Isaiah: *In its time, I will hasten it* (Isa. 60:22). Similarly, Habakkuk notes: *He shall speak of the end, and it shall not fail. Although it tarry, wait for it, for it shall surely come. It shall not delay* (Hab. 2:3).

It therefore appears that if we merit it, God will hasten the end. If we do not, it will occur at its appointed time, whenever that may be! One way to merit the end, when prophecy is universal, is to be deserving of it. While the Hebrew Bible advises adherence to God's precepts as conducing to that time, medieval Jewish philosophers expand upon this concept by teaching that we become deserving by perfecting our imaginative and rational faculties. Up until now, we could hasten the end only through study and virtue. Now we have the additional tools of psychedelic pharmacology and biology.

It is likely that at some point in the future we will have obtained as detailed as possible an understanding of the biological changes conducing to prophecy, to the extent that they actually do so. A further step in the direction of making prophecy and other spiritual experiences universally available would then be through genetic engineering.[7] We may be able to turn on the production of endogenous compounds that stimulate the imaginative and rational faculties. The religious, ethical, and moral questions that this technology would raise are myriad, but it is not too early to begin considering the implications of such a project. If we can modify brain function in this manner, we will, and doing so wisely and for the greatest good will be more of a challenge than accomplishing the science itself. The question then is not: Can we perfect our faculties by whatever means at our disposal? Rather, it is: To what purpose?*

PRACTICAL APPLICATIONS

Now that we have examined the possible mechanisms, both biological and metaphysical, that may underlie the prophetic and DMT states, let's turn our attention to the practical implications of the theoneurological model.

---

*In Olaf Stapledon's novel *Last and First Men,* the author chronicles two billion years of human evolution, beginning with the present day. One human species, simply a massively proportioned brain that the previous race develops through genetic engineering, fails to survive not because of its lack of knowledge but due to its lack of empathy.

In the Research Center

A rich research agenda emerges from the above discussion. One avenue is to characterize the effects of endogenous and exogenous psychoactive compounds on the rational and imaginative faculties using state-of-the-art biological and psychological methodologies.

Another avenue of inquiry is to determine the role of endogenous DMT and related compounds in those experiencing prophecy-like states resulting from any method: study of the Hebrew Bible, dreams, prayer, ritual observance, chant, dance, and kabbalistic meditation. If such individuals demonstrate greater DMT activity than that found in normal waking consciousness, such data would support a role for this endogenous psychedelic compound in mediating the states these methods elicit.

In addition to establishing how particular agents modify the imagination and intellect, the more salient issue is to determine to what extent they actually elicit prophecy-like experiences and not simply their individual constituents. To answer this question, it will be necessary to develop suitable metrics for determining how "prophetic" a particular state is. Maimonides' hierarchy of prophecy that I noted in chapter 8, Prophet and Prophecy, may help researchers address this question.

Approaching this issue from the other direction, we may wish to more rigorously determine the "psychedelic" properties of prophecy. One approach to this task is to apply the rating scale I developed in quantifying the DMT effect to records of biblical prophetic experience. This would involve using the same statistical tests of reliability and validity we applied to the DMT data. In the context of our project of reclaiming prophecy, both these sets of data comparing the DMT and prophetic states will aid in designing research intended to develop the imagination and intellect so as to make prophecy more likely.

It is important to reiterate that similar phenomenology is not equivalent to a similar message, despite the phenomenology being necessary for the transmission of that message. Maimonides' hierarchy and my rating scale both emphasize elements of the imaginative faculty and not the information content of the experiences. The goal of this project is not to resurrect a certain set of experiences but rather to reestablish access to the reservoir of information that flows through true prophecy. Here the metrics for the "true" and "false" prophetic message are considerably less quantifiable. This is a potentially fruitful area of collaboration for scientific researchers and enlightened clerics.

Finally, in the context of clinical research that directly elicits spiritual experience, we may build on historical precedent. The Good Friday Experiment at Boston University's Marsh Chapel in the 1960s demonstrated that psilocybin administration to divinity school students brought about mystical experiences more often than did a placebo.[8] A more sophisticated study recently replicated these findings.[9] However, both groups emphasized mystical-unitive states rather than interactive-relational ones. Future studies must look for and characterize differences in phenomenology, message, and impact between these two types.

In the House of Worship

A house of worship refers to any religious environment: a synagogue, church, or mosque; a site of communal study; or one's private quarters. In this context, one is seeking a deeper understanding of the prophetic text contained in the Hebrew Bible.

PSYCHEDELICS IN THE HOUSE OF WORSHIP

Using psychedelics to strengthen the imaginative faculty while studying the Hebrew Bible may provide access to more cogent and highly articulated imaginal experiences of scripture than would occur in normal waking consciousness. This enhancement of imaginative forms—visual, auditory, emotional, and others—may prove useful in working with the entire text and not only with records of ostensible prophetic experiences. This material includes law, ritual, prayers, songs, wisdom, and even the seemingly banal genealogies and narratives.*

---

*Josephus believes that only a true prophet is capable of being an accurate historian. Thus, even the narratives and genealogies in the Hebrew Bible reflect the activity of a prophetic mind.

Here, the principle of dose and response will play an important role. Lower doses of a psychedelic substance may allow someone to sit in a chair, read the text, associate new meanings with it, and converse with study partners or fellow congregants. Higher doses would necessitate laying down the text and attending to the visions it has elicited in a more private, internalized manner.

Judicious use of psychedelics also may aid in the effectiveness of other activities one engages in with the intent of drawing down divine influence. For example, most of the prayers of the Jewish liturgy were composed by rabbis in an inspired, prophecy-like state; thus, using a psychedelic substance during prayer may bring one closer to that state. This is conceptually akin to the use of psychedelics to aid meditation, another spiritual technology. However, rather than meditating on the nature of the mind, body, or phenomenal existence in order to free oneself from the cycle of birth and death, one prays to YHVH of the Hebrew Bible for mercy, love, healing, and wisdom.

The Hebrew Bible ranks the Sabbath, Friday sunset to Saturday sunset, as the holiest day of the week. It is a time of rest, rejuvenation, prayer, study, and communal activities, all intended to increase one's intimacy with God. Just as certain places may be more conducive to spiritual experience, including prophecy, certain times may be as well.[10] The Sabbath and its associated activities, in addition to other holy days in the Jewish liturgical calendar such as the New Year and Day of Atonement, may thus be an especially auspicious time for working with the psychedelic drug experience.

The *mitzvot** are the behavioral and attitudinal precepts that the Hebrew Bible records God instructing us to perform. They serve to demonstrate and strengthen our love and awe of God, in addition to providing intrinsic social and individual benefits. In the social sphere, they revolve around the Golden Rule. With respect to our relationship with God, their intent is to abolish idolatry. The rabbis have added many mitzvot to those already in the Hebrew Bible, such as lighting

---

*Plural of *mitzvah,* from the root *Tz-V-H*—to command or enjoin.

the Sabbath candles, celebrating the holiday of Hanukkah, and using the traditional prayer shawl.

The mitzvot are concrete examples of the prophetic message "in action." Judah Halevi believes that they affect the soul, and we feel this subjectively. We might consider enhancing our subjective experience of performing mitzvot through the psychedelic drug state. Doing so may allow us to approach closer to prophecy, inasmuch as those who received these precepts did so through the aegis of that spiritual experience.

RECENT DEVELOPMENTS IN PSYCHEDELICS AND WORSHIP

Two syncretic religions in the West with U.S. government protection now use a psychedelic sacrament within a model that includes biblical notions and sensibilities. These are the Native American Church, in whose ceremonies participants consume the mescaline-containing peyote cactus,[11] and the Brazilian Christian-spiritist syncretic churches, which use DMT-containing ayahuasca.[12] These two churches, neither older than two hundred years, amalgamate Christian and indigenous religious beliefs and practices and have begun to bridge psychedelic consciousness with Western spirituality.

The next stage in this evolution of joining Western religious models with the psychedelic drug experience would more explicitly incorporate these substances into an extant Western religion, rather than developing a new tradition around the substance. Within the context of our project, this could occur in an established Jewish denomination in which crucial clerical and scholarly expertise in text, history, ethics, and rituals would be available. In addition, such a modification of preexisting Jewish religious practice would be more amenable to peer-review and consensus development than creating a new religion out of whole cloth.

In the Field

Most people take and will continue to take psychedelic drugs, including DMT, in non-research and non-religious settings. From my observations, it appears that these substances' effects on the imaginative function are channeled primarily toward hedonic purposes such as increasing aesthetic, emotional, and related experiences. The minority who do attempt to utilize these drugs' potential to elicit spiritual effects do not have access to a suitable Western intellectual scaffolding—a Western psychedelic theology—upon which to stand for this task. To use the metaphysical concept, their rational faculty lacks proper notions. As a result, they have turned to Eastern religious or Latin American shamanic systems, or they may invoke a mélange of New Age ideas, combining them with a similarly eclectic infusion of psychotherapeutic concepts and practices.

The ideas this book contains provide an alternative model. I encourage those who take psychedelic drugs for spiritual purposes to turn to the Hebrew Bible for guidance in strengthening their rational faculty in order to infuse the relatively message-poor but imagination-rich drug state with additional meaning. This Western prophetic text presents a culturally resonant model, employing Western "indigenous" concepts, vocabulary, narratives, and figures. One may view the contents of the psychedelic state through the lenses of the Golden Rule and its corollaries, God's nature and activities, the events at Mount Sinai, Adam and Eve's experience in the Garden of Eden, and so on. With respect to "psychedelic wisdom," Proverbs, Job, and Ecclesiastes may similarly engage the Western mind at a more culturally resonant level than analogous Buddhist philosophical texts.

While recognizing the shortcomings of Buddhism for providing a fully cogent model for the spiritual properties of the psychedelic state, it is also important to acknowledge the value of Eastern religious meditation practices *qua* practices. They may assist our attempts to attain prophecy with or without psychedelic drug augmentation by helping us concentrate and step away from personal preoccupations and temporary upsets that interfere with a clear apprehension of any experience.

The prophetic model of the Hebrew Bible also may help us incorporate and evolve beyond shamanism's invoking and manipulating noncorporeal spirits and forces of nature. This, for example, would provide the basis for asking a being we behold who is *its* God, or seeking healing and wisdom from the highest possible source, the creator and sustainer of that spirit. In addition, the Hebrew Bible provides welcome ethical and moral guidelines regarding how to apply the powers and insights resulting from these states, something the shamanic model to a great degree presently lacks.

Dream interpretation is another potentially fruitful application of this method that combines knowledge of prophecy with the ability of psychedelic drugs to stimulate the imaginative faculty. While such work might take place in a research setting or a religious one, it is broad enough to include in our present discussion. The Hebrew Bible and the medieval Jewish philosophers consider accurate dream interpretation to be a variety of prophecy; i.e., God communicating His message to humans. As Joseph states, when beginning to interpret the Egyptian king's dream: *It is God who will respond to Pharaoh's welfare* (Gen. 41:16). If psychedelics help us attain a prophecy-like state, they may thus facilitate our ability to interpret dreams more accurately.

RISKS

Attempting to restore the prophetic stream by utilizing the psychedelic drug state is not without potential risks. These risks are clinical, legal, and spiritual.

Clinical and Legal

Psychedelic drugs are extraordinarily powerful mind-altering substances, and their use can lead to serious psychological problems,[13] even in religious settings.[14] While it is possible to minimize the occurrence of these adverse effects with careful screening, preparation, supervision, and follow-up of drug sessions, it is impossible to avoid them entirely. Thus, it behooves anyone embarking on this venture to prepare to the utmost extent to maximize potential benefits and minimize potential risks.[15] And except for a very small number of research projects and religious settings, possession of these drugs is illegal in most of the world.

False Prophecy

While clinical and legal adverse effects may result from possession or misguided use of psychedelics for spiritual purposes, their adverse spiritual effects are more subtle. These lead us again into the realm of false prophecy, a notion that somehow we simply cannot avoid. If we are to use the power of the psychedelic drug state for prophetic purposes, we need guidelines to determine the truth or falsity of the message we receive, either from our own experiences of "experimental prophecy" or those of others. Are we apprehending God's overflow upon us or our wishful thinking and projections? If there are elements of both, which will most likely the case, how do we distinguish between them? Because medical scientists know as little about prophecy as religious authorities know about DMT, false prophecy, like the true variety, is a critical point of shared concern and collaboration.

While the Hebrew Bible and the medieval Jewish philosophers give examples of true and false prophecy, provide guidelines in assessing the putative prophet and his or her message, and speculate regarding mechanisms, there are unfortunately no hard and fast rules for distinguishing between the two types. One critical factor all agree on is the nature of the message. Is it consistent with the ethos pervading the Hebrew Bible? In particular, does it conform to the text's two primary messages? These are the practice of the Golden Rule, the essential revealed teaching of the Hebrew Bible. The other is the love and awe of God and God alone; that is, the abolition of idolatry. Various intellectual, cultural, and spiritual forces have lulled many of us into moral and spiritual relativism; for example, "right and wrong are relative" or "God is simply one experience among many." However, the prophetic message is anything but insipid, and its contemporary application anything but facile.[16]

We must also examine carefully the character of anyone, including ourselves, who claims prophetic inspiration. What are the person's motivations, the degree to which that individual wishes to serve him- or herself or the larger world? And how consistent is that person's life with the message he or she is expressing?

23 Concluding Remarks

Two related questions motivated me to write both *DMT: The Spirit Molecule* and *DMT and the Soul of Prophecy:* What is the DMT effect? And why does the DMT state matter? The first question led me to "enlarge the discussion" regarding the DMT experience. However, enlarging the discussion by taking it into the furthest reaches of science did not immediately answer the second question, which we may also express by our familiar refrain: "If so, so what?" To determine the meaning of the DMT state, I needed to expand the scope of my investigations even further than I had anticipated. This then led me to the Hebrew Bible's notion of prophecy. There I found a solution to the task of determining the personal and social meaning of the results of my drug studies as well as novel metaphysical mechanisms to explain them. Both charges combined to push me out of the familiar and relatively well-circumscribed confines of the scientific worldview and into the religious one that takes such a prominent place in this book.

My initial intuition that the Hebrew Bible contained the model I was seeking impelled me to pursue various topics as they appeared. Some were dead ends, and others resulted in valuable discoveries, either in and of themselves or for where they subsequently pointed. During the course of this project, I have immersed myself in the twenty-four books of the Hebrew Bible; learned the astonishing power of the biblical Hebrew language; and gained insights into the social, historical, theological, and metaphysical worlds of both the original text and the medieval Jewish philosophers who labored so mightily to explain it.

The final outcome has been the development of a new model—theoneurology—for a particular type of spiritual experience with striking similarities to the DMT effect: Hebrew biblical prophecy. In this model, the contemporary scientific and the medieval metaphysical-religious worldviews meet as equals. It provides a theoretical framework for certain practical applications for students of the Hebrew Bible and for those who use psychedelic drugs for spiritual purposes.

Let me now close this book by summarizing its main findings.

1. The effects of administering the endogenous psychedelic substance DMT in a controlled clinical research setting replicated many of the features we read about in the Hebrew Bible's accounts of prophetic experience. These resemblances are especially pronounced in the perceptual sphere, but emotional, physical, cognitive, and volitional similarities also are quite striking.

2. The interactive-relational properties of the two states also are highly congruent. In this they differ profoundly from the unitive-mystical state which has become the default position for much of contemporary clinical research into spirituality as well as the goal for those who use psychedelic drugs for spiritual purposes.

3. While the informational content of the DMT and prophetic states overlap to some degree, that of the canonical prophets is much more highly articulated, profound, and meaningful. We can easily determine this by noting the enduring and pervasive effects of the prophetic message on world civilization. While the message of the non-canonical prophets is substantially less voluble, it also possesses a truth value that also far outshines the DMT one. Herein lies the essential meaning of any spiritual experience, prophetic or psychedelic. That meaning resides in the truth and beneficial effects of its message.

4. Utilizing the medieval Jewish philosophers' model of God, God's intermediaries, emanation, and the rational and imaginative

faculties of the human mind, I have proposed mechanisms by which to explain the similarities and differences between the DMT and prophetic states. The DMT experience predominantly reflects enhancement of the imaginative faculty, whereas the prophetic one also includes the operation of a highly developed rational faculty as well as God's will to bestow the state.

5. This model suggests both pharmacological and educational approaches to enhancing the likelihood of contemporary prophetic experience. Study of the Hebrew Bible and the natural sciences will enhance the rational faculty, and the judicious use of psychedelic drugs will enhance the imaginative one. True prophecy—bestowal of divine emanation—is more likely to take place in someone who is qualified, one in whom exists the highest possible development of these two vital mental functions.

For an educated, contemporary Western secularist, the most challenging aspect of the theoneurological model's reliance on medieval Jewish metaphysics is the role that God plays in it. According to this model, God created and sustains all the natural and moral laws of the universe, and prophecy is nothing other than a direct relationship with that God. Any model for prophecy that relies on the Hebrew Bible must either accept this theocentric orientation or not. By rejecting it, the text immediately becomes metaphoric, and the medieval Jewish philosophers rarely approach the text metaphorically to derive their sophisticated metaphysics. The value of their model is that, paradoxically, we can study it using modern science.

Thoughtfully grafting the medieval model on the biological one leads to a God-based theoneurology that provides a counterpoint to a brain-based neurotheology. The biological concomitants of prophecy are how God communicates with us, rather than how the brain creates the impression of that communication. A faith-based individual may find confirmation of his or her beliefs in such a proposition, whereas a secularist may find it of value to conduct a thought experiment exploring the implications of such a model.

The disproportionate aesthetic features of the psychedelic drug state relative to its intellectual ones is of critical importance, as it reflects its primary effects on the imaginative rather than the rational faculty. While biblical aesthetics are at least as impressive as those of the DMT experience, it is the prophetic message that has exerted the more profound and enduring effect on the world. The verbal teachings of the Hebrew Bible's God and His angels gave birth to and continue to sustain Western law, theology, ethics and morality, psychology, natural and social science, history, finance, and government. In contrast, a uniquely psychedelic influence on these foundations of Western civilization as yet is nowhere near as visible.

This minimal non-aesthetic impact may be due to the relative paucity of the psychedelic experience's message or the lack of a culturally appropriate religious and intellectual model for understanding and communicating it. The theoneurological model provides potential solutions to these challenges. It suggests strengthening the rational faculty through appropriate education in addition to using the Hebrew Bible's vocabulary and concepts to mine the psychedelic state for its message.

For those intent on attaining a deeper understanding of the Hebrew Bible, studying it with the judicious assistance of the psychedelic drug state may provide greater resonance with the mind out of which the text emerged; that is, the mind of prophecy. And for those seeking an intellectual and religious foundation upon which to interpret and apply the contemporary Western psychedelic drug experience, Hebrew biblical prophecy, sharing as many features as it does with the DMT state, may provide just that foundation.

Appendix
Sacred Texts: Translations, Commentaries, Philosophical Works, and Scholars

I have organized the three sections of this appendix chronologically. The earliest stratum consists of the Hebrew Bible translations, followed by post-biblical writings, and finally medieval commentaries and philosophical treatises, further organized by biblical scholar. Some of these references also appear in the bibliography, but many do not. However, these latter works also made a significant contribution to my understanding of the Hebrew Bible and its notions of prophecy.

HEBREW BIBLE TRANSLATIONS

JPS Hebrew-English Tanakh. 2nd ed. Jewish Publication Society, ed. Philadelphia: Jewish Publication Society, 1999. All twenty-four books of the Hebrew Bible in one volume. An authoritative translation for the Conservative movement of Judaism and most contemporary academic and/or scholarly research.

Rosenberg, A. J., ed. New York: Judaica Press, various dates. The twenty-four books of the Hebrew Bible in separate volumes. Provides an orientation to Modern Orthodox Judaism.

Tanach: The Stone Edition. Scherman, Nosson, ed. Brooklyn: Mesorah, 1997. In addition to this one-volume set of all twenty-four books of the Hebrew Bible, ArtScroll/Mesorah has published many single-volume editions of individual books, such as Genesis, Jonah, Daniel, 1 and 2 Samuel, Proverbs, etc. Their perspective is slightly more conservative/ traditional than Modern Orthodox.

POSTBIBLICAL WRITINGS

Rabbinic Texts

Freedman, H., and Maurice Simon, eds. *Midrash Rabbah*. 10 vols. New York: Soncino Press, 1983. Rabbinic collection of metaphoric, allegoric, and ethical interpretations of the Hebrew Bible, generally in the form of a running commentary on the text.

Friedlander, Gerald, ed. *Pirkê de Rabbi Eliezer*. New York: Hermon Press, 1965. Highly novel interpretations of selected topics from the Hebrew Bible, such as Jonah, Adam in Eden, and the creation in "seven days."

Simon, Maurice, ed. *The Zohar*. 5 vols. 2nd ed. New York: Soncino Press, 1984. Foundational text of Kabbalah. Highly abstract exegetical approach to the Hebrew Bible in the form of a running commentary to the text. This edition is minimally footnoted. Daniel C. Matt's ongoing translation and commentary: *The Zohar* (Stanford, Ca: Stanford University Press) is massively footnoted and as of May 2014, the 8th volume has reached the beginning of Numbers.

Zlotowitz, Gedaliah, Yisroel Simcha Schorr, Chaim Malinowitz, Asher Dicker, and Nesanel Kasnett, eds. *Schottenstein Edition of the Talmud*. 73 vols. Brooklyn: Mesorah, various dates. Mostly legal discussions, but also voluminous ethical, philological, and some mystical exegeses. This version is the Babylonian Talmud, whose compilation was completed in about 500 CE. The shorter Jerusalem (or Palestinian) Talmud was compiled approximately 150 years earlier.

Non-rabbinic Deuterocanonical Texts

Late Second Temple period works such as Enoch, Maccabees, Jubilees, and Additions to Daniel. Authors include Jewish and early Jewish

Christians. While several Christian versions of the "Old Testament" include these books, the Jewish Hebrew Bible does not.

Charles, R. H., ed. *The Apocrypha and Pseudepigrapha of the Old Testament.* 2 vols. London: Oxford University Press, 1913.

Charlesworth, James H., ed. *The Old Testament Pseudepigrapha.* 2 vols. Peabody, Mass.: Hendrickson, 1983.

CLASSICAL BIBLICAL COMMENTATORS AND PHILOSOPHERS

Isaac Abravanel (also Abarabanel, Abrabanel)   Portuguese rabbi, statesman, philosopher, financier for Queen Isabella and King Ferdinand, lived 1437–1508.

bar Eitan, Zev, ed., trans. *Abravanel's World of Torah. Genesis.* Park City, Utah: Renaissance Torah Press, 2013.

Joseph Albo   Spanish philosopher and rabbi, lived 1380–1444.

Albo, Joseph. *Sefer Ha-'Ikkarim (The Book of Principles).* Translated by Isaac Husik. 4 vols. Philadelphia: Jewish Publication Society of America, 1929–1930.

Abraham ibn Ezra   Peripatetic Spanish rabbi, poet, grammarian, and astrologer, lived 1089–1164.

ibn Ezra, Abraham. *Ibn Ezra's Commentary on the Pentateuch.* Translated by H. Norman Strickman and Arthur M. Silver. 5 vols. Menorah: New York, 1988–2004.

———. *The Commentary of Ibn Ezra on Isaiah.* Translated by M. Friedländer. Vol. 1. New York: Feldheim, 1873.

———. *The Secret of the Torah.* Translated by H. Norman Strickman. Northvale, N.J.: Jason Aronson, 1995.

Saadiah Gaon   Babylonian rabbi and academy head, Talmudist, and Bible commentator, lived 882/892–942.

Gaon, Saadia. *The Book of Beliefs and Opinions.* Translated by Samuel Rosenblatt. New Haven, Conn.: Yale University Press, 1948.

Gersonides   Levi ben Gershom or Ralbag. French rabbi and philosopher, lived 1288–1344.

> Gersonides. *The Wars of the Lord*. Translated by Seymour Feldman. 3 vols. Philadelphia: Jewish Publication Society, 1984–1999.

Judah Halevi   Spanish philosopher and poet, lived 1075–1141.

> Halevi, Judah. *Book of Kuzari*. Translated by Hartwig Hirschfeld. New York: Bloch, 1946.
>
> ———. *The Kuzari*. Translated by N. Daniel Korobkin. New York: Feldheim, 2009.

Maimonides   Moses ben Maimon, Spanish/Egyptian rabbi, physician, philosopher, lived 1135–1204.

> Halkin, Abraham S., trans. *Moses Maimonides' Epistle to Yemen*. New York: American Academy for Jewish Research, 1952. Addresses questions regarding the nature and activities of the messiah.
>
> Maimonides, Moses. *The Commandments*. Translated by Charles B. Chavel. 2 vols. New York: Soncino Press, 1967.
>
> ———. *The Guide of the Perplexed*. Translated by M. Friedländer. New York: Hebrew Publishing, 1881.
>
> ———. *The Guide of the Perplexed*. Translated by Shlomo Pines. Introduction by Leo Strauss. Chicago: University of Chicago Press, 1963.
>
> Rosner, Fred, trans. *Moses Maimonides' Treatise on Resurrection*. New York: Ktav, 1982. Distinguishes between messianic era and the world to come.

Nachmanides   Moses ben Nachman or Ramban; Spanish rabbi and Kabbalist, lived 1194–1270.

> Chavel, Charles B., ed. *Ramban (Nachmanides): Commentary on the Torah*. 5 vols. New York: Shilo, 1973–1999.
>
> Nachmanides. *Writings and Discourses*. Translated by Charles B. Chavel. 2 vols. New York: Shilo, 1978.

Rashbam   Samuel ben Meir, grandson of Rashi; lived 1080–1160, rabbi and grammarian.

Lockshin, Martin I., ed. *Rabbi Samuel Ben Meir's Commentary on Genesis.* Lewiston, N.Y.: Edwin Mellen Press, 1989.

———. *Rashbam's Commentary on Deuteronomy. An Annotated Translation.* Providence, R.I.: Brown University Press, 2004.

———. *Rashbam's Commentary on Exodus.* Atlanta, Ga.: Scholars Press, 1997.

———. *Rashbam's Commentary on Leviticus and Numbers.* Providence, R.I.: Brown University Press, 2001.

Rashi   Solomon ben Isaac, rabbi and Talmudist of southern France, lived 1040–1105.

Herczeg, Yisrael Isser Zvi, ed. *Sapirstein Edition Rashi: The Torah with Rashi's Commentary Translated, Annotated and Elucidated.* Brooklyn, N.Y.: Mesorah, 1994–1998.

Benedict de/Baruch Spinoza   Dutch lens grinder, author of monumental *Ethics*, lived 1632–1677.

Spinoza, Benedict de. *Tractatus Theologico-Politicus, Tractatus Politicus.* Translated by R. H. M. Elwes. London: George Routledge and Sons, 1895.

Notes

PROLOGUE.
A HEBREW PROPHET IN BABYLONIA
AND A DMT VOLUNTEER IN NEW MEXICO

1. Strassman, *DMT*.
2. Newberg, *How God Changes Your Brain*.

CHAPTER 1.
SETTING THE STAGE

1. Freedman, "Hallucinogenic Drug Research."
2. Harman, McKim, Mogar, et al., "Psychedelic Agents in Creative Problem Solving."
3. Forte, ed., *Entheogens and the Future of Religion*, 5.
4. Freud, *Moses and Monotheism*, 43.

CHAPTER 2.
DEFINING OUR TERMS

1. Tart, ed., *Altered States of Consciousness*.
2. James, *Varieties of Religious Experience*.
3. MacLean, Leoutsakos, Johnson, and Griffiths, "Factor Analysis of the Mystical Experience Questionnaire."

CHAPTER 3.
THE PATH TO DMT:
PSYCHEDELIC DRUGS, MEDITATION,
AND THE PINEAL GLAND

1. Moody, *Life after Life.*

2. Hofmann, *LSD: My Problem Child.*

3. Cleary, *Flower Ornament Scripture,* 55.

4. Badiner and Grey, eds., *Zig Zag Zen.*

5. Gyatso, *A Flash of Lightning in the Dark of Night.*

6. Benson and Klipper, *The Relaxation Response.*

7. Barker, Borjigin, Lomnicka, and Strassman, "LC/MS/MS Analysis of the Endogenous Dimethyltryptamine Hallucinogens."

8. Sai-Halász, Brunecker, and Szára, "Dimethyltryptamin: Ein Neues Psychoticum."

9. Rätsch, *Encyclopedia of Psychoactive Plants.*

10. Barker, McIlhenny, and Strassman, "A Critical Review of Reports of Endogenous Psychedelic N,N-Dimethyltryptamines in Humans."

11. Takahashi, Takahashi, Ido, et al., "^{11}C-Labeling of Indolealkylamine Alkaloids and the Comparative Study of Their Tissue Distribution," 965–69; and Yanai, Ido, Ishiwata, et al., "In Vivo Kinetics and Displacement Study of Carbon-11-Labeled Hallucinogen, N,N-[^{11}C] Dimethyltryptamine."

12. Thompson and Weinshilboum, "Rabbit Lung Indolethylamine N-Methyltransferase."

13. Thompson, Moon, Kim, et al., "Human Indolethylamine N-Methyltransferase."

14. Ibid.

CHAPTER 4.
THE DMT WORLD:
WHERE IS THIS?

1. Strassman and Qualls, "Dose-Response Study of N,N-Dimethyltryptamine in Humans. I."

2. Strassman, Qualls, Uhlenhuth, and Kellner, "Dose-Response Study of N,N-Dimethyltryptamine in Humans. II."

3. Newberg, *Principles of Neurotheology.*

CHAPTER 5.
CANDIDATE RELIGIOUS SYSTEMS

1. Metzner, Alpert, and Leary, *Psychedelic Experience.*

2. Teitsworth, *Krishna in the Sky with Diamonds.*

3. Aung, *Folk Elements in Burmese Buddhism.*

4. Harner, *Way of the Shaman.*

5. Beyer, *Singing to the Plants.*

6. Dobkin de Rios, *Visionary Vine.*

CHAPTER 6.
INTRODUCTION TO THE HEBREW BIBLE:
WHAT IT IS AND HOW TO STUDY IT

1. Strassman, "DMT and the Dharma."

2. Bonder, *The Kabbalah of Envy,* 27.

3. Ibid.

4. Specifically, the Babylonian Talmud, Tractate Yoma, folio 23a. The Babylonian Talmud is the reference text, in that its opinions usually supersede those of its Jerusalem counterpart. It possesses sixty-three tractates or volumes. Yoma is a tractate, and this excerpt appears in chapter 23, folio a. My reference copy of the Babylonian Talmud is: Zlotowitz, Schorr, Malinowitz, Dicker, and Kasnett, eds., *Schottenstein Edition of the Talmud.*

5. Spinoza, *Tractatus Theologico-Politicus, Tractatus Politicus.*

6. Saadia, *The Book of Beliefs and Opinions.*

7. Anton, *Rashi's Daughters.*

8. There are innumerable editions of Rashi's Torah commentary. The version in my library is the Sapirstein edition: Rashi, *The Torah with Rashi's Commentary.*

9. ibn Ezra, *Commentary on the Pentateuch.*

10. Strickman, *The Secret of the Torah*.

11. Ramban (Nachmanides), *Writings and Discourses*, 651–96.

12. Ramban (Nachmanides), *Commentary on the Torah*.

13. Numerous translations and commentaries exist. A recent and readable edition is Korobkin's: Yehudah Halevi, *The Kuzari*.

14. Maimonides, *The Guide of the Perplexed*. My favorite translation is Friedländer's annotated edition from 1881. A more recent but less annotated and thus less readable translation published in 1963 is by Pines.

CHAPTER 7. GOD

1. *Stone Edition Tanach*.

2. *JPS Hebrew-English Tanakh*.

3. Kreisel, "R. Moses ben Maimon (Maimonides), *The Guide of the Perplexed*," in *Prophecy*, 148–315.

CHAPTER 8.
PROPHET AND PROPHECY:
THE BIBLICAL RECORD

1. Hieronimus, *Kabbalistic Teachings of the Female Prophets*.

2. Bennett and McQueen, *Sex, Drugs, Violence, and the Bible*.

3. Shanon, "Biblical Entheogens."

4. Merkur, *Mystery of Manna*.

5. van Dam, *Urim and Thummim*.

CHAPTER 9. OVERVIEW

1. Strassman, Qualls, Uhlenhuth, and Kellner, "Dose-Response Study of N,N-Dimethyltryptamine in Humans. II."

2. Maimonides, *Guide of the Perplexed* 2:36; this refers to part 2, chapter 36.

3. Idel, *Studies in Ecstatic Kabbalah*.

4. Maimonides, *Guide of the Perplexed*, 2:45.

CHAPTER 10. THE BODY

1. Pine, *Heart Sutra*.

CHAPTER 11. EMOTIONS

1. Strassman, "Contact Through the Veil: 2," in *DMT,* 202–19.

CHAPTER 13. COGNITION

1. Kugel, *God of Old,* 5–36.

CHAPTER 15.
RELATEDNESS: A UNIQUE PROPHETIC CATEGORY

1. Gupta, "Twelve-Membered Dependent Origination."

CHAPTER 16. KAVOD: GOD'S GLORY

1. Such as the Jewish Publication Society, *JPS Hebrew-English Tanakh*.
2. Wolfson, *Through a Speculum That Shines*.

CHAPTER 17.
MESSAGE AND MEANING I: BELIEF AND BEHAVIOR

1. Grof, *Beyond the Brain*.
2. Funkenstein, *Maimonides,* 20–25.
3. Buber, *Eclipse of God,* 77–78.
4. Maimonides, *The Commandments*.

CHAPTER 18.
MESSAGE AND MEANING II:
HISTORY, THE WORLD TO COME, THE MESSIAH,
RESURRECTION, FALSE PROPHECY, WISDOM, AND POETRY

1. Kuenen, *Prophets and Prophecy in Israel*.
2. Barton, *Oracles of God*.

3. *Funk & Wagnalls Standard Dictionary*, s.v. "eschatology."

4. Maimonides, *Treatise on Resurrection*.

5. For example, Jer. 6:13; 26:7, 8, 11, 16; 27:9; 28:1; 29:1, 8; Zech. 13:2.

6. Glasov, *The Bridling of the Tongue*.

7. Fox, *Proverbs 1–9*, 30–43.

8. Kaiser, *How the Hippies Saved Physics*.

9. Isaacson, *Steve Jobs*.

CHAPTER 19. THE METAPHYSICS OF PROPHECY

1. MacLean, Leoutsakos, Johnson, and Griffiths, "Factor Analysis of the Mystical Experience Questionnaire."

2. For example, Ball, *All Is One*.

3. Heschel, "Hosea," in *The Prophets*, 39–60.

4. Kreisel, *Prophecy*.

5. Maimonides, *Guide of the Perplexed*, 2:36.

6. Ibid., Introduction.

7. Spinoza, *Tractatus*.

CHAPTER 20.
THE METAPHYSICS OF DMT:
A THEONEUROLOGICAL MODEL OF PROPHECY

1. Maimonides, *Treatise on Resurrection*.

2. Thompson, Moon, Kim, Xu, et al., "Human Indolethylamine *N*-Methyltransferase."

3. Maimonides, *Laws of Repentance*, 174.

4. Rose, *The Soul After Death*.

5. Cozzi, Mavlyutov, Thompson, and Ruoho, "Indolethylamine *N*-Methyltransferase Expression in Primate Nervous Tissue."

CHAPTER 21. THE END OF PROPHECY

1. Maimonides, *Guide of the Perplexed*, 3:17.

2. Ibid., 2:32.

3. Strauss, *Spinoza's Critique of Religion.*

4. Freud, *Future of an Illusion.*

5. Jaynes, *Origin of Consciousness in the Breakdown of the Bicameral Mind.*

6. Greenspahn, "Why Prophecy Ceased."

7. Deist, "The Prophets," 584.

8. Halevi, *The Kuzari,* 3:67 (chapter 3, verse 67).

9. Gray, *Prophetic Figures in the Late Second Temple Jewish Palestine,* 8.

10. Charles, *The Apocrypha and Pseudepigrapha of the Old Testament;* and Charlesworth, *The Old Testament Pseudepigrapha.*

11. Levenson, *Creation and the Persistence of Evil,* 33.

12. Heschel, *Prophetic Inspiration after the Prophets.*

13. Maimonides, *Guide of the Perplexed,* 3:22.

14. Idel, *Studies in Ecstatic Kabbalah.*

15. Faierstein, *Jewish Mystical Autobiographies,* 41–263.

16. Buber, *Legend of the Baal-Shem.*

17. Brueggemann, *Prophetic Imagination.*

CHAPTER 22.
THE ONCE AND FUTURE PROPHET

1. Flacker and Wei, "Endogenous Anticholinergic Substances May Exist during Acute Illness in Elderly Medical Patients."

2. Oroc, *Tryptamine Palace.*

3. Beaton and Christian, "Stress Induced Changes in Whole Brain Indolealkylamine Levels in the Rat."

4. Maimonides, *Epistle to Yemen.*

5. Sotnikova, Caron, and Gainetdinov, "Trace Amine-Associated Receptors as Emerging Therapeutic Targets."

6. Eisner, "Influence of LSD on Unconscious Activity"; and Fisher, "Some Comments Concerning Dosage Levels of Psychedelic Compounds for Psychotherapeutic Experiences."

7. Charlton, "Genospirituality."

8. Pahnke and Richards, "Implications of LSD and Experimental Mysticism."

9. Griffiths, Richards, McCann, and Jesse, "Psilocybin Can Occasion Mystical-Type Experiences Having Substantial and Sustained Personal Meaning and Spiritual Significance."

10. Heschel, *The Sabbath.*

11. La Barre, *The Peyote Cult.*

12. Labate, de Rose, and dos Santos, *Ayahuasca Religions.*

13. Strassman, "Adverse Reactions to Psychedelic Drugs."

14. dos Santos, "Critical Evaluation of Reports Associating Ayahuasca with Life-Threatening Adverse Reactions."

15. Strassman, "Preparation for the Journey;" and Fadiman, *Psychedelic Explorer's Guide.*

16. Podhoretz, *The Prophets.*

Bibliography

Anton, Maggie. *Rashi's Daughters. Book I, Joheved*. New York: Plume, 2007.

Aung, Htin. *Folk Elements in Burmese Buddhism*. Westport, Conn.: Greenwood Press, 1978.

Badiner, Allan Hunt, and Alex Grey, eds. *Zig Zag Zen: Buddhism and Psychedelics*. San Francisco: Chronicle Books, 2002.

Ball, Martin W. *All Is One: Understanding Entheogens and Nonduality*. Ashland, Ore.: Kyandra, 2012.

Barker, Steven A., Jimo Borjigin, I. Lomnicka, and Rick J. Strassman. "LC/MS/MS Analysis of the Endogenous Dimethyltryptamine Hallucinogens, Their Precursors, and Major Metabolites in Rat Pineal Gland Microdialysate." *Biomedical Chromatography* 27, no. 12 (December 2013): 1690–1700.

Barker, Steven A., Ethan H. McIlhenny, and Rick Strassman. "A Critical Review of Reports of Endogenous Psychedelic N,N-Dimethyltryptamines in Humans: 1955–2010." *Drug Testing and Analysis* 4 (2012): 617–35.

Baron, David. *The Visions and Prophecies of Zechariah*. 3rd ed. London: Morgan and Scott, 1919. Thorough analysis of Zechariah's visions.

Barton, John. *Oracles of God*. Oxford: Oxford University Press, 2007.

Beaton, John M., and Samuel T. Christian. "Stress Induced Changes in Whole Brain Indolealkylamine Levels in the Rat: Using Gas Liquid Chromatography-Mass Spectrometry." *Society for Neuroscience Abstracts* 4 (1978): 419.

Benisch, A. "The Sons of the Prophets and the Prophetic Schools." In *Miscellany of Hebrew Literature,* edited by A. Löwy, 97–128. London: Society of Hebrew Literature, 1877.

Bennett, Chris, and Neil McQueen. *Sex, Drugs, Violence, and the Bible.* Gibsons, Canada: Forbidden Fruit, 2001.

Benson, Herbert, and Miriam Z. Klipper. *The Relaxation Response.* New York: Harper, 2000.

Beyer, Stephan. *Singing to the Plants: A Guide to Mestizo Shamanism in the Upper Amazon.* Albuquerque: University of New Mexico Press, 2010.

Blank, Sheldon H. *"Of a Truth the Lord Hath Sent Me."* The Goldenson Lectures. Cincinnati, Ohio: Hebrew Union College, 1955. False prophecy.

Bonder, Nilton. *The Kabbalah of Envy.* Boston: Shambhala, 1997.

Brown, Francis, S. R. Driver, and C. A. Briggs. *A Hebrew and English Lexicon of the Old Testament, with an Appendix Containing the Biblical Aramaic, Based on the Lexicon of William Gesenius.* Translated by Edward Robinson. Oxford: Clarendon Press, 1966.

Brueggemann, Walter. *The Prophetic Imagination.* 2nd ed. Minneapolis, Minn.: Fortress Press, 2001.

Buber, Martin. *Eclipse of God: Studies in the Relations between Religion and Philosophy.* New York: Harper and Brothers, 1952.

———. *I and Thou.* Translated by Walter Kaufmann. New York: Touchstone, 1996.

———. *The Legend of the Baal-Shem.* Translated by Maurice Friedman. Princeton, N.J.: Princeton University Press, 1995.

———. *Moses.* Oxford: East and West Library, 1946. Theologically oriented biography.

———. *The Prophetic Faith.* New York: MacMillan, 1949. Discusses unique message of individual prophets.

Cassuto, Umberto. *A Commentary on the Book of Exodus.* Translated by Israel Abrahams. Skokie, Ill.: Varda Books, 2005.

———. *A Commentary on the Book of Genesis.* 2 vols. Translated by Israel Abrahams. Skokie, Ill.: Varda Books, 2005. Cassuto contributes his knowledge of how Ancient Near Eastern cultures impacted the Hebrew biblical mind.

———. *The Documentary Hypothesis and the Composition of the Pentateuch.* Translated by Israel Abrahams. New York: Shalem Press, 2006. Argues for one source of the text, rather than multiple competing sources.

Charles, R. H., ed. *The Apocrypha and Pseudepigrapha of the Old Testament.* 2 vols. London: Oxford University Press, 1913.

Charlesworth, James H., ed. *The Old Testament Pseudepigrapha.* 2 vols. Peabody, Mass.: Hendrickson, 1983.

Charlton, Bruce G. "Genospirituality: Genetic Engineering for Spiritual and Religious Enhancement." *Medical Hypotheses* 71 (2008): 825–28.

Cleary, Thomas. *The Flower Ornament Scripture: A Translation of the Avatamsaka Sutra.* Boston: Shambhala, 1993.

Cozzi, Nicholas V., Mavlyutov A. Timur, Michael A. Thompson, and Arnold E. Ruoho. "Indolethylamine *N*-Methyltransferase Expression in Primate Nervous Tissue." *Society for Neuroscience Abstracts* 37 (2011): 840.19.

Crenshaw, James L. *Defending God: Biblical Responses to the Problem of Evil.* New York: Oxford University Press, 2005. Theodicy.

———. *Prophetic Conflict: Its Effect Upon Israelite Religion.* Atlanta, Ga.: Society of Biblical Literature, 2007. False prophecy.

Cunningham, Eric. "Ecstatic Treks in the Demon Regions: Zen and the *Satori* of the Psychedelic Experience." E-AsPac.com. http://mcel.pacificu.edu/easpac/2005/cunningham.php3. Accessed May 27, 2014. Cogent analysis.

Davidson, Benjamin. *The Analytical Hebrew and Chaldee Lexicon.* Peabody, Mass.: Hendrickson, 2000.

Deist, Frederick E. "The Prophets: Are We Heading for a Paradigm Switch?" In *The Place Is Too Small for Us,* edited by Robert P. Gordon, 584. Winona Lake, Ind.: Einsenbrauns, 1995.

Dobkin de Rios, Marlene. *Visionary Vine: Hallucinogenic Healing in the Peruvian Amazon.* San Francisco: Chandler, 1972. Classic early treatment.

dos Santos, Rafael Guimarães. "A Critical Evaluation of Reports Associating Ayahuasca with Life-Threatening Adverse Reactions." *Journal of Psychoactive Drugs* 45 (2013): 179–88.

Eisner, Betty G. "The Influence of LSD on Unconscious Activity." *Proceedings of the Quarterly Meeting of the Royal Medico-Psychological Association* (February 1963): 141–45.

Fadiman, James. *The Psychedelic Explorer's Guide.* Rochester, Vt.: Park Street Press, 2011.

Faierstein, Morris M., trans. *Jewish Mystical Autobiographies.* New York: Paulist Press, 1999.

Fields, Rick. *How the Swans Came to the Lake.* 3rd ed. Boston: Shambhala, 1992. How Asian Buddhism came to the West.

Fisher, Gary. "Some Comments Concerning Dosage Levels of Psychedelic Compounds for Psychotherapeutic Experiences." In *The Psychedelic Reader,* edited by Gunther M. Weil, Ralph Metzner, and Timothy Leary. New Hyde Park, N.Y.: University Books, 1965.

Flacker, Jonathan M., and Jeanne Y. Wei. "Endogenous Anticholinergic Substances May Exist during Acute Illness in Elderly Medical Patients." *Journal of Gerontology: Medical Sciences* 56A (2001): M353–M55.

Forte, Robert, ed. *Entheogens and the Future of Religion.* San Francisco: Council on Spiritual Practices, 1997.

Fox, Michael V. *Proverbs 1–9. The Anchor Yale Bible Commentaries.* New Haven, Conn.: Yale University Press, 2000.

Freedman, Daniel X. "Hallucinogenic Drug Research. If So, So What?" *Pharmacology Biochemistry and Behavior* 24 (1986): 407–15.

Freedman, H., and Maurice Simon, eds. *Midrash Rabbah.* 10 vols. New York: Soncino Press, 1983. Metaphoric, allegoric folk interpretation of Hebrew Bible.

Freud, Sigmund. *The Future of an Illusion.* Translated by James Strachey. New York: W. W. Norton, 1961.

———. *Moses and Monotheism.* Translated by Katherine Jones. New York: Alfred A. Knopf, 1939.

Friedlaender, M. *Essays on the Writings of Abraham Ibn Ezra.* London: Society of Hebrew Literature, 1877. Valuable collection.

Friedländer, M. "Ibn Ezra in England." *Jewish Quarterly Review* 8 (1895): 140–54. Apocryphal tales.

Funkenstein, Amos. *Maimonides: Nature, History and Messianic Beliefs.* Tel Aviv: MOD Books, 1997.

———. "Maimonides: Political Theory and Realistic Messianism." *Miscellanea Mediaevalia* 11 (1977): 81–103. Different views of the possible messiah's characteristics.

Glas, Garrit, Moshe Halevi Spero, Peter J. Verhagen, and Herman M. van Praag, eds. *Hearing Voices and Seeing Visions: Psychological Aspects of Biblical Concepts and Personalities.* Dordrecht, Netherlands: Springer, 2007. Psychological and neurotheological approach.

Glazov, Gregory Yuri. *The Bridling of the Tongue and the Opening of the Mouth in Biblical Prophecy.* Sheffield, England: Sheffield Academic Press, 2001.

Gray, Rebecca. *Prophetic Figures in the Late Second Temple Jewish Palestine: The Evidence from Josephus.* Oxford: Oxford University Press, 1993.

Greenspahn, Frederick E. "Why Prophecy Ceased." *Journal of Biblical Literature* 108 (1989): 37–49.

Griffiths, R. R., W. A. Richards, U. McCann, and R. Jesse. "Psilocybin Can Occasion Mystical-Type Experiences Having Substantial and Sustained

Personal Meaning and Spiritual Significance." *Psychopharmacology* 187 (2006): 268–83.

Grinspoon, Lester, and James B. Bakalar. *Psychedelic Drugs Reconsidered.* New York: Basic Books, 1979. Classic.

Grob, Charles S. "The Psychology of Ayahuasca." In *Ayahuasca: Human Consciousness, and the Spirits of Nature,* edited by Ralph Metzner, 214–49. New York: Thunder's Mouth Press, 1999. Overview of psychological and biological effects.

Grof, Stanislav. *Beyond the Brain: Birth, Death, and Transcendence in Psychotherapy.* Albany: State University of New York Press, 1985.

Gupta, Rita. "'Twelve-Membered Dependent Origination.' An Attempted Reappraisal." *Journal of Indian Philosophy* 5 (1977–1978): 163–86.

Gyatso, Tenzin. *A Flash of Lightning in the Dark of Night.* Boston: Shambhala, 1994.

Halevi, Yehudah, *The Kuzari.* Translated by N. Daniel Korobkin. New York: Feldheim, 2009.

Harman, Willis W., Robert H. McKim, Robert E. Mogar, et al. "Psychedelic Agents in Creative Problem Solving: A Pilot Study." *Psychological Reports* 19 (1966): 211–27. One of the only scientific papers on psychedelics and creativity.

Harner, Michael J. *The Way of the Shaman.* New York: HarperSanFrancisco, 1990.

Heschel, Abraham J. *Maimonides.* Translated by Joachim Neugroschel. New York: Farrar, Straus and Giroux, 1982. Biography.

———. *Prophetic Inspiration after the Prophets: Maimonides and Other Medieval Authorities.* Hoboken, N.J.: Ktav, 1996.

———. *The Prophets.* New York: Jewish Publication Society of America, 1962.

———. *The Sabbath.* New York: Farrar, Straus and Giroux, 1975.

Hieronimus, J. Zohara Meyerhoff. *Kabbalistic Teachings of the Female Prophets.* Rochester, Vt.: Inner Traditions, 2008.

Hoffer, Abram, and Humphrey Osmond. *The Hallucinogens.* New York: Academic Press, 1967. Classic and encyclopedic.

Hofmann, Albert. *LSD: My Problem Child.* New York: McGraw Hill, 1980.

Husik, Isaac. *A History of Medieval Jewish Philosophy.* New York: MacMillan, 1916. Overview.

ibn Ezra, Abraham. *Commentary on the Pentateuch,* 5 vols. Translated by

H. Norman Strickman and Arthur M. Silver. New York: Menorah, 1988–2004.

———. *The Commentary of Ibn Ezra on Isaiah*. Translated by M. Friedländer. Vol. 1. New York: Feldheim, 1873. Similar exegetical approach as his Torah commentary.

Idel, Moshe. *Studies in Ecstatic Kabbalah*. Albany: State University of New York Press, 1988.

Isaacson, Walter. *Steve Jobs*. New York: Simon and Schuster, 2011.

James, William. *The Varieties of Religious Experience*. New York: Triumph Books, 1991.

Jaynes, Julian. *The Origin of Consciousness in the Breakdown of the Bicameral Mind*. Boston: Houghton Mifflin, 1976.

Jewish Publication Society, *JPS Hebrew-English Tanakh*. 2nd ed. Philadelphia: Jewish Publication Society, 1999.

Joseph, Elder. *Monastic Wisdom: The Letters of Elder Joseph the Hesychast*. Florence, Ariz.: Saint Anthony's Orthodox Greek Monastery, 1998. Greek Orthodox Christian approach to non-drug induced visions.

Kaiser, David. *How the Hippies Saved Physics: Science, Counterculture, and the Quantum Revival*. New York: W. W. Norton, 2012.

Knight, Harold. *The Hebrew Prophetic Consciousness*. London: Lutterworth Press, 1947. Psychological approach.

Kreisel, Howard. "Medieval Jewish Philosophical Interpretations of the Bible." In *Cambridge History of Jewish Philosophy*, edited by Steven Nadler and T. M. Rudavsky, 88–120. New York: Cambridge University Press, 2009. Review.

———. *Prophecy: The History of an Idea in Medieval Jewish Philosophy*. Dordrecht, Netherlands: Kluwer Academic Publishers, 2001.

Kuenen, Abraham. *The Prophets and Prophecy in Israel*. London: Longmans, Green, and Co., 1877.

Kugel, James L. *The God of Old*. New York: Free Press, 2003.

La Barre, Weston. *The Peyote Cult*. 5th ed. Norman, Ok.: University of Oklahoma Press, 1989.

Labate, Beatriz C., Isabel S. de Rose, and Rafael G. dos Santos. *Ayahuasca Religions: A Comprehensive Bibliography and Critical Essays*. Santa Cruz, Calif.: Multidisciplinary Association for Psychedelic Studies, 2009.

Lancaster, Irene. *Deconstructing the Bible: Abraham Ibn Ezra's Introduction to the Torah*. London: RoutledgeCurzon, 2003. How ibn Ezra approaches exegesis.

Levenson, Jon D. *Creation and the Persistence of Evil*. San Francisco: Harper and Row, 1988.

Lew, Alan. *One God Clapping: The Spiritual Path of a Zen Rabbi*. Woodstock, Vt.: LongHill Partners, 2009. Zen student becomes Jewish rabbi.

MacLean, Katherine A., Jeannie-Marie S. Leoutsakos, Matthew W. Johnson, and Roland R. Griffiths. "Factor Analysis of the Mystical Experience Questionnaire: A Study of Experiences Occasioned by the Hallucinogen Psilocybin." *Journal for the Scientific Study of Religion* 51 (2012): 721–37.

Maimonides. *The Commandments*, 2 vols. Translated by Charles B. Chavel. New York: Soncino Press, 1967.

———. *Epistle to Yemen*. Translated by Abraham S. Halkin. New York: American Academy for Jewish Research, 1952.

———. *The Guide of the Perplexed*. Translated by M. Friedländer. New York: Hebrew Publishing, 1881.

———. *The Guide of the Perplexed*. Translated by Shlomo Pines. Chicago: University of Chicago Press, 1963.

———. *The Laws of Repentance*. Translated by Eliyahu Touger. New York: Moznaim, 1990. One of the volumes of *Mishneh Torah*, Maimonides' summary of Talmudic law.

———. *Treatise on Resurrection*. Translated by Fred Rosner. New York: Ktav, 1982.

Mandel, David. *Who's Who in the Jewish Bible*. Philadelphia: Jewish Publication Society, 2007. Encyclopedic and valuable.

Marin, Juan Miguel. "'Mysticism' in Quantum Mechanics: The Forgotten Controversy." *European Journal of Physics* 30 (2009): 807–22. The further reaches of science.

McKane, William. *Prophets and Wise Men*. Vol. 44 of *Studies in Biblical Theology*. London: SCM Press, 1965. Conflict between revelation and reason, especially in affairs of state.

Merkur, Dan. *The Mystery of Manna: The Psychedelic Sacrament of the Bible*. Rochester, Vt.: Park Street Press, 2000.

Metzner, Ralph, Richard Alpert, and Timothy F. Leary. *The Psychedelic Experience: A Manual Based on the Tibetan Book of the Dead*. New York: Citadel Underground, 1995.

Moody, Raymond A. *Life after Life*. New York: Bantam Books, 1988.

Munk, S. *Philosophy and Philosophical Authors of the Jews*. Translated by Isidor Kalisch. Cincinnati, Ohio: Bloch and Company, 1881. Review.

Munn, Henry. "The Mushrooms of Language." In *Hallucinogens and Shamanism*, edited by Michael Harner, 86–113. New York: Oxford University Press, 1973. Obscure.

Newberg, Andrew B. *How God Changes Your Brain*. New York: Ballantine, 2010.

———. *Principles of Neurotheology*. Burlington, Vt.: Ashgate, 2010.

Newberg, Andrew B., Eugene D'Aquili, and Vince Raus. *Why God Won't Go Away*. New York: Ballantine, 2002. First cogent summary of neurotheological findings and theories.

Nichols, David E. "Hallucinogens." *Pharmacology and Therapeutics* 101 (2004): 131–81. Review.

Oroc, James. *Tryptamine Palace*. Rochester, Vt.: Park Street Press, 2009.

Ott, Jonathan. *Pharmacotheon: Entheogenic Drugs, Their Plant Sources and History*. 2nd ed. Kennewick, Wash.: Natural Products, 1996. Encyclopedic.

Pahnke, Walter N., and William A. Richards. "Implications of LSD and Experimental Mysticism." *Journal of Religion and Health* 5 (1966): 175–208.

Pendell, Dale. *Pharmako/Gnosis: Plant Teachers and the Poison Path*. San Francisco: Mercury House, 2005. Poetry and pharmacology.

Pine, Red. *The Heart Sutra*. Berkeley, Calif.: Counterpoint, 2005.

Podhoretz, Norman. *The Prophets*. New York: Free Press, 2002.

Ramban (Nachmanides). *Writings and Discourses*, 2 vols. Edited by Charles B. Chavel. New York: Shilo, 1978.

———. *Commentary on the Torah*, 5 vols. Edited by Charles B. Chavel. New York: Shilo, 1974–1976.

Rashi. *The Torah with Rashi's Commentary. Translated, Annotated and Elucidated*, 5 vols. Edited by Yisrael Isser Zvi Herczeg. Brooklyn, N.Y.: Mesorah, 1994–1998.

Rätsch, Christian. *The Encyclopedia of Psychoactive Plants*. Rochester, Vt.: Park Street Press, 2005. Essential reference.

Reines, Alvin Jay. *Maimonides and Abrabanel on Prophecy*. Cincinnati, Ohio: Hebrew Union College, 1970. Abrabanel challenges Maimonides' Aristotelianism.

Robinson, Theodore H. *Prophecy and the Prophets in Ancient Israel*. London: Duckworth, 1953. Valuable treatment.

Rose, Seraphim. *The Soul after Death*. Platina, Calif.: Saint Herman of Alaska Brotherhood, 1980.

Rosenberg, A. J., trans. *Torah/Bible, Prophets, Writings*. New York: Judaica Press, various dates.

Saadia, *The Book of Beliefs and Opinions*. Translated by Samuel Rosenblatt. New Haven, Conn.: Yale University Press, 1948.

Sai-Halász, A., G. Brunecker, and S. I. Szára. "Dimethyltryptamin: Ein Neues Psychoticum." *Psychiatria et Neurologia* (Basel) 135 (1958): 285–301. First report of human psychoactivity.

Shanon, Benny. "Biblical Entheogens: A Speculative Hypothesis." *Time and Mind* 1 (2008): 51–74.

———. "The Biblical Merkava Vision and Ayahuasca Visions." *Studies in Spirituality* 13 (2003): 31–43. Relates Ezekiel's vision and ayahuasca phenomenology.

Shemesh, Yael. "Lies by Prophets and Other Lies in the Hebrew Bible." *Journal of Ancient Near Eastern Studies* 29 (2002): 81–95. True prophets may lie.

Shulgin, Alexander T., and Ann Shulgin. *TiHKAL: The Continuation*. Berkeley, Calif.: Transform Press, 1997. Encyclopedic treatment of chemistry and subjective effects of tryptamine psychedelics.

Siegman, Edward F. *The False Prophets of the Old Testament*. Washington, D.C.: Catholic University of America, 1939. False prophecy.

Simon, Uriel. *Reading Prophetic Narratives*. Translated by Lenn J. Schramm. Bloomington: Indiana University Press, 1997. Penetrating analysis.

Smith, Houston. "Do Drugs Have Religious Import?" *Journal of Philosophy* 61 (1964): 517–30. Classic treatment.

Snyder, Solomon H. "Seeking God in the Brain—Efforts to Localize Higher Brain Functions." *New England Journal of Medicine* 358 (2008): 6–7. Neurotheological approach by Nobel Prize winner.

Sotnikova, Tatyana D., Marc G. Caron, and Raul R. Gainetdinov. "Trace Amine-Associated Receptors as Emerging Therapeutic Targets." *Molecular Pharmacology* 72 (2009): 229–35.

Spinoza, Benedict de. *Tractatus Theologico-Politicus, Tractatus Politicus*. Translated by R. H. M. Elwes. London: George Routledge and Sons, 1895.

Stapledon, Olaf. *Last and First Men*. Los Angeles: Jeremy P. Tarcher, 1988.

Stevens, Jay. *Storming Heaven: LSD and the American Dream.* New York: Grove Press, 1998. LSD and the 60s.

Stiegman, Edward F. *The False Prophets of the Old Testament.* Carthagena, Ohio: Messenger Press, 1939. False prophets.

Stone Edition Tanach. Edited by Nosson Scherman. Brooklyn: Mesorah, 1997.

Strassman, Rick J. "Adverse Reactions to Psychedelic Drugs: A Review of the Literature." *Journal of Nervous and Mental Disease* 172 (1984): 577–95.

———. "DMT and the Dharma." *Tricycle: The Buddhist Review* 6 (1996): 81–88.

———. *DMT: The Spirit Molecule.* Rochester, Vt.: Park Street Press, 2001.

———. "Preparation for the Journey." In *Inner Paths to Outer Space,* edited by Rick Strassman, Slawek Wojtowicz, Luis Eduardo Luna, and Ede Frecksa, 268–98. Rochester, Vt.: Park Street Press, 2008.

Strassman, Rick J., Glenn T. Peake, Clifford R. Qualls, and E. Jonathan Lisanksy. "A Model for the Study of the Acute Effects of Melatonin in Man." *Journal of Clinical Endocrinology and Metabolism* 65 (1987): 847–52. Initial findings from 1980s melatonin research.

Strassman, Rick J., and Clifford R. Qualls. "Dose-Response Study of N,N-Dimethyltryptamine in Humans. I: Neuroendocrine, Autonomic, and Cardiovascular Effects." *Archives of General Psychiatry* 51 (1994): 85–97.

Strassman, Rick J., Clifford R. Qualls, Eberhard H. Uhlenhuth, and Robert Kellner. "Dose-Response Study of N,N-Dimethyltryptamine in Humans. II: Subjective Effects and Preliminary Results of a New Rating Scale." *Archives of General Psychiatry* 51 (1994): 98–108.

Strauss, Leo. *Persecution and the Art of Writing.* Chicago: University of Chicago Press, 1952. How medieval Jewish philosophers couched their revolutionary ideas.

———. *Spinoza's Critique of Religion.* New York: Schocken Books, 1965.

Strickman, H. Norman. *The Secret of the Torah. A Translation of Abraham ibn Ezra's Sefer Yesod Mora Ve-Sod Ha-Torah.* Northvale, N.J.: Jason Aaronson, 1995.

Takahashi, Toshihiro, Kazuhiro Takahashi, Tatsuo Ido et al. "11C-Labeling of Indolealkylamine Alkaloids and the Comparative Study of Their Tissue Distributions." *International Journal of Applied Radiation and Isotopes* 36 (1985): 965–69.

Tart, Charles T., ed. *Altered States of Consciousness.* New York: John Wiley and Sons, 1969.

————. "States of Consciousness and State-Specific Sciences." *Science* 176 (1972): 1203–10. A revolutionary paper.

Teitsworth, Scott. *Krishna in the Sky with Diamonds: The Bhagavad Gita as Psychedelic Guide.* Rochester, Vt.: Inner Traditions, 2011.

Thompson, Michael A., Eunpyo Moon, Ung-Jin Kim et al. "Human Indolethylamine *N*-Methyltransferase: cDNA Cloning and Expression, Gene Cloning, and Chromosomal Localization." *Genomics* 61 (1999): 285–97.

Thompson, Michael A., and Richard M. Weinshilboum. "Rabbit Lung Indolethylamine *N*-Methyltransferase." *Biological Chemistry* 273 (1998): 34502–10.

Twersky, Isadore, and Jay M. Harris, eds. *Rabbi Abraham Ibn Ezra: Studies in the Writings of a Twelfth-Century Jewish Polymath.* Cambridge, Mass.: Harvard University Press, 1993. Collected essays.

van Dam, Cornelis. *The Urim and Thummim.* Winona Lake, Ind.: Eisenbrauns, 1997.

Whedbee, J. William. *Isaiah and Wisdom.* Nashville, Tenn.: Abingdon Press, 1971. Wisdom in the Book of Isaiah.

Wolfson, Elliot R. *Through a Speculum That Shines.* Princeton, N.J.: Princeton University Press, 1994.

Yanai, Kazuhiko, Tatsuo Ido, Kiichi Ishiwata et al. "In Vivo Kinetics and Displacement Study of Carbon-11-Labeled Hallucinogen, N,N-[^{11}C] Dimethyltryptamine." *European Journal of Nuclear Medicine* 12 (1986): 141–46.

Zeitlin, Solomon. "Dreams and Their Interpretation from the Biblical Period to the Tannaitic Time: An Historical Study." *Jewish Quarterly Review* 66 (1975): 1–18. Cogent review.

————. "An Historical Study of the Canonization of the Hebrew Scriptures." *Proceedings of the American Academy for Jewish Research* 3 (1931): 121–58.

————. *Maimonides: A Biography.* 2nd ed. New York: Bloch, 1955.

Zimmerli, Walther. *The Law and the Prophets.* Oxford: Blackwell, 1965. Christian view that prophetic standards of conduct are unattainable.

Zlotowitz, Gedaliah, Yisroel Simcha Schorr, Chaim Malinowitz, Asher Dicker, and Nesanel Kasnett, eds. *Schottenstein Edition of the Talmud.* 73 vols. Brooklyn: Mesorah, various dates.

Biblical Index

THE TORAH
(FIRST FIVE BOOKS OF THE HEBREW BIBLE)

OTHER BOOKS OF THE HEBREW BIBLE

Index